*The*
# KINGDOM of GOD
## as LITURGICAL
## EMPIRE

*The*
# KINGDOM of GOD
# as LITURGICAL
# EMPIRE

## A THEOLOGICAL COMMENTARY
## ON 1–2 CHRONICLES

# Scott W. Hahn

**Baker Academic**
*a division of Baker Publishing Group*
Grand Rapids, Michigan

© 2012 by Scott W. Hahn

Published by Baker Academic
a division of Baker Publishing Group
P.O. Box 6287, Grand Rapids, MI 49516-6287
www.bakeracademic.com

Printed in the United States of America

Library of Congress Cataloging-in-Publication Data

Hahn, Scott.
    The kindgom of God as liturgical empire : a theological commentary on 1–2 Chronicles / Scott W. Hahn.
        p.   cm.
    Includes bibliographical references (p.    ) and indexes.
    ISBN 978-0-8010-3947-8 (pbk.)
    1. Bible. O.T. Chronicles—Commentaries. 2. Bible. O.T. Chronicles—Theology. I. Title.
BS1345.53.H34 2012
222′.607—dc23                                                                 2011041161

12   13   14   15   16   17   18        7   6   5   4   3   2   1

To David Scott
and Rusty Reno,
my colleagues and friends,
whose conversations help to shape me—
and shaped this book
(Proverbs 27:17)

# Contents

# Abbreviations

| | | | |
|---|---|---|---|
| Amos | Amos | 1 Kgs. | 1 Kings |
| Bar. | Baruch | 2 Kgs. | 2 Kings |
| 1 Chr. | 1 Chronicles | Lam. | Lamentations |
| 2 Chr. | 2 Chronicles | Lev. | Leviticus |
| Dan. | Daniel | 1 Macc. | 1 Maccabees |
| Deut. | Deuteronomy | 2 Macc. | 2 Maccabees |
| Eccl. | Ecclesiastes | Mal. | Malachi |
| Esth. | Esther | Mic. | Micah |
| Exod. | Exodus | Nah. | Nahum |
| Ezek. | Ezekiel | Neh. | Nehemiah |
| Ezra | Ezra | Num. | Numbers |
| Gen. | Genesis | Obad. | Obadiah |
| Hab. | Habakkuk | Prov. | Proverbs |
| Hag. | Haggai | Ps. | Psalms |
| Hos. | Hosea | Ruth | Ruth |
| Isa. | Isaiah | 1 Sam. | 1 Samuel |
| Jdt. | Judith | 2 Sam. | 2 Samuel |
| Jer. | Jeremiah | Sir. | Sirach |
| Job | Job | Song | Song of Songs |
| Joel | Joel | Tob. | Tobit |
| Jonah | Jonah | Wis. | Wisdom of Solomon |
| Josh. | Joshua | Zech. | Zechariah |
| Judg. | Judges | Zeph. | Zephaniah |

# "Now the Records Are Ancient"

*An Introduction to Chronicles*

## The Book of the Events of the Days

Reading the books of 1–2 Chronicles, we are confronted right away with questions about the meaning and practice of history and prophecy. The Chronicler obviously understands himself to be writing history in some sense. With his first word, "Adam," he signals his ambition to tell the world's story from the beginning—from the creation of the first man—to the end—his own time in the late sixth or early fifth century BC, possibly within a generation of the decree of King Cyrus of Persia that concludes his work.

At the time of the original composition of Chronicles, the people of Israel were being restored from their captivity in Babylon; they had returned home to rebuild the temple and again worship the living God at Jerusalem. The Chronicler wrote in a time of disorientation and uncertainty, when there was a real need for a remembrance of things past in order to make sense of the present and prepare for the future. And the rabbinic tradition placed his resulting work at the end of the canon of authoritative scripture—as the final book of Ketuvim, or "Writings," and the close of the Tanak, the entire Hebrew Bible (Ackroyd 1991; Steins 1995: 415; Klein 2006: 2n15; Kalimi 2009: 17–33).[1]

The Hebrew title, *dibrê hayyāmîm* (The Events [*or* Words] of the Days), suggests the provenance of Chronicles as historical writing. As we begin our study, we need to remember that Chronicles was written originally as one book. The current division of the text into 1 Chronicles and 2 Chronicles in

---

1. The rabbinic canon does exhibit some wide variations, however, as Chronicles comes first in the Ketuvim in both the Aleppo and Leningrad Codexes. Our canonical approach is similar to Steins, who (like Ackroyd) sees the Chronicler as "the first theologian of the canon," except for his complex redactional theory of multiple layers and a late dating to the Maccabean period.

both the Jewish and Christian canons is an innovation begun with the ancient Greek translation, the Septuagint.

Chronicles takes a fairly straightforward chronological approach to Israel's story. The basic outline of Chronicles looks like this: the Chronicler begins with a long list of the family of nations and ancestors of Israel (1 Chr. 1–9). He picks up Israel's national story during the last days of its ill-fated first king (1 Chr. 10). The narrative pivots on the reigns of the great King David (1 Chr. 11–29) and his son and successor, Solomon (2 Chr. 1–9). The breakup of the monarchy into northern and southern kingdoms in the years after Solomon and the reigns of the post-Solomonic kings are detailed in the rest of the work (2 Chr. 10–36). He traces the fortunes of the southern kingdom, which preserves the house of David, through nineteen kings, until 586 BC, when invading Babylonian forces seize Jerusalem, destroy the temple, and drive the southerners into exile. Chronicles ends with King Cyrus of Persia's decree announcing the end of the exile and the beginnings of their restoration and return to Judea (36:17–28).

The Chronicler aims at a recapitulation of the history of the people Israel. But the reader notices that there is more than history at work here. Chronicles strains the categories and definitions of traditional historiography, secular or biblical. First, there is the matter of tone: it simply does not read like history. Chronicles is a commentary, maybe even a series of homilies on Israel's national story as told in its sacred scripture. Second, there is the question of selection, of why the Chronicler includes so much material omitted from other biblical sources, while excluding so much material that other biblical writers counted as essential to Israel's national story. Finally, there is the matter of the Chronicler's perspective. More than a summary or overview, Chronicles is a theological and liturgical interpretation of Israel's history that answers key questions: Who are we? How did we get here? What must we do, and why?

The writing of Chronicles is an act of what the Hebrews called zākhôr, an act of remembrance that is liturgical, that aims to bring one into a living and vital contact with events recalled. Among their contemporaries in the ancient Near East, none was as preoccupied with historical remembrance as the children of Israel. Reif says:

> The Hebrews were often commanded to remember and not to forget, and this kind of religious imperative is unique to Israel. . . . It was not all facts that were to be remembered but those that specifically documented God's intervention and man's response since in this way human history could be interpreted as the revelation of God's will. Memory was a central element in ritual and recital, and the festivals manifestly had historical as well as religious and agricultural dimensions. The biblical narrative revolves around the reality of everyday life rather than having its focus on the exclusively spiritual. . . . Thus, Israel's history was incorporated—even transformed—into its Scripture. The whole process was maintained and nurtured by transmission, recitation, and education. (2006: 322)

In Chronicles too we see Israel's history being transformed into scripture. We wonder to what extent the Chronicler felt himself to be writing an authoritative text. If Chronicles demands to be understood in some sense as history, we must acknowledge that it is history told in a prophetic key. There are more than a dozen original prophetic speeches in Chronicles found nowhere else in the canon. Prophets, seers, and divine emissaries play a prominent role in his recasting of Israel's history: warning kings, delivering God's covenant word, and—significantly—prophesying in the context of the temple liturgy.

Scholars have shown how the prophetic discourses in Chronicles reflect fundamental theological concerns of the author (Schniedewind 1997; Beentjes 2001). But this dimension of the work raises a set of further questions: To what extent did the Chronicler understand his own writing of Israel's history to be a prophetic and even liturgical act—receiving the word of God, interpreting and applying it, and delivering it to God's people in their concrete historical moment? To what extent is the Chronicler himself prophesying in the context of the temple liturgy?

At the outset of this commentary, my assumption is that Chronicles can best be understood as a work of *prophetic historiography* characterized by the author's profound assimilation and interpretation of the covenantal and liturgical worldview of the Hebrew Bible. Josephus, the Jewish historian who wrote in the first century AD, said that the historical records found in the Bible are unique because "only prophets have written the original and earliest accounts of things as they learned them from God himself by inspiration" (*Against Apion* 1.37). Thus the rabbis described the Historical Books, such as Samuel and Kings, as the "Former Prophets."

We detect this prophetic sensibility in the Chronicler, who aims to do far more than retell Israel's national story. He is delivering a word of divine assurance. He wants his readers to understand that the history he is retelling is not finished: it is ongoing. God's divine purposes are still unfolding in the lives of his people—despite the catastrophe of the exile and the hesitant and anticlimactic beginnings of the people's return from exile and their restoration to Jerusalem. The Chronicler's intent is to remind Judah's people of God's original intentions—not only for Israel, but also for creation—and to help align their hearts and lives more faithfully with that divine plan. A prophetic exhortation attributed to King Jehoshaphat could serve as a summary of his authorial purposes in this book: "Hear me, Judah and inhabitants of Jerusalem! Believe in the LORD your God, and you will be established; believe his prophets and you will succeed" (2 Chr. 20:20).

"The Book of Chronicles was given only to be expounded upon homiletically," we hear in *Leviticus Rabbah* 1.3, a midrash that dates to about the fifth century AD but contains material centuries older (ArtScroll 1987: xvi–xvii; Knoppers and Harvey 2002: 230–31). According to the Mishnah, Chronicles was among the books read by the high priest during the solemn evening vigil preceding Yom Kippur, the Day of Atonement—along with the books of Ezra, Job, Zechariah, and sometimes Daniel (*Yoma* 1.6). And generally in Jewish tradition, Chronicles was read spiritually, as a divinely inspired commentary on the history of the children of Israel.

The content and the form of the book are intensely liturgical. Many years ago Gerhard von Rad surmised that it was structured around a series of Levitical sermons (1966: 267–80). More recently, De Vries (1997) identified the Jewish liturgical festivals as the organizing principle of the book. My own sense is that Chronicles may have been originally composed as a series of interconnected homilies on Israel's historical scripture, intended to be read in the liturgy.

The "style is very strongly homiletic," Ackroyd observes (1991: 276), and its many repetitions suggest a strong catechetical intent. This is history told for didactic and deeply spiritual reasons. Ackroyd is surely correct in describing the Chronicler as "the first theologian of the canon" (1991: 285; cf. 280). And Selman, who wrote one of the best modern commentaries, identifies a unique feature of the work: "Chronicles stands apart in its attempt to interpret the Old Testament from beginning to end" (1994a: 42).

Before beginning our close reading of 1–2 Chronicles, I want to identify some of the distinctive features of the work's theological interpretation of the canon. I will inquire into the worldview we find in Chronicles: What does the Chronicler believe about history, how does he come to those beliefs, and how do his beliefs guide his selection of materials to include and exclude from his work? Second, I will look at the literary tools and narrative methods he employs for interpreting his sources and telling his story.

## The Chronicler's Covenantal Worldview

The pivotal feature of the Chronicler's prophetic historiography is his sense of the covenant and the covenantal structure of the divine economy. Of crucial significance for interpreting Chronicles is the biblical notion that God's covenant establishes sacred kinship, setting God, Israel, and humanity in a familial relationship (Hahn 2009b; 2005a). This relationship is not metaphorical or a sort of legal fiction. The covenant points to a kind of sacramental consanguinity, a blood bond, calling Israel to be "one flesh and bone" with God—a nuptial-covenantal image we hear in the Chronicler (1 Chr. 11:1; also Exod. 24:6). At the heart of the covenant is the divine word, an oath sworn by God himself. The Chronicler will speak of the covenant as "the word that he commanded, for a thousand generations," as a divine oath that can never be broken (1 Chr. 16:15). The identity of God himself is defined by his keeping of his covenant oath, as King Solomon sings: "O LORD, God of Israel, there is no God like thee, in heaven or on earth, keeping covenant" (2 Chr. 6:14).

The sequence of biblical covenants is central to the Chronicler's understanding of the divine economy. This can be traced from the early pages of his work. Beginning with Adam and the covenant of creation, his genealogy follows the path of God's covenant through Noah, Abraham, Israel, and, finally and cumulatively, David, with whom God makes a "covenant of salt," meaning a new and everlasting covenant (2 Chr. 13:5; 21:7).

His work focuses on David and the kingdom and temple liturgy established by the Davidic covenant. The making of this covenant is the climax of the Chronicler's history, with the covenant presented as the fulfillment of God's purposes for creation. The Davidic covenant is a *novum*, something unprecedented and radically new. But in the Chronicler's presentation is a profound unity in salvation history, reflected in the continuity of God's covenants. This is another way of saying that, for the Chronicler, the Davidic covenant advances the fulfillment of God's purposes in all the covenants that came before, especially the covenant with Moses and Israel at Sinai and the foundational covenant—the covenant with Abraham.

The Mosaic and Abrahamic covenants illuminate the Chronicler's understanding of salvation history. Indeed, these covenants provide a kind of typological substructure for the history that unfolds in the Chronicler's work. The telos of history for the Chronicler is the fulfillment of God's threefold promise to Abraham—to make Abraham's descendants a great nation, to give him a great name, and to make him the source of blessing for all the nations of the world (Gen. 12:1–3; 15:7–21; 17:1–8; 22:16–18). And the Chronicler's ideal of Israel is drawn implicitly from the mandate given to Moses and Israel at Sinai—to be God's "firstborn son" (Exod. 4:22) and "my own possession among all the peoples, . . . a kingdom of priests and a holy nation" (19:5–6; Hahn 2009b: 101–35).

In Chronicles, David's kingdom fulfills the "covenant with the people of Israel, when they came out of Egypt" (2 Chr. 5:10; 6:11). The law of the kingdom is the *tôrâ* given at Mount Sinai, "the book of the covenant" (2 Chr. 34:30), now transformed at Zion into a law for all humanity. Further, the Chronicler depicts David as a new Moses and describes the kingdom of David and Solomon in terms that make clear the kingdom's dependence on the covenant institutions established at Sinai—the ark of the covenant of God, the central role of the law and the Levitical priesthood, and the liturgical assembly or *qāhāl* (Greek *ekklēsia*).

Yet, in contrast to the other historical works in the canon where the Mosaic covenant is dominant, the Chronicler seems to insist on the priority of the Abrahamic covenant. This again reflects a sound interpretation of the canonical record, where the Abrahamic covenant is foundational and Israel's liberation from Egypt and exodus to Sinai are brought about because "God remembered his covenant with Abraham" (Exod. 2:24; 6:5). The Chronicler may also feel that, following the ordeal of the exile, the people need a return to their roots—to understand that long before the exodus and Sinai there was Moriah, the site of Abraham's binding of Isaac and, in God's plan, the site of the temple at Zion (2 Chr. 3:1).

The Chronicler wants his readers to see the inner unity of salvation history—running from Adam to Abraham, to the covenant with Abraham's descendants at Sinai, and finally to the kingdom of David at Zion and his son Solomon, in which salvation history reaches its zenith (Ackroyd 1991: 265). The kingdom of David is the fulfillment of Israel's mission to be a kingdom of priests—but again for the sake of God's original covenant purposes with Abraham—to bring blessings to all the nations of the world through Abraham's "seed."

The Chronicler's God is a God of the covenant, and the economy of salvation is for the sake of this covenant. When David finally brings the ark of the covenant to rest in Jerusalem, the great historical psalm he composes for the occasion declares: "He is mindful of his covenant for ever, . . . the covenant which he made with Abraham, . . . an everlasting covenant to Israel" (1 Chr. 16:15–17; cf. Ps. 105:8–10).

## Typological Interpretation of History in Chronicles

The Chronicler's history represents a deep reading of the canon of Israel's scripture. Beginning in the Torah and continuing through the historical and prophetic books of the Nevi'im, as well as the liturgical and Wisdom literature of the Ketuvim, the Hebrew canon is filled with examples of inner-biblical exegesis. Later texts rewrite, comment upon, or reinterpret earlier ones; new situations and people are understood and characterized by analogy to earlier texts. The large measure of what scholars call the Chronicler's *Vorlage*, or source material, is drawn from the biblical books of Samuel and Kings. But in addition to his rewriting and reinterpreting his *Vorlage*, his work is shot through with scriptural references and allusions, in addition to direct quotations and citations. For instance, in describing David's ill-fated census, the Chronicler builds his account on his source in 2 Samuel while integrating allusions to earlier scenes in Israel's history—Abraham's acquisition of burial ground in Canaan, Gideon's encounter with an angel, the deadly angel of the exodus, the heavenly fire of Aaron's time, and maybe even the temptation of Adam. This is not clever literary styling, but biblical theology being practiced at a very deep level.

Like any good historian, the Chronicler provides a record of past figures, places, and events; but his accounting is written in such a way that these figures, places, and events often appear as types—signs, patterns, and precursors—intended to show his readers not only the past but also their present reality from God's perspective. David is sketched as both a new Adam and a new Moses; the temple is a new creation and a new tabernacle and altar. In the Chronicler's account, the faithlessness and failures of Israel's first king, Saul, are replayed by kings centuries later. Saul is more than a failed monarch: he becomes the type of the unrighteous king who leads God's people to ruin and exile. In the same way, good kings in Chronicles do the things that David did—because David is a prototype of the righteous king.

Acknowledging this intensely inner-biblical and typological narrative technique is not to deny the historical reliability of the Chronicler's account. Rather, I am suggesting that reporting history "as it happened" is not the Chronicler's sole interest. What happened in the past is crucial for the Chronicler, but only because in the *what* of history he sees the patterns of divine intention and intervention revealed—the *why* of history. The why of history is the reason for the Chronicler's work, which seeks not only to document past events but also to interpret these events in light of his readers' present needs for guidance and hope in the face of an uncertain future.

The way the Chronicler comes to understand, interpret, and explain the why of salvation history is through typology. As an intensely typological work, Chronicles gives us a typological interpretation of history (Hahn 2005c: 19–25). Typology for the Chronicler is a way to shed light on the unity of God's plan in history and to show the meaning of people, places, and events in light of God's covenant promises and redemptive acts.

Trompf suggests (1979) that the typological patterns of "recurrence" found in Chronicles and elsewhere in the Bible are related to the use of these scriptures in the rhythms of Israel's cult and worship (also G. Wright 1962). Others, beginning with the rabbis, noticed an archetypal pattern of creation/blessing, sin/exile, repentance/restoration running through the canon. The creation of Adam and Eve is followed immediately by their sin and consequent exile from paradise; Israel is created as God's chosen people in the Sinai covenant and immediately falls into the golden-calf apostasy, which leaves them wandering in the wilderness until a new generation comes along. Similar patterns can be traced in the period of the judges, and these patterns run throughout the Chronicler's retelling of Israel's history, especially in his accounts of the divided monarchy and the destruction of the temple. In turn, Israel's sacrificial liturgy and priesthood grows out of this archetypal story and orient the prayer and worship of the people toward repenting for sin and seeking atonement.

All of this has an important bearing on our reading of the Chronicler's work. These overarching biblical archetypes are at work in his liturgical historiography, and this helps us to understand how certain features that scholars have long identified as peculiar to the Chronicler, such as his supposed theology of immediate retribution, have not always been fully or accurately understood.

What we find in the Chronicler fits the definition of what Fishbane terms "aggadic historiography." It is a kind of inner-biblical exegesis in which the Chronicler reinterprets key elements of Israel's "received historical *traditum*" (Fishbane 1985: 381). Fishbane, however, does not think that the Chronicler

presumed his readers to know this *traditum* so intimately that they would recognize the reinterpretations and historical revisionism going on in his text. He
argues that Chronicles does not present itself as an interpretive commentary
on earlier scriptures but rather as an authoritative "final document" that "pur-
ports to tell the past 'wie es eigentlich gewesen,'" as it actually was (1985: 382).

This characterization of the Chronicler's project is not as self-evident as
Fishbane supposes, although he is surely correct to caution us against projecting
our modern historical and literary-critical hypotheses back onto the Chronicler
and his audience. But it may perhaps be another kind of modern projection to
assume that the Chronicler's audience was as unaware or unmindful of Israel's
national story as many moderns are about their own traditions. After all, one
can hardly speak of a *traditum* unless one presumes that these works are not
only known by the people but also bear some normative authority in their
lives and worship. Fishbane's own close readings confirm that the Chronicler
is often consciously retelling and reshaping a story that he presumes his audience already knows from the liturgy. The original placement of Chronicles
as the final book in the Hebrew Bible further suggests an awareness among
the Chronicler's first readers that his work is intended less as a stand-alone
historical text than as haggadah, a theological homily on all of Israel's history.

In any event, what is clear is that the Chronicler is often making haggadic—
theological and homiletic—rereadings of Israel's *traditum*, often utilizing various
forms of typology. In general, his narrative is shaped by a typological outlook
that is characteristic of the biblical worldview and sees the divine hand at work
in Israel's history. As Fishbane notes, typology is far more than a literary device:

> Typological exegesis . . . celebrates new historical events in so far as they can
> be correlated with older ones. By this means it also reveals *unexpected unity in
> historical experience and providential continuity* in its new patterns and shapes.
> Accordingly, the perception of typologies is not solely an exegetical activity, it
> is, at the same time, a religious activity of the first magnitude. . . . Typological
> exegesis is . . . a disclosure of the plenitude and mysterious workings of divine
> activity in history. (1985: 352)

For the Chronicler, the typological key to "the plenitude and mysterious
workings of divine activity in history" is the kingdom of David. Chronicles
is the world's family history written in a Davidic key, beginning in the deceptively simple genealogical lists, which are actually careful compositions that
progressively narrow the world's family tree into a single branch—the line of
the family of David.

Typology for the Chronicler is a way to shed light on the unity of God's
plan in history and to show the meaning of people, places, and events in light
of God's covenant promises and redemptive acts. Williamson offers a helpful
clarification of the Chronicler's use of typology: "Typology . . . is not used to

point to one incident or institution as the fulfillment of its shadowlike predecessor; rather, it serves as a cross-reference from one incident to another, inviting the reader to draw parallels and conclusions that go beyond the immediate statement of the text" (1991: 21).

In the Chronicler we do find a profound belief in the unity and continuity of the history of God's people. This is the point of the genealogies that open the work. The Chronicler's audience is the same people of God born to Abraham and Israel. They are all members of the same family, sharing a common ancestry, a common covenant, and a common story. That means that what God did for their ancestors he did, in a certain way, for them; what was written earlier in the scriptural story was meant for them too. "All that happened to the fathers was a sign for their sons," the thirteenth-century scholar and poet, Immanuel of Rome, famously wrote (quoted from Fishbane 1985: 350).

This is the principle at work in Israel's liturgy. Rabbi Gamaliel used to say of the Passover celebration:

> In every generation a person is duty-bound to regard himself as if he personally has gone forth from Egypt, since it is said, *And you shall tell your son in that day saying, It is because of that which the Lord did for me when I came forth out of Egypt* (Ex. 13:8). Therefore we are duty-bound to thank, praise, glorify, honor, exalt, extol, and bless him who did for our forefathers and for us all these miracles. He brought us forth from slavery to freedom, anguish to joy, mourning to festival, darkness to great light, subjugation to redemption, so we should say before him, Hallelujah. (Mishnah, *Pesaḥim* 10.5, quoted from Neusner 1988: 250, emphasis original)

This same principle of liturgical historiography is at work in Chronicles. History is being brought into the present tense, as it is in the liturgy. "The Chronicler . . . shared a common hermeneutic with the Jewish community who composed the Targum," according to Duke's rhetorical analysis. "Scripture was actualized. The message of the text was contemporary; it spoke to the present; 'revelation' was continuous. . . . The Chronicler interpreted his tradition both in light of contemporary cultic praxis and according to the need of the present situation" (1990: 115).

In the Chronicler we are often brought to the point where scripture and the liturgy intersect as mutual projects of *zākhôr* or *anamnēsis*—as "remembrances" of the *mirabilia Dei* that in a certain sense actualize these miraculous works of God, bringing the people of today into living contact with them. Cult and history are inseparable in Israel's covenant relationship with God. For Israel, liturgy was historical and history was liturgical. Cultic prayers such as Pss. 77, 78, 105, 106, and 136 are essentially meditations on history. The great feasts of Passover and Weeks are memorials rooted in historical events that God has commanded his people to remember liturgically (Exod. 12:1–13:4; 23:14–16; Lev. 23:4–22).

## The Twofold Pattern of the Canon

In its own way Chronicles fits into the scheme of the biblical canon. Reading the Bible canonically, we see a larger twofold pattern in the canon, and this larger pattern helps us to interpret the Chronicler's purpose. The Hebrew canon presents us with two distinctly different perspectives on Israel's history: one decidedly more secular, and the other more liturgical or priestly. Yet these are not hard and fast divisions, and we should be cautious in labeling texts as "secular" or "priestly." For instance, what scholars identify as the "Deuteronomistic History"—the history recorded in Joshua, Judges, 1–2 Samuel, and 1–2 Kings—lays more stress on secular concerns, such as law, society, and royal government, than does Chronicles. And we can trace this pattern backward and forward in the canon. Within the Pentateuch, Deuteronomy is preoccupied with the Deuteronomic covenant establishing the twelve tribes as a holy yet secular nation-state. Leviticus, on the other hand, is concerned with the priestly and liturgical life of the nation.

I am not suggesting mutually exclusive viewpoints here. Deuteronomy does not stress the secular to the exclusion of the liturgical any more than Leviticus stresses the liturgical to the exclusion of the secular. What I am arguing is that, read from a canonical and synchronic perspective, the final redactor of the canon appears to intend for readers to see certain dialectical tensions within Israel's history and an overriding concern for the proper coordination of the secular and the liturgical, the royal and the priestly. Thus the Deuteronomist focuses our attention on the lay governance of the twelve tribes and how the national order is to be related to the priestly ministry of the Levites. Leviticus, on the other hand, focuses on the training, sanctification, and ministry of the Levitical priests—on how their ministry is ordered to the twelve tribes.

Throughout the so-called Deuteronomistic History, Israel is constantly tempted to follow the secular model of the surrounding nations, which would exalt the political and military concerns above the priestly and religious service of God. These temptations culminate in Israel's desire for "a king to govern us like all the nations," a desire that is interpreted as a rejection of God's rule (1 Sam. 8:4–22). Such a king, Samuel warns, will demand the best of everything from the people—their children, their money, their crops; that is, he will demand a tithe as the priests do. In other words, the royal will supplant the priestly: the kingdom will be ordered to the earthly king and not the true king in heaven.

Running through the canon, this tension between the pull of the secular and the call of the divine is expressed in the tensions between the royal and the priestly concerns of Israel. This twofold pattern appears even within the Ketuvim. The so-called Wisdom literature reflects more secular concerns of daily life—morals, ethics, and the like. The Psalter, on the other hand, points to the sacred, the liturgical concerns of the priestly and the temple. In the later histories of 1–2 Maccabees, we again detect this pattern: 1 Maccabees looks at Israel's restoration entirely in political or military terms, whereas 2 Maccabees is written by a different author, who while covering the same general period, writes from the perspective of the priesthood and the temple.

Again, I am not suggesting any kind of antithesis or opposition within the canon. Only the modern, post-Enlightenment mind finds these viewpoints irreconcilable. In the biblical canon, the secular and the sacred are not distinguished to be opposed: they are distinguished to be united. In the canon we find a duality of complementary perspectives rather than a dualism of contradictory viewpoints. Chronicles must be understood in light of this wider canonical pattern. A canonical and synchronic reading of Chronicles enables us to see that what Leviticus is to Deuteronomy, Chronicles is to the so-called Deuteronomistic History. The Chronicler retells Israel's story, not from the standpoint of secular and lay concerns, but from the perspective of the sacred historiography of liturgy. Some scholars consider it to be a kind of rewritten Bible. Others consider it to be a work of primitive political theology, a literary work of "utopia" or "ideology," in which the author seeks to portray an idealized Israelite society or an "alternative reality" (Schweitzer 2007: 415; also Dyck 1988).

Although there is much to be learned from a political-theological or utopian reading of the text, this type of viewpoint can have the tendency to downgrade or relativize the historicity of the Chronicler's account. Scholars continue to debate to what extent Chronicles depicts events that actually happened, and they have produced a steady stream of more or less plausible arguments. But such discussions can never transcend the merely hypothetical; hence they are not necessarily useful for helping us to understand the text as handed on to us in the Jewish and later Christian tradition.

In addition to reading Chronicles in its final form as presented to us in the canon, a Christian theological commentary must take into account the findings of literary and historical research in order to understand the work's intent and its reception by its original audience. We also need to read it in light of Jewish and later Christian interpretive tradition. Jewish tradition, while acknowledging a certain midrashic quality to the work, never received it as a work of historical fiction or as a statement of a religious or political ideal. Chronicles was understood to be a commentary on history, on events that in fact did happen in Israel's past.

## "A Chronicle of All Divine History"

The editors of the Septuagint, the Greek translation of Hebrew scripture, grouped Chronicles as the last of the Historical Books, following the books of Kings. The Septuagint title, *Paraleipomena*, indicates the editors' apparent belief that it contained mostly supplemental "things omitted or left behind" in those earlier historical accounts.

Yet contrary to the implications of its Septuagint title, Chronicles is far from a gathering of fragments or things left over. It is a coherent and compelling theology of history. Chronicles is more than a "rewritten Bible" (Pitre 2003), and the Chronicler is doing more than biblical interpretation. His prophetic historiography is guided by a prayerful and profound biblical worldview—based on an understanding of what he believes scripture reveals about God's ways and means and his purposes for Israel and the world.

The Chronicler's narrative is pervaded by a sense of what Paul and later Christian tradition would call the *oikonomia*, the divine economy through which God works out his saving purposes. For the Chronicler, history has a telos—a definite direction and goal toward which it is driving, a goal established through the intention of God. This does not mean that in Chronicles history is reducible to eschatology. Chronicles is not an eschatological work or a species of apocalyptic literature. It is prophetic historiography that looks forward not to the end of history, but to the fullness of time and the fulfillment of what is anticipated in Israel's liturgy, which is always open to what God holds in store for the future. It is typological in its look at Israel's past.

Rabbi David Kimchi, also known by the acronym RaDaK, prefaced his thirteenth-century commentary on Chronicles with an affirmation that "this book is a historical account" (Berger 2007: 26). This basic understanding remains consistent throughout the early Christian interpretive tradition. The first full-fledged Christian commentary, written by Bishop Theodoret of Cyrus in the fifth century, begins: "What the royal scribe [the redactor of Samuel and Kings] omitted, the author who took up this specific task set down, using as sources many of the books of prophecy. Much of what was written in those books he harmonized with these events [in 1–2 Chronicles], so that he might demonstrate historical consistency" (quoted from Knoppers and Harvey 2002: 234).

This recognition about Chronicles was made early in the Christian interpretive tradition. In the preface to his translation of Samuel and Kings, Jerome called it "a chronicle of all divine history" (Klein 2006: 1). For the Chronicler, human history is divine history: in human events we see signs of divine purpose; history is salvation history. History in Chronicles is a kind of dialogic and filial encounter between the Creator and his creation and especially his chosen "firstborn," the children of Israel.

Chronicles, quite simply, begs to be read as it is written—as the history of a people. "Now the records are ancient," the Chronicler tells us (1 Chr. 4:22), and his work includes a wide variety of these records—straight historical narratives, official correspondence, legislation and legislative history, private prayers and ritual practices, speeches, homilies, poetry, prophecies, and genealogies. This is the stuff, the raw data of human remembrance, and the Chronicler uses it all to preserve for us a rich historical record. Chronicles is a family history, with Israel understood to be a family of families—fathers and mothers, sons and daughters, uncles and aunts, and cousins and distant relations, all tied by blood and bound by divine-human covenant in a special kinship with God.

Chronicles is also the history of a people that understands itself to be God's agent in the world, the chosen vessel of the Almighty for bringing about his divine purposes for creation. It is an account of God's revelation of himself in the history of his people, a history in which the human and the divine are intertwined. One of the author's chief aims is to make the case that God is still in charge, that his divine purposes are still unfolding in the lives of his people—despite the catastrophe of the exile and the hesitant and anticlimactic beginnings of the restoration. A prayer of David preserved by the Chronicler could serve as a summary of his authorial purposes in this book: "O LORD, the God of Abraham, Isaac, and Israel, our fathers, keep for ever such purposes and thoughts in the hearts of thy people, and direct their hearts toward thee" (1 Chr. 29:18).

The Chronicler's homiletic intent is to remind the people of God's plan and to align their hearts more faithfully to that plan. Thus the Chronicler does not write only a historical account. He also sets out to interpret events in light of what later Christian interpreters call the *oikonomia*, the divine economy through which God works out his saving purposes.

Chronicles tells Israel's history backward, from the perspective of the end, the *qēṣ*, the zenith of history foretold by the prophets. Then the people will be definitively restored from exile and the kingdom of David will finally be established by God's Anointed One, the Messiah, who will rebuild the temple at Zion to be the font for the blessings that God wants to pour out upon the families of the world from the beginning of time.

In the Chronicler's prophetic historiography we see what Daniélou notices in the Old Testament prophets—a profoundly "typological interpretation of history," in which the basis of present hope and the vision for the future is based upon a deep reading of God's patterns of dealing with his covenant people in the past (1960: 157). For the Chronicler, the key to history is the kingdom of David, established by divine covenant and embodied in the temple at Zion and its liturgy. As the rise of this liturgical empire in the past triggered blessings for God's chosen people and for the world, so its future restoration will bring to fulfillment God's plan for history.

# 1 Chronicles

# 1

## Chronicle of All Divine History

*A Genealogy of Grace in a Time of Exile and Restoration
(1 Chr. 1–9)*

**Major Divisions of the Text**

1. Line of descent from Adam to Israel (1:1–2:2)
2. Tribes of Israel: Royal line of Judah (2:3–4:23)
   Royal family of David (3:1–24)
3. Tribes of Israel: Simeon (4:24–43)
4. Tribes of Israel: Transjordanian tribes (5:1–26)
   Reuben (5:1–10)
   Gad (5:11–22)
   Half-tribe of Manasseh (5:23–26)
5. Tribes of Israel: Priestly line of Levi (6:1–81)
   High-priestly line of Aaron (6:1–15)
   Genealogy of the Levites (6:16–30)
   Genealogy of the Levitical musicians (6:31–48)
   Duties of the Aaronic high priests (6:49–53)
   Settlements of the Levites (6:54–81)
6. Tribes of Israel: West Jordan tribes (7:1–40)
   Issachar (7:1–5)
   Benjamin (7:6–12a)
   Dan (7:12b)
   Naphtali (7:13)
   Half-tribe of Manasseh (7:14–19)

## Synopsis of the Text

The Chronicler begins his work with a long list of the ancestry of Israel, which he traces back to Adam, considered by Israel's scriptural tradition to be the primordial human. The listing is deceptively simple and initially may not make for compelling reading. Closer scrutiny, however, reveals that this genealogical prologue contains a wealth of insights into the Chronicler's motives and concerns. In these initial lists we see the Chronicler's covenantal understanding of history as he traces Israel's heritage through individuals who spoke with God and entered into covenant with him—Adam, Noah, Abraham, and finally David. As a work of historical memory, the genealogies focus attention on the royal tribe of Judah and the priestly tribe of Levi, while establishing Jerusalem and the temple as the geographical and cultic locus of concern. Israel's national history is outlined from the creation of the world, focusing on the divine oath sworn to Abraham and its progressive fulfillment: first in Israel's establishment as a nation in the exodus and later as an imperial kingdom under David and his son Solomon. These initial genealogies extend into the present for the Chronicler's first audience, tracing the lines of descent through the division and eventual collapse of the kingdom, the people's exile, and the beginnings of their restoration in Jerusalem.

## Theological Exegesis and Commentary

### The Genesis of Election and Mission

In the Aramaic paraphrase, the Targum on Chronicles, the work is titled "the book of the genealogies, the Chronicles from earliest times." In the Babylonian Talmud it is also called "the book of the genealogies" (*Pesaḥim* 62b).

The genealogies that begin Chronicles distinguish the work both within the Bible and among historical writings in the wider Mediterranean world. By some scholarly estimates, genealogies and other lists make up roughly one-quarter of the Chronicler's work (Knoppers 2004: 1.251–52).

These genealogies are integral to the Chronicler's intentions, functioning as a kind of overture to the work, sounding the author's worldview and intentions and establishing narrative patterns that will continue throughout—law, liturgy, covenant, kingdom, temple, sin, and redemption—all set in the context of an understanding of Israel as the firstborn among the nations, with a divinely given royal and priestly mission to the other nations of the world.

The genealogies culminate in the experience of exile and return, a seventy-year period expressed with the Chronicler's characteristically compact understatement: "And Judah was taken into exile in Babylon because of their unfaithfulness. Now the first to dwell again in their possessions in their cities were Israel, the priests, the Levites, and the temple servants" (1 Chr. 9:1–2).

As the exile and return mark the culmination of the Chronicler's genealogies, they also mark the culmination of his entire work. In the poignant expression "to dwell again" is expressed all of the Chronicler's hope. This hope is both historical and eschatological. For the Chronicler and for his readers, "to dwell again" evokes the hope of rebuilding the temple, reestablishing the liturgy of Jerusalem, and restoring the everlasting dynasty of David as promised by God.

It is impossible to date with specificity when Chronicles was written, and I am not sure that hypothetical reconstructions help us much in interpreting the text. The canonical text, read in a way that respects what Frei calls the "history-like" quality of the biblical narrative (1974: 14), gives us perhaps our best insights. Reading the text on its own terms, we have a history of Israel from the beginning of the world to the decree of King Cyrus of Persia. It seems reasonable to presume that the author writes in the early postexilic period, perhaps within a generation of Cyrus's decree and the beginnings of the restoration from exile. Interpreting the author on his own terms, we can presume that he writes with the purpose of persuading the people both in Jerusalem and in the Diaspora that the return from exile is the work of God and that this is how the promised kingdom of David will be restored.

The Chronicler draws on "the book of the generations" (Hebrew *sēper tôlĕdōt*, Greek *hē biblos geneseōs*) found in Gen. 5 and the listing of "the generations of the sons of Noah" in Gen. 10. These sources are themselves intriguing and unique among the genealogical literature of the ancient world. While other peoples were intensely interested in the lines of descent of their kings, heroes, and even gods, no other people in antiquity can be found attempting to compile a genealogical record of the entire human race. This is a key to understanding Israel's national and ethnic self-consciousness as well as the intentions of the Chronicler.

The genealogies reflect a familial vision of the human race. The Chronicler's genealogies, like those of Genesis, reveal Israel's solidarity with the entire human family. They also reflect Israel's deep sense of its own "election" (*bāḥar*), of its being a people set apart, specially chosen by God to be his "firstborn" (*bĕkôr*) among the peoples of the world (Exod. 4:22). Israel's identity is totally shaped by this awareness of its primogeniture among the nations, a kinship with God established by God's own "covenant" (*bĕrît*). This covenant was the source of life, law, and liturgy for Israel (Hahn 2009b: 1–31). The anchor was Israel's establishment as God's firstborn. This divine sonship was the seed from which Israel's twofold royal and priestly vocation to the world grew, reaching full flower in the kingdom of David, which is established by a "covenant of salt"—a new and everlasting covenant (2 Chr. 13:5; 21:7).

The Chronicler's genealogical consciousness is a part of this covenantal worldview, in which Israel experiences itself as the one people out of all the peoples of the earth to have been chosen by God to be his own possession, a holy people (Deut. 7:6–7; 10:15; 14:2; cf. Exod. 19:6). His genealogy reflects what others have detected: covenant provides the narrative framework for the story of Israel told in the Bible. Beginning with Adam and the covenant of creation, his genealogy follows the path of God's covenant through Noah, Abraham, Israel, and David. The purposes of God's covenant—the blessing of the world—are gradually unfolded in the biblical narrative and are centered in the history of his firstborn.

Israel's sense of chosenness, though badly shaken by the national traumas of the divided kingdom and later the sack of Jerusalem and the exile to Babylon, nonetheless persisted. It was the backbone of the faith of the Chronicler's audience, the people who have returned to the land and begun to rebuild the temple. The prophets of the exile leaned heavily on the promise of God's covenant, and they taught the people to hope for the same. Isaiah taught them to look for the day when God will "again choose Israel, and will set them in their own land, and aliens will join them and will cleave to the house of Jacob" (Isa. 14:1). This promise of an internationalized Israel will prove to be important to the Chronicler. The importance of Israel's awareness of its special relationship with God is well expressed by the prophet Jeremiah: "Thus says the LORD: If I have not established my covenant with day and night and the ordinances of heaven and earth, then I will reject the descendants of Jacob and David my servant and will not choose one of his descendants to rule over the seed of Abraham, Isaac, and Jacob. For I will restore their fortunes, and will have mercy upon them" (Jer. 33:25–26; cf. 31:35–36).

In Chronicles the notion of election is subtle but unmistakable. The Chronicler nowhere speaks of Israel as "chosen" or "elected," but he does depict the fulfillment of Israel's election in David's kingdom and the cult of the temple. God "chooses" (*bḥr*) David to be king (1 Chr. 28:4), Jerusalem to be the center of his kingdom (2 Chr. 12:13) and the site of his temple (7:12, 16; 33:7), and the Levites to be his priests (1 Chr. 15:2). A consciousness of election pervades the text. Throughout, God calls Israel "my people," frequently in contexts where he is recalling his faithfulness to his covenant (1 Chr. 11:2; 17:6–7, 9–10; 2 Chr. 6:5–6; 7:13–14). At the climactic moment of the Davidic covenant, King David responds with a prayer of gratitude and wonder: "What other nation on earth is like thy people Israel? . . . Thou didst make thy people Israel to be thy people for ever; and thou, O Lord, didst become their God" (1 Chr. 17:21–22).

By his initial genealogy, the Chronicler establishes that Israel's election "was implicit already in Adam," according to Williamson (1982: 41). Von Rad observes that the Chronicler "portrays history from Adam onwards as taking place all for [Israel's] own sake" (1962–65: 1.347). Here we touch on a related strain of thought that is critical for appreciating the Chronicler's biblical worldview—Israel's belief that the world was created *for* Israel, to provide a sacred space for its special covenant relationship with God.

This is already implied in the quotation from Jeremiah. God's covenant with Israel is associated with his primordial covenant in the creation of heaven and earth (Jer. 31:35–36; 33:25–26; cf. 2 Chr. 6:14). This sensibility becomes more explicit in later Judaism. "He created the world on behalf of his people," according to the first-century AD *Testament of Moses* 1.12–13 (cf. 12.4). Closer to the Chronicler's concern is the exilic lament registered in *4 Ezra* 6.55–59, written in the late first century:

> It was for us that you created this world. As for the other nations which have descended from Adam, you have said that they are nothing. . . . And now, O Lord, behold, these nations . . . domineer over us and devour us. But we your people, whom you have called your firstborn, only begotten, zealous for you, and most dear, have been given into their hands. If the world has indeed been created for us, why do we not possess our world as an inheritance? How long will this be so?

These anguished questions lie behind the words of Chronicles, as the Chronicler seeks to address the quite similar concerns of his initial audience, those who have returned from exile to a shattered land and a temple in ruins. What can election mean when the elected people remain scattered throughout the world, living under foreign domination? What can it mean when there is no son of David on the throne of Israel? These are the anxious concerns of the Chronicler's audience in a period of grave uncertainty, at a time when Israel has returned from its exile among the domineering and devouring nations to reclaim a now rather dubious looking inheritance. Yet the Chronicler responds with a calm, quiet confidence that some commentators have mistaken for quietism or indifference.

The Chronicler starts with a different set of questions: Why was Israel elected? To ask that question is to beg a series of bigger, prior questions: What did God have in mind? What was his purpose? What was his plan? Where does Israel fit into it? He begins by directing his readers' attention to the foundation of the world, to the first man, Adam. In this, he is reminding Israel that its national destiny cannot be separated from the destiny of the world. To put it another way, God's purposes for the world depend on Israel. This point is worth underlining here at the start of our study.

Chronicles is a fiercely nationalist document. It tells the tale of a proud nation. But we cannot forget that it is also a work that reflects a broadly internationalist, even cosmic outlook. From the initial genealogies, Israel's gaze is being directed outward, *ad gentes* (to the nations). Israel is asked to understand itself in light of the world's beginnings and in light of the history of the world's peoples.

The few lines of commentary interspersed among the otherwise unembellished listing of names in these early chapters reinforce this universalist, internationalistic perspective. The first of these comments regards Nimrod, who "began to be a mighty one [*gibbôr*] on the earth" (1 Chr. 1:10). The second refers to Peleg, whose name symbolizes that "in his days the earth was divided" (1:19). The next people the Chronicler describes are "the kings who reigned in the land of Edom before any king reigned over the Israelites" (1:43).

In these narrative asides, the Chronicler signals three notes that will recur in his book: *monarchy* in Israel and its place among the wider community of nations; *division*, which characterizes the effects of covenant unfaithfulness in Chronicles and leads to the kingdom's demise; and *foreign domination* (*gibbôr* can mean "tyrant" or "despot"), which will be the fate of the people under the divided kingdom. There may even be, as Johnstone suggests, a subtle allusion to the Babylonian captivity in the reference to Nimrod. In Gen. 10:10 he is "identified with Babylon . . . and thus with the power that is ultimately to be responsible for the downfall of Israel" (1997: 1.30–31). This interpretation would be in line with the Targum on 1 Chr. 1:10, which associates Nimrod with Babylon and calls him "a mighty man in sin, shedding innocent blood and a rebel before the Lord" (McIvor 1994: 38n3).

We might also pause for a moment longer over the Chronicler's introduction of a long list of foreign kings in his genealogy (1:43–51). For the most part, he has simply inserted the list from his source material in Gen. 36, with the apparent purpose of reporting that there were kings in the land before David came to the throne in Israel. In the context of his genealogy and later work, the eightfold use of the word "died" is striking. Do we have here a subtle commentary on the kingdoms of the nations—that they are destined to die, while the covenant kingdom of David, which will become the focus of the Chronicler's work, is promised to rule forever? It is at least a suggestive juxtaposition that the listing of the kings and chiefs of Edom immediately precedes the introduction of "the sons of Israel" (1 Chr. 2:1).

### The Liturgical Destiny of History

In drawing from the Table of Nations in Gen. 10:1–29, the Chronicler sets his work in a global context. As in Genesis, the seventy sons of Noah that he lists are meant to symbolize all the nations of the world and to illustrate their filial relationship to a common father, Adam (Knoppers 2004: 1.273; Johnson 1969: 232). This gives a familial cast to the story that the Chronicler is about to tell. David, Solomon, and others in Chronicles frequently invoke "the God of our fathers" or the "God of Abraham, Isaac, and Israel, our fathers" (1 Chr. 29:18).[1] Chronicles is biblical history as family history, the story of humanity as a single family, a family of families with a common father, Adam.

At the center of this family of nations is the tribal family of Israel. In these introductory genealogies, the Chronicler is making a statement about his ultimate concerns and intentions. Klein observes: "This is a history of all days, a universal history, beginning with Adam and extending to Israel. . . . The chapter [1 Chr. 1] implies the diversity *and* the unity of the world and it suggests that Israel understood its role within the family of nations and as a witness to all humanity" (2006: 81).

If Israel understands itself as the key player in God's plan for the world, it is initially puzzling that God himself is not introduced by name until the fifty-seventh verse (1 Chr. 2:3). The Chronicler apparently presumes his readers' knowledge of scripture's testimony that the descent of the nations from Adam is steered by God's fatherly hand and purposes.

The question will still remain: What is God's plan all about, and what are his divine purposes in creation? The Chronicler, as a biblical theologian, is working with a story told in Israel's canon of scripture. This story has been honed in the period of exile among the prophets, and it shaped the writing down of Israel's history in the books of the Pentateuch. In these writings a simple summary answer emerges: the world was made to be the space for God's covenant with his people, for human worship and God's bestowing of his divine blessings on his children. Israel's mission is to bear witness to that truth and to lead the rest of the world's families to serve and worship the living God and receive his blessings.

This basic set of beliefs and assumptions underlies what most commentators identify as the unique perspective of the Chronicler—his focus on worship, sacrifice, prayer, and the priesthood; and his preoccupation with the ark, temple, and liturgical assembly of all Israel, the *qāhāl*. The Chronicler indeed presents us with a utopia. It is not an ideal political economy or kingdom, but a liturgical empire, a multinational kingdom ordered to offer sacrifice and praise to the living God.

That is why the Chronicler begins with the name "Adam" (*'ādām*). Adam is far more than the first name in a list, more even than the founding genetic

---

1. Such expressions are used some thirty times throughout the work; see Allen 2003.

father of the human family. Especially in the genealogies, the Chronicler presumes that his audience knows scripture and the stories of Israel's past. Thus, as Johnstone says, the Chronicler is able to write in "a kind of shorthand: the allusion to a name is enough to conjure up incidents in the earlier works in which the individual is involved" (1997: 1.11, 25).

In beginning with the name "Adam," the Chronicler conjures up all that Adam had come to symbolize in the Jewish imagination. There was no unified or consistent Adam myth during the period in which the Chronicler was writing. Nonetheless, surveying a wide swath of evidence from the Second Temple era, Marcus rightly concludes that there was considerable and fertile interest in "the biblical figure of the primordial man" (2003: 51). Adam was considered to be the archetype and prototype of the human person, the icon in which we glimpse God's purposes and expectations for humanity.

These Second Temple traditions concerning Adam and creation help illuminate the Chronicler's understanding of Israel's vocation to the nations as well as his treatment of David, temple, and kingdom. Beginning within the canon and intensifying in the extrabiblical tradition, Adam is understood in terms that elsewhere are applied only to Israel and Israel's monarch—as the firstborn son of God, as a priest, and as a king. Not coincidentally, these become key categories in the Chronicler's account of Israel's history and mission.

The Chronicler would have been familiar with the deep "liturgical flavor" (Levenson 1988: 58) and motivation in the creation accounts. Westermann and others identify in Gen. 1 a solemn, rhythmical pattern of repetitions and a precise structure of sevens and multiples of sevens, beginning in the first verse, which is precisely seven words long, preceding through seven divine declarations ("Let there be . . ."), and concluding with the Sabbath of the seventh day. What these patterns indicate is that the biblical account is narrating a kind of cosmic covenant liturgy (citations and analysis in Hahn 2005d: 106n12).

As in his account of the building of the temple, the author was not unique among biblical writers in being deeply impressed by the Genesis account of the universe being created as a kind of cosmic temple-palace, with the garden of Eden as a sort of holy of holies. In the temple of creation, Adam is pictured as having been created as the firstborn son of God and as a king and royal high priest of creation—created to be on earth as the living image of God, the sign of the Creator's lordship over all the earth (von Rad 1961: 60). The language of the *imago Dei* ("the image of God"; Hebrew ṣelem ʾĕlōhîm) is royal and filial language. In Wis. 10:1, Adam is described as "the first-formed father of the world," much as the later rabbis described him as the "firstborn of the world" (*Numbers Rabbah* 4.8; in Marcus 2003: 54n69).

The Gospel of Luke's genealogy gives a fine interpretive summary of the biblical record when it asserts that Adam is "the son of God" (3:38). This conclusion flows naturally from a close reading of the biblical text. As God created Adam in his image (Gen. 1:26–28), Adam begets Seth "in his likeness, after his image" (5:3). And God the Father's blessing Adam establishes a pattern of paternal blessing (9:26; 27:27; 48:15; 49:28) that runs through Genesis and parallels the frequent reiteration of God's own blessings (1:28; 5:2; 9:1; 12:3; 24:1).

As the son of God and the image of God, Adam is the king of creation or the earthly vice-regent of the heavenly king (Clines 1998: 488–93). He is given royal prerogatives and a mandate to rule: "Be fruitful and multiply, and fill the earth and subdue it; and have dominion over . . . the earth" (Gen. 1:28; cf. 1:26; Batto 2004: 179). This royal understanding of Adam's vocation is found throughout the Old Testament and can be traced through intertestamental and rabbinic sources (numerous sources cited in Marcus 2003: 53, 59n82). For instance, in Ps. 8 we have what amounts to an inner-biblical exegesis of Gen. 1:26–28. "The son of man [*'ādām*]" is described as "made . . . little less than God" and is "crown[ed] . . . with glory" and "given . . . dominion" over all God's "works."

In the Jewish tradition, Adam is also understood in priestly terms. Wenham observes: "If Eden is seen as an ideal sanctuary, then perhaps Adam should be described as an archetypal Levite" (1986: 21). The Chronicler will depict the task of the Levitical priesthood in the same language used to describe the mandate given to Adam in creation. As Adam was "put . . . in the garden of Eden to till [*'ābad*] and keep [*šāmar*] it" (Gen. 2:15), the priests "keep charge" (*šāmar*) of the "service" (*'ābad*) of the house of God. The Levitical priests are described as "guardians" (*šōměrîm*) of the temple (1 Chr. 9:19; 23:32). In this the Chronicler is following an Old Testament pattern of usage. When *'ābad* and *šāmar* appear in the same context, they are usually translated "serve and guard [or keep]"; more often than not, the reference is to liturgical service in the temple or tabernacle (Num. 3:7–8; 8:26; 18:5–6; Ezek. 44:14; discussion in Beale 2004: 66–70).

Again, what is implicit in the ancient tradition is stated as a matter of course in the later tradition. Thus the Targums and midrashim presume that Adam was created on the site where Israel's temple would be built, even created with "dust from the site of the sanctuary" (*Targum Pseudo-Jonathan* on Gen. 2:7; 3:23; citations in Beale 2004: 67n90). A midrash on Genesis describes Adam as offering sacrifices (*Genesis Rabbah* 16.5), and later texts describe Adam as a priest in the temple (2 *Baruch* 4.3; *Jubilees* 3.27; Beale 2004: 77–78). But this interpretive tradition begins already within the pages of scripture.

In the prophet Ezekiel's oracles against the prince of Tyre, these themes are brought together powerfully, as the prophecy takes the form of an allegory of the creation and fall of the first man in Eden. The prince is called "the signet of perfection," a symbol elsewhere associated with royal likeness and authority (Ezek. 28:12; Gen. 41:42; Jer. 22:24–25; Hahn 2005d: 108; Batto 2004: 162–63). He is also described in images that evoke Israel's high priest. His breastplate is adorned with the same precious stones found in Havilah, one of the lands watered by the river of Eden (Ezek. 28:13; Exod. 28:17–20; Gen. 2:12; for a thorough review of the ancient sources, see Beale 2004: 67–70). According to Callender, Ezekiel is drawing from a tradition that "understands the primal human in priestly terms, or, perhaps better put, in 'intermediary' terms. The imagery he employs is consonant with that of the sacral king, endowed for service as vice-regent of God and mediator between human and divine" (2000: 29).

All of this tradition sets us up to understand the Chronicler's preoccupations. The Chronicler too is informed by this tradition of Adam as "the archetypal priest-king in the primal paradise-garden" (J. Davies 2004: 202). The Chronicler's understanding of Israel and the Davidic kingdom is expressed in terms that evoke this Adamic tradition. Indeed, already in his genealogy of Israel, he narrows his focus to two lines—the royal line of Judah and the priestly line of Levi.

For the Chronicler, Israel is the heir to the mission given to Adam, called to be a holy firstborn son of God among the nations, a royal and priestly people who fill all the earth with the divine blessings. Indeed, the Chronicler's biblical theology is rooted in this understanding of an Adamic vocation. Johnstone describes the Chronicler's project this way:

> Chronicles is a theological work: it is concerned with the universal relationship between God and humanity, and the vocation of Israel within that relationship. . . . The human race was created in Adam for fellowship with God but the history of that relationship has, from the beginning, been marked by false starts and unsuccessful restarts. . . . Israel takes its place with its vocation to become what all else had hitherto failed to become, a people dedicated to God and the agent of the restoration of the relationship between God and humanity. . . . The question with which the Chronicler's whole work is concerned is the relation between God and his human creation, the recognition of God's dominion on earth. The ideal lost under Adam is to be recovered, after several false starts, through Israel. (1997: 1.10, 12, 38)

Israel's vocation is seen in its ideal form in the kingdom of David and in his son Solomon. And in the Chronicler's portrait of the Davidic kingdom, we see the intended destiny of the human family, the reason for creation. He envisions a liturgical destiny for the human family, as all men and women come to worship the God of Israel at the temple in Jerusalem. What the Chronicler sees is hinted at in the beautiful psalm that David composes to be sung by Asaph (1 Chr. 16:8–36).

This psalm is a call to worship and praise issued to the nations, to all the "families of the peoples," and indeed to all creation—the sea, the sky, and the earth. In singing God's faithfulness to his covenant with Abraham, God will bless the nations. And for "his marvelous works among all the peoples," the nations will give him glory. The Chronicler's sense that Israel, and humankind in general, was made to give thanks and praise to God for the wonders of creation is already anticipated in the Chronicler's genealogy—which begins with the creation of Adam and concludes with the beginnings of renewed worship in the temple. Selman observes that the Chronicler also ends his work with the call to rebuild the temple, suggesting that this rebuilding is somehow a fulfillment of God's intentions with Adam:

> These two passages [the beginning and the end of the genealogies] bring together the creation of the human race in Adam and the restoration of Temple worship, a connection that also applies to the beginning and end of the book. In other words, the genealogies and outer framework of the book demonstrate that the rebuilt Temple represented in some way the continuation or restoration of the work that God had begun in creating Adam. The Temple could therefore be no optional extra, but was a central element in God's intentions for Israel and for humanity itself. (1994a: 39)

### The God of Our Fathers

The trajectory of the Chronicler's genealogy moves from Adam to Israel, from the temple of creation to the temple at Jerusalem. At the outset of his work, he is tracing bloodlines, but also lines of election and mission. Israel does not appear until thirty-four verses into the book. There is a certain humility in this. Israel is not portrayed as the first among nations; it is just one among many, with the seventy or seventy-two nations listed in 1 Chr. 1:5–23 symbolizing all the known peoples of the world.

In this, however, we also have an expression of one of the Chronicler's key underlying themes—God's providential guidance of history. If Israel is his firstborn, as God told Moses (Exod. 4:22), this is not a statement of historical or anthropological fact but of divine election. God determines history and destinies in the Chronicler's worldview. And during the course of his narrative, this obscure people, born amid the family of nations, will be made the center of a worldwide kingdom of God, with all the kings of the earth desiring to make pilgrimage to its temple (2 Chr. 9:23).

In the genealogical introduction, we detect a deliberate, divinely guided narrowing of the channels as history moves from its beginnings to the concerns of the Chronicler's moment, the age of exile and restoration. In his first verses, the author takes us from the first man and father of all the earth's families, Adam, to Noah, a kind of new Adam, in whom humanity was reborn after the great flood. One of Noah's sons, Shem, becomes the focus of the Chronicler's portrait of the postdiluvian era; the pathway of election winds its way through Shem's descendant, Eber, from whom the Hebrew people take their name, before coming to rest—ten generations after Noah and twenty after Adam—in "Abram, that is, Abraham" (1 Chr. 1:27).

In that slight turn of phrase, "Abram, that is, Abraham" lies all the mystery of Israel's election and its covenant relationship with God. We need to keep in mind, especially in these early genealogies, the principle identified earlier in discussing the figure of Adam, a principle well described by Ackroyd: "Often we may observe that [the Chronicler] assumes that his readers know the story being told, or that they know the form in which the story existed in the older presentations; by an allusion, by a brief summary, by a comment, he invites a particular kind of understanding, pointing in the direction of a particular moral or theological insight" (1991: 276). In this case, "Abram, that is, Abraham" is a kind of historical-theological shorthand meant to evoke the moment when God made his covenant with Abram and gave him a new name: "No longer shall your name be Abram, but your name shall be Abraham; for I have made you the father of a multitude of nations" (Gen. 17:5).

But the Chronicler is doing more than looking back into the mists of time. Like Adam—and indeed his story is integrally related to Adam's—the story of Abraham helps makes sense of Israel's present. The Chronicler is quite aware of Abraham as the founding father of Israel and as essential to the people's identity and self-understanding of its mission. Late in his book, he will recount the prayer of King Jehosaphat, in which "thy people Israel" is parallel to "the descendants of Abraham, thy friend" (2 Chr. 20:7).

In the familiar story of Israel's beginnings assumed by the Chronicler, Abraham appears after the great sin and scattering of the world's peoples at the Tower of Babel. His role in salvation history is well expressed in a rabbinic dictum: "I will make Adam first, and if he goes astray I will send Abraham to sort it all out" (*Genesis Rabbah* 14.6). Starting in the pages of Genesis, Jewish tradition has understood that it is "Abraham's task to restore what Adam has done," Wells writes (2000: 187). Abraham, like Noah before him, is a new Adam. In him humanity is given another chance to extract itself from chaos and failure and to live in the presence of God. Abraham hears and obeys God's call where Adam would not, where the peoples at Babel would not. Called to go out from his "father's house" (Gen. 12:1), Abraham is to father a chosen people, who will build a "house" for the Father of heaven and earth, a temple that will serve as a house of God and a house of prayer for all peoples.

Again, in his spare, minimalist genealogy, the Chronicler is summoning deep traditions and historical associations. There is a continuity in the national-family story that the Chronicler is retelling. To say that Abraham is a new-Adam figure is not to reduce him to the status of a literary sign or metaphor. It is to say that with Abraham, God's purposes in creation are restated and amplified. The theme of divine blessing, present in the commission to Adam, comes to the fore in Abraham. God's desire and work is described as one of blessing his people. And this work of blessing is to proceed through Abraham and his children. "But henceforth you shall confer blessings," *Midrash Tanḥuma-Yelammedenu* 84 says of Abraham.

Throughout the canonical narrative with which the Chronicler is working, the words of God's original blessing and commission of Adam are a constant refrain (Gen. 1:26–28). These words form the foundation for the covenant relationship that God establishes with Abraham and his descendants. The covenant with Abraham is threefold and is built on the three promises that God makes to Abraham in their initial encounter—to make him a great nation, to give him a great name, and to make him the source of blessing for all the world (12:1–3). God later upgrades each of these promises by making a covenant with Abraham.

As a result of this covenant, not only will Abraham be a great nation; his descendants are also promised to be delivered from oppression and to be given a new land and possession of "the gate of their enemies" (Gen. 15:7–21; 22:17). Not only will Abraham's name be great, but he will also become "the father of a multitude of nations" and of a royal dynastic line: "Kings shall come forth from you" (17:1–8). God will "multiply" Abraham's descendants, until they are as many as "the stars of heaven and as the sand which is on the seashore." And by Abraham's "descendants shall all the nations of the earth bless themselves" (22:16–18).

These covenant oaths form the narrative structure for the salvation history told in the Pentateuch. And as Jewish tradition has recognized, these covenant promises mark the extension of the Adamic mandate to be fruitful and multiply and to fill and rule over the earth. The language and intention of the Adamic mandate and the Abrahamic commission are strikingly similar. God blesses Abraham as he did Adam. He promises to multiply Abraham's seed past all counting—as Adam was called to be fruitful, multiply, and fill the earth. As Adam was given the command to subdue and rule over the earth, Abraham's descendants are to possess and rule the land and to bring God's blessings to the families of the earth.

We can trace this same language in God's revelations and instructions to the patriarchs descended from Abraham. God appears to Abraham's son, Isaac, and promises to bless and multiply him and to give him the land (Gen. 26:3–5, 23–24). Isaac in turn blesses his son, Jacob, with these same words of promise (28:1, 3). Later God appears to Isaac and affirms that his descendants "shall be like the dust of the earth, and you shall spread abroad to the west and to the east and to the north and to the south; and by you and your descendants shall all the families of the earth bless themselves" (28:12–15). "Thus at major turning points in the story . . . the narrative quietly insists that Abraham and his progeny inherit the role of Adam and Eve," N. Wright observes (1992: 263).

What most commentators miss, however, is the centrality of cult, liturgy, and sacrifice in this role inherited from Adam. As Abraham's descendants explicitly inherit Adam's "kingship" over creation, the scriptural narrative is also quietly insistent that they assume Adam's "priestly" mantle as well. Beale is among the few who notice that in the patriarchal narratives "the Adamic commission is repeated in direct connection with what looks to be the building of small sanctuaries" (2004: 96; e.g., Gen. 26:25; 28:18). This can be seen most vividly in the account of the establishment of the sanctuary at Bethel:

> And God said to him, ". . . No longer shall your name be called Jacob, but Israel shall be your name." So his name was called Israel. And God said to him, "I am God Almighty: be fruitful and multiply; a nation and a company of nations shall come from you, and kings shall spring from you. The land that I gave to Abraham and Isaac I will give to you, and I will give the land to your descendants after you." Then God went up from him in the place where he had spoken with him. And Jacob set up a pillar in the place where he had spoken with him, a pillar of stone; and he poured out a drink offering on it, and poured oil on it. So Jacob called the place where God had spoken with him, Bethel. (35:10–15)

Again in this passage we hear the words of the Adamic commission—the promises of fertility, possession of the land, and kingship. But we notice something more. Israel's response to his encounter with God is liturgical and sacrificial. He erects a "pillar"—elsewhere a symbol of the divine presence and even of "God's house" (28:22)—and makes a sacrificial offering to God. This pattern can be detected throughout the patriarchal narratives. The response to the vision of God leads Abraham and his descendants to establish primitive altars or sanctuaries and to offer sacrifices, cultic work later associated only with Israel's priests (Pagolu 1998).

Later Jewish tradition saw these altars and pillars built by Abraham, Isaac, and Jacob as prefigurements of the future temple at Jerusalem. Some of these sources claimed that the patriarchs were granted visions of Solomon's temple, while others claimed that the temple was literally built on the site of these ancient patriarchal shrines (sources cited in Beale 2004: 99n36). Here two points are important for our efforts to enter into the Chronicler's worldview. First, the commission of Abraham and his descendants involves both kingly and priestly prerogatives and responsibilities—to be fruitful and multiply, to be the source of his blessing to the nations, and to offer fitting worship to God. Second, Jewish tradition sees a seamless continuity between the priestly sacrifices offered by the patriarch under the Abrahamic covenant and the later worship of the temple in the kingdom of David.

The Chronicler clearly stands within this understanding of the covenant with Abraham. He describes David's faith that his kingdom fulfills God's promise "to make Israel as many as the stars of heaven" (1 Chr. 27:23; Gen. 22:17; 26:4; Beentjes 2006: 69–70). Even more dramatically, the Chronicler locates the temple as being built on Mount Moriah—the site of the Akedah, Abraham's binding and "offering" of Isaac (2 Chr. 3:1; Gen. 22:2). This detail, found nowhere else in Hebrew scripture, serves to bind the Davidic covenant with the Abrahamic covenant, as well as the worship of the patriarchs with the sacrifices of the temple.

### A Kingdom of Priests and a Holy Nation

Beginning in his genealogy, the Chronicler is subtly insisting on the central-ity of the Abrahamic covenant. This helps explain a distinctive feature of his work that most scholars notice but have a hard time explaining adequately: the Chronicler's supposed lack of concern for the exodus and the covenant with Israel at Sinai. In my opinion, the Chronicler's presumed silence on Sinai and the exodus has been greatly exaggerated by scholars. What E. P. Sanders says about the absence of explicit references to Israel's covenant traditions in later rabbinic writings applies here: "Word studies are not always deceptive, but they can be, and this one is. . . . I venture to say that it is the *fundamental nature of the covenant conception which largely accounts for the relative scarcity of appear-ance of the term 'covenant' in rabbinic literature*" (1977: 420, emphasis added).

Something similar is at work in Chronicles. The exodus and Sinai experience is so fundamental to Israel's self-identity that it hardly needs explicit mention by the Chronicler. Even so, at key moments in the narrative it is punctuated with important references to them. The Chronicler refers twice to the "cov-enant with the people of Israel when they came out of Egypt" (2 Chr. 5:10; 6:11) and also to the Torah as "the book of the covenant" (34:30).

Further, the Chronicler depicts David as a new-Moses figure and describes the kingdom of David and Solomon in terms that make clear the kingdom's dependence on the covenant institutions established at Sinai—the "ark of the covenant of God," the central role of the law, the Levitical priesthood, and the liturgical assembly of the *qāhāl*.

It is surprising, given the Chronicler's emphasis on the royal and priestly character of the Davidic kingdom, that he never once refers to the fundamental terms of Israel's covenant at Sinai—the people's establishment as God's "first-born son," "my own possession among all peoples, . . . a kingdom of priests and a holy nation" (Exod. 4:22; 19:5–6). J. Davies, in his close and fine reading of this covenant language, rightly sees that Israel "at Sinai was constituted as the new humanity, the true successors to Adam" (2004: 202; also Wells 2000: 34–35). From his canonical reading of Exodus, the Chronicler would surely have appreciated that the Sinai covenant is the culmination of God's purposes in creation. N. Wright expresses this fulfillment well:

> Israel's covenantal vocation caused her to think of herself as the Creator's true humanity. If Abraham and his family are understood as the Creator's means of dealing with the sin of Adam, and hence with the evil in the world, Israel herself becomes the true Adamic humanity. . . . Israel is to be the nation of priests (Exod. 19), the people through whom the Creator will bless his creation once more. (1992: 262, 263)

If all this is true, then how do we account for the Chronicler's omission of this pivotal point in the formation of Israel's identity? We could again appeal to Sanders's insight—that the "covenant conception" of Israel as a kingdom of priests is so fundamental that it needs little explicit restatement. Indeed, we could say that the entire work of the Chronicler is a sort of long midrash on Exod. 19:5–6, seen as the fulfillment of God's covenant plan from the beginning. And perhaps the Chronicler feels that at this stage in Israel's history, after the ordeal of the exile, the people need to return to their roots, to understand that long before the exodus and Sinai there was Eden and Moriah. Ackroyd rightly remarks of the Chronicler's downplaying of Sinai:

> The real foundation of God's relationship with his people is rooted much further back, in the Abrahamic covenant, and this itself in the context of the primeval history. God's purpose for his people begins in creation, not at the Exodus. . . . The list of names, so easily read as a mere catalogue, is in fact an assurance of the ultimate origin of the relationship. "Adam, Seth, Enoch"—that is where Israel, the true Israel begins. (1991: 265)

The Chronicler wants his readers to see the inner unity of salvation history—running from Adam to Abraham, to the covenant with Abraham's descendants at Sinai, and finally to Zion and the kingdom of David and his son Solomon, in which salvation history reaches its zenith. In this presentation the Chronicler is not straying far from his scriptural sources. Read in canonical context, Israel's liberation from Egypt is for the sake of God's covenant with Abraham: "And God heard their groaning, and God remembered his covenant with Abraham, with Isaac, and with Jacob" (Exod. 2:24; 6:5; 1 Chr. 16:15–17).

Both the exodus and the Sinai covenant were made with the Abrahamic covenant in view. "At Sinai, the revelation made to Moses is not said to introduce a new covenant, but is presented rather as the fulfillment of the promises made to Abraham," writes Clements (1967: 74–75); "the basic covenant of Israel was that made with Abraham. . . . It is the foundation stone upon which the whole of Israel's religious and national life is built" (Exod. 33:1; Num. 32:11; Deut. 1:8; 9:5; 30:20).

Reading canonically, we hear many echoes of the Adamic-Abrahamic promise and commission in Israel's national story. The people Israel are clearly understood as heirs to the mission of being fruitful and multiplying, of subduing the land and bringing God's blessing to the nations (Exod. 32:13; Lev. 26:9; Deut. 1:10; 7:13; 8:1; 28:63; 30:5, 16). The Chronicler presents the kingdom of David as the fulfillment of Israel's mission—but again for the sake of God's original covenant with Abraham. David himself recognizes this in his great historical psalm: "He is mindful of his covenant for ever, . . . the covenant which he made with Abraham, . . . an everlasting covenant to Israel" (1 Chr. 16:15–17; cf. Ps. 105:8–10).

In the Chronicler's presentation of the covenant with David, we also hear deliberate repetitions and echoes of the exodus narrative. Throughout the

exodus story, God refers to the descendants of Abraham as "my people Israel."
He uses the same language in making his covenant with David, repeating that
the covenant is for "my people Israel" (1 Chr. 17:6, 7, 9, 10; cf. 2 Sam. 7:8, 10,
11; Exod. 3:7, 10; 5:1; 6:7; 7:16; 9:1; Lev. 26:12).

### The True Identity of All Israel

In the Chronicler's portrait, the Davidic kingdom is the ideal image of
the priestly kingdom that God envisioned for Israel, his firstborn, at Sinai,
in remembrance of his covenant with Abraham and the mandate given to
Adam at the beginning of the world. In the persons of the Davidic king and
the Aaronic high priest, God is to rule over and bless his creation and receive
the worship that is his due as Creator.

Although his opening genealogies hint at that glorious reality, they also
serve to set down markers for the authentic identity of Israel as the people
of God. For the Chronicler, the true people of God is one and holy, even
though the kingdom of Israel has long been broken and divided. "So all Israel
was enrolled by genealogies" is how the Chronicler signals that he is wrap-
ping up his genealogical introduction (1 Chr. 9:1). The expression "all Israel"
is repeated throughout Chronicles—especially at key moments such as the
coronations of David and Solomon (11:1; 29:20–22) and the dedication of
the temple (2 Chr. 7:8)—and speaks of the author's ideal, his understanding
that "Israel" means all twelve tribes of Abraham's grandson Jacob, or Israel.
It is another distinctive mark of Chronicles that Israel is never referred to as
Jacob, the name given to him at birth and the name to which he is most often
referred throughout the rest of the Hebrew Bible. For the Chronicler, Jacob
is always Israel, the name given to him by God that announces his role in the
divine economy (Gen. 32:24–30; 35:10).

His invocation of "all Israel" is poignant because the Chronicler's audience
never knew this unity, having grown up in the period after the schism and the
splitting off of the northern tribes. But beginning in his genealogy, in which he
includes mention of all twelve tribes, even the northern tribes, the Chronicler
makes clear that he considers these breakaway tribes to be still a part of Israel.
In the first decisive confrontation between Judah and the northern rebels, the
Chronicler records King Abijah of Judah as affirming that these rebels remain
"sons of Israel" (2 Chr. 13:12). And there does seem to be a kind of apologetic
of reunification going on in the Chronicler's pages, especially in the second
part of the work, which can be read as one long appeal for the northern "sons
of Israel" to repent and return to the covenant worship established by the God
of their fathers at Jerusalem.

The division of the kingdom, while a sad historical fact, is not determinative.
The Chronicler rejects the division of Israel as temporary and contrary to the
will of God. We see this starting in the genealogy and carrying through the

rest of the book. His is not a remnant theology. He intentionally demonstrates to the remnant that has returned and rebuilt the temple that they are part of the larger theological reality that he calls "all Israel" (*kōl yiśrā'ēl*).

Ackroyd makes the fertile suggestion that there is an affinity between the Chronicler's purposes and the purposes of Jonah and other works of the later exile and restoration era. Zechariah, for instance, looked forward to the day when "many nations" would join themselves to Israel's God and be called his people (Zech. 2:11; 8:22–23). Jonah personifies Israel's reluctance to carry out its mission to the surrounding nations. And the Chronicler, perhaps responding to a similar disinclination or even a loss of missionary sensibility altogether, seems to be making the same didactic point as the author of Jonah. Ackroyd puts it:

> Restoration is not for Israel alone, but is related to the wider purposes of God for the nations. . . . The people is restored, as the prophet Jonah is restored, by being brought back to a starting point, the point from which the fulfillment of the divine commission is to be undertaken. Just as the prophet is shown as endeavoring to escape from his true mission, so the people, through historic experience, is brought to a deepened understanding of its mediating role to the nations. (1991: 78)

Closely related to this deepened understanding is the Chronicler's concern to promote a universalistic or internationalistic understanding of Israel's identity. Thus, against tendencies toward ethnic exclusivism in evidence in restoration-era works such as Ezra and Nehemiah, the Chronicler's genealogies show that all Israel—especially Judah—has always been ethnically mixed, not to mention at times ethically mixed up. For instance, while other contemporary works show a strong polemic against intermarriage (Ezra 9:14; 10:2–3; Neh. 10:28–31; 13:23–27), the Chronicler records without comment and hence with tacit approval at least six cases of intermarriage in the genealogy of Judah.

Knoppers notes that in the Chronicler's genealogies the line of Judah includes such non-Israelite groups as Canaanites, Ishmaelites, Arameans, Egyptians, Moabites, Calebites, Midianites, Jerahmeelites, Maacathites, Qenizzites, and Qenites, among others: "By hinting at kinship relationships with other tribes . . . and mixed marriages with other peoples, . . . and by incorporating members of other groups . . . into Judah's lineages, the [Chronicler] presents a Judah that is very much connected with its neighbors. The descendants of the patriarch . . . do not appear as an unadulterated, homogeneous, and internally fixed entity" (2000; also Knoppers 2001; 2003b; Riley 1993: 193; Japhet 1997: 350; 1993: 46; Klein 2006: 46).

Emphasizing these historical and genealogical facts also serves a theological purpose for the Chronicler. It hints that Israel's mission to bless the nations has already begun: sojourners and strangers have already begun identifying

themselves with Israel's God—through intermarriage and through their worship of Israel's God. The implication is that God's people is to be understood,
not as a political, geographic, or ethnic reality, but as a religious or liturgical
one. Israel, the kingdom of God, is a liturgical empire, an empire of prayer.
In this kingdom, life is liturgy, and worship is aimed at the transformation of
the world into a temple of the living God. The Chronicler, according to Tuell,
"reclaims the flow of Israel's ancient narrative, recalling that what made them
a people was not politics, but liturgy" (2001: 207).

### A Covenant of Perpetual Priesthood

The simple architecture of the introductory genealogies establishes this notion of Israel as a liturgical empire. The Chronicler keeps narrowing his lines
of descent until he is building the house of Israel on two pillars—the royal line
of Judah and the priestly line of Levi. The sons of Levi are at the center of the
genealogies—both literally and symbolically. For the Chronicler, the priesthood of the Levites is at the heart of Israel's identity as a priestly kingdom.

Sparks contends that the genealogies are structured in the form of a chias-
mus that pivots on the appointment of the Levites for "all the service of the
tabernacle of the house of God" and on the superiority of the sons of Aaron
as priests (1 Chr. 6:48–53). This chiastic structure signals what Sparks sees as
the Chronicler's central theme: "The Chronicler's purpose is to ensure that
the proper cultic officials are offering the proper cultic offerings in the proper
cultic place, and that the people are supporting the cult so as to maintain its
proper functioning" (2008: 32, 362).

The Chronicler's purposes should not be characterized in such essentially
reductionist or functionalistic terms because the Chronicler has much more
on his mind than the proper organization and working of the liturgical cult.
Nevertheless, I can acknowledge Sparks's finding that in the very literary
structure of his genealogies, the Chronicler is identifying prayer, worship, the
cultic liturgy, and the temple priesthood as central to his concerns and vision.

His Levitical genealogy is long, stretching some twenty-five generations,
from the patriarch Levi to the period of the exile. For the Chronicler's audience, this serves to connect in an unbroken line the priesthood of the newly
built or soon-to-be built second temple with the original Levitical and Aaronic
priesthood. We know from other biblical sources that Joshua son of Jehozadak
was the high priest in the years after the restoration (Ezra 3:2; Hag. 1:1; Zech.
6:9–13). Thus, in ending the high-priestly line with Jehozadak's deportation
to Babylon along with the rest of Jerusalem and Judah, the Chronicler is
establishing the legitimacy of the postexilic temple establishment, as well as
its continuity with the preexilic priesthood.

The Chronicler's focus is on the high-priestly line, which he says twice,
presumably for emphasis (1 Chr. 6:3–15, 50–53). Japhet (1993: 150) and

Williamson (1982: 70–71) here detect a typological rather than a strictly historical pattern of chronology. Exactly twelve generations stretch from the first high priest, Aaron, to Azariah, priest of Solomon's temple. With each generation accounted typologically as forty years long, the genealogy corresponds to the claim that the temple was built 480 years after the exodus (1 Kgs. 6:1). Further, according to this genealogy, the first postexilic high priest, Joshua, would be the twenty-fourth from Aaron, another typological signal of the "divine orderliness" that the Chronicler sees in history (Williamson 1982: 71). Indeed, this pattern prefigures the twenty-four priestly rotations that will serve in the temple (1 Chr. 23–27).

The genealogy of the Levites follows on the heels of the sad tale of the children of the half-tribe of Manasseh, who "transgressed [*māʿal*] against the God of their fathers, . . . played the harlot after the gods of the peoples of the land," and were punished by exile (1 Chr. 5:25). *Māʿal* is a key word in Chronicles to indicate unfaithfulness to the covenant. It is probably no coincidence that, historically speaking, the Levites, and later the high-priestly line of Phineas, were established in the wake of similar episodes of covenant infidelity and "playing the harlot" (Exod. 34:15–16; Num. 25:1) in the period after the exodus and the Sinai covenant.

"The sons of Levi" were the only tribe to remain "on the LORD's side" in the aftermath of the golden-calf apostasy (Exod. 32:25–29). Jewish tradition seems to assume that the people of Israel forfeited its covenant status as "a kingdom of priests" during this episode. In the Babylonian Talmud, Rabbi Simlai says that two crowns had been awarded to each Israelite at Sinai— one the crown of kingship and the other the crown of priesthood. Following the golden-calf affair, each was taken away (*Šabbat* 88a; cited in Smolar and Aberbach 1968: 107n19). Perhaps this tradition explains the question raised earlier as to why the Chronicler passes over the Sinai establishment of Israel's royal and priestly identity.

In the scriptural story that the Chronicler's audience would have known well, the Levites through their faithfulness "ordained themselves" for the liturgical service of Israel (Exod. 32:29). There is much evidence of a pre-Levitical priesthood in Israel: before the Levitical appointment, the firstborn males of Israelite families performed priestly tasks of offering sacrifices and bestowing blessings (sources in Hahn 2009b: 206, 209). After the golden-calf episode, and probably because the Israelite firstborns were involved in the idolatrous worship, these priestly tasks became the exclusive responsibility of the Levites.

The Chronicler also presumes knowledge of the canonical story of "Phinehas the son of Eleazar, son of Aaron the priest." At Baal-peor, in circumstances remarkably similar to that of the Levites and the golden calf, Phinehas earned for himself and his descendants "the covenant of a perpetual priesthood" (Num. 25:11, 13). This covenant has important implications for the Chronicler's understanding of the Davidic kingdom. Phinehas's descendant, Zadok, is anointed as the first high priest in Solomon's temple. The Chronicler, like the prophets Ezekiel and Zechariah, seems keen on establishing the Zadokite line as the only true and authentic heir to the Aaronic high priesthood in the postexilic era (Ezek. 40:46; 43:19; 44:15; Zech. 3).

The Chronicler's vision of Israel as the kingdom of God draws on a deep understanding of the priesthood as the source and model of holiness. In this tradition, as J. Davies notes, the priest "is to serve as a visual model of what ideal humanity is to look like, humankind in their original created dignity and honor in relation to God and the world around them" (2004: 156–57).

### The Scepter Shall Not Depart from Judah

The Chronicler's genealogy also emphasizes the royal prophecy made to the line of Judah, that "the scepter shall not depart from Judah" (Gen. 49:8–12). The Chronicler's genealogy of Judah narrows to focus on the line of David; he thereby establishes David's direct descent from the royal line of Judah, while at the same time he traces David's line into the Chronicler's own day, after the exile (1 Chr. 3:17–24).

But more than biology and bloodlines are at work. Unlike 1 Sam. 16:10–11 and 17:12, where he is said to be Jesse's eighth son, David is here described as "the seventh" (1 Chr. 2:15). The meaning is no doubt theological, associating David with the holy number symbolic of the covenant and the Sabbath of the seventh day, which marked the perfection of God's work of creation. The kingdom and covenant of David "the seventh" thus marks the perfection of God's plans and purposes for Israel and for creation. "All 'sevens' are beloved [by God]. . . . [The seventh] son [is beloved] as it is written, 'And David was the seventh,'" according to *Leviticus Rabbah* 29.9. Yet as surely as David is beloved and his covenant-kingdom marks the completion of God's purposes, his background is far from neat in the Chronicler's telling. A closer look at his genealogy of Judah and David reveals the Chronicler's overturning expectations or rather depicting a God whose covenant purposes defy all human conventions and expectations.

At the beginning of David's ancestral line, we hear how Judah's firstborn son, Er, is slain for an unspecified wickedness (*māʿal*). This is the first reference to "the LORD" in the Chronicler's work, and he is shown as exacting justice in upholding his covenant (1 Chr. 2:3; cf. Gen. 38:7). To Judah are borne three sons by a foreign woman, a Canaanite, and David's direct line stems from Judah's illicit relationship with his daughter-in-law Tamar (Gen. 38; cf. Lev. 18:15; 20:12). The Chronicler is again pressing his theological points—that, against the ethnic exclusivists, even the royal line is not ethnically pure; in this case it contains Canaanite blood. He also seems to emphasize to his readers that God's ways are not our ways, that even out of human weakness and moral failure, God continues to work his purposes.

This seems also to be the point of another unique detail that he introduces in his genealogy—the rather lengthy explanation of Judah's preeminence, despite Judah not being the "firstborn" (*bĕkôr*), but the fourth-born son of Israel. In Israel, as throughout the cultures of the ancient Near East, the firstborn son was privileged and obligated in special ways and within the household had priestly functions of blessing and offering. He also was entitled to his father's blessings and a double portion of his inheritance (Gen. 43:33; 48:5–20; Deut. 21:15–17).

Much of the drama of the chosen people in the book of Genesis plays out against the backdrop of these cultural expectations concerning primogeniture—the firstborn Cain slays his brother, Abel, over sacrifice; Esau, the firstborn, sells his birthright to his younger brother, Jacob; Ishmael and Isaac are at odds; Joseph, the younger son, is sold by his brothers into slavery, only to be reunited in an emotional scene that involves them all sitting at a table according to their birth order (Gen. 43:33).

These instances of fraternal conflict foreshadow God's election of Israel as his "firstborn son" among the nations (Exod. 4:22; cf. Sir. 36:12; Jer. 31:9). Israel's confrontation with Pharaoh reaches its climax in the destruction of Egypt's firstborn sons and the liberation of God's "firstborn" in the exodus. Israel's subsequent covenant, including its covenant liturgy, is marked by numerous provisions for the offering of its firstborn. The firstlings—of flocks, fields, and family—are all to be dedicated to God (Exod. 13:2, 12, 15; 22:29; 34:19; Lev. 27:26; Num. 3:40–51; 18:15, 17). In this we see a recognition that will become important in the Chronicler's understanding of worship—that everything comes from God and that the only fitting way to pay the debt of gratitude we owe to God is through a joyful liturgy of thanksgiving and praise expressed in the sacrificial offering of firstfruits.

In the years of the exile, and based on the covenant promise made to David, Israel began to hope for a Messiah who would be a firstborn son of God. We hear in *Exodus Rabbah* 19.7: "Rabbi Natan said: 'The Holy One, blessed be he, told Moses: "Just as I have made Jacob a firstborn, for it says: Israel is my son, my firstborn, so will I make the King Messiah a firstborn, as it says: I also will appoint him firstborn"' [Ps. 89:27]."

This hope is heard in the Psalter and gives a certain shape to the Chronicler's ideas about David and his mission (Pss. 2:7–8; 89:26–27; cf. 1 Chr. 17:13; 2 Sam. 7:14). And this long tradition of the firstborn lies behind the Chronicler's curious parenthetical remarks on the genealogy of Reuben, the firstborn son of Israel (1 Chr. 5:1–2). The Chronicler goes out of his way to provide an interpretation found nowhere else in the Hebrew Bible for the preeminence of the tribe of the younger Judah and the relative obscurity of Reuben's tribe. In effect, he is offering an interpretation of three events at the end of the patriarch Israel's life: Israel's adoption of Joseph's Egyptian-born sons, Manasseh and Ephraim (Gen. 48), his denunciation of Reuben (49:3–4), and his prediction of an everlasting dynasty for Judah (49:8–12).

As the Chronicler sees it, Reuben lost his birthright because of his sinful intercourse with Israel's concubine (Gen. 35:22), and his birthright was transferred to Joseph. The promise to Judah he sees fulfilled in David. The Chronicler's reading of these events seems to draw from a Jewish interpretive tradition that finds its fullest expression in the Targums. In this tradition, Reuben's transgression leads to a loss of the three pillars of primogeniture: his status as the firstborn, his priesthood, and his kingship.

For instance, the *Targum Pseudo-Jonathan* on Gen. 49:3 offers this interpretation of Israel's denunciation: "Reuben, you are my firstborn; . . . you would have been worthy of the birthright, the dignity of the priesthood and the kingship. But because you sinned, my son, the birthright was given to Joseph, the kingship to Judah, and the priesthood to Levi" (Maher 1992: 157; cf. McNamara 1992: 217). The Targum on Chronicles makes the same interpretation:

> The sons of Reuben, the firstborn of Israel: he was indeed the firstborn, but when he desecrated his sanctity by going up to his father's bed, his birthright was taken away from him and given to the sons of Joseph. . . . Because Judah was the strongest of his brethren, the kingship was taken away from Reuben and given to Judah. . . . As for Levi, he was a godly man, . . . so the high priesthood was taken away from the sons of Reuben and . . . given to Aaron and his sons, . . . but the birthright was given to Joseph. (McIvor 1994: 64)

The larger theological point is that biology and birth order do not determine destiny: God does. This no doubt was heard with a certain double-edged meaning by the Chronicler's original audience. It means that, contrary to the claims of ethnic exclusivists within the returning community, reliance on tribal ties and ethnic descent is not enough. The Chronicler stresses that God wants faithfulness and worship, men and women who seek the Lord.

### The Genealogy of Grace

On the other hand, there is a distinct outlook of hope in the Chronicler's genealogy. Israel, the children of Abraham, called to be God's firstborn among the nations, has been laid low by its sinfulness, divided, and scattered. And yet God's purposes are not mocked. His will is not frustrated by human failure. This already is the unmistakable subtext of the Chronicler's genealogy, which will be borne out in the narrative that follows. The God of the Chronicler is the God of surprises, the God of the unexpected. Israel's history, preserved and amplified in this introductory genealogy, proves that firstborns and others can fail, beginning with the firstborn of creation, Adam. But that same history proves that God does not fail: he remains faithful to his covenant promises.

Chronicles begins with a genealogy of grace that opens to a narrative of eschatological hope. The God who created Adam, Abraham, Israel, and David is still at work in history. God's reign on earth, realized provisionally in the Davidic-Solomonic kingdom, will be established once and for all. The Chronicler's faith is not based on the righteousness or merit of the people, but on God's faithfulness to his covenant, to his promise of an everlasting kingdom to the descendants of David. With the prophets of the captivity—Hosea, Isaiah, Micah, Jeremiah, Ezekiel—and the postexilic prophets Haggai and Zechariah, the Chronicler looks forward to the restoration of the Davidic kingdom (Freedman 1961: 438–39).

Again, this kingdom is not a kingdom based only on blood or tribal descent; it is based on faith in the God of Israel. The blessings of God are destined for all the families of the world. From beginning to end, the Chronicler tells a story of unmerited grace and the possibilities of forgiveness. Again and again, sins are forgiven, and out of sin and repentance, God brings even greater works. This, finally, is the homiletic point that the Chronicler is seeking to make: "If you seek [dāraš] him, he will be found by you; but if you forsake him, he will cast you off for ever" (1 Chr. 28:9). It is a point delivered as both a warning and a promise.

All of this gives meaning to the short and mysterious passage in the genealogy about Jabez (4:9–10). Jabez appears as if out of nowhere in the Chronicler's genealogy—in the middle of a list of Judahites but without any reference to his father. His name is unique to the Chronicler's account. It does not come from any of the genealogical lists he is working from. Is he of the tribe of Judah? The text does not tell us. Reference is made to his brothers—he is said to be more "honorable" than them—but who they are is never said.

Jabez's mother is said to have named him after the "pain" or "affliction" (ʿōṣeb) she experienced in giving birth to him (the Hebrew name yaʿbēṣ is a play on ʿṣb). Could this be a reference to the consequences of original sin that God announced to Eve in the garden of Eden: "In pain [b ʿṣb] you shall bring forth children" (Gen. 3:16)? It probably is, and this detail helps to explain Jabez's prayer.

The prayer is the point of the anecdote. Jabez is the first one in Chronicles to "call on [qrʾ] the God of Israel" by name. This divine title is used often in Chronicles and reflects the deep affinity between God and the people. As Japhet observes, the epithet "testifies to a direct bond between YHWH and his people. By virtue of his very essence, YHWH is the God of Israel" (1997: 20). In recognizing the God of Israel as his God, Jabez's prayer is a fourfold request: for divine blessing in abundance (Klein 2006: 132 translates the Hebrew as "Oh that you would thoroughly bless me"), for a larger share of land, for God's divine strength, and for freedom from evil and harm:

> Oh that thou wouldst bless me
>   and enlarge my border,
> and that thy hand might be with me,
> and that thou wouldst keep me from harm
>   so that it might not hurt me! (1 Chr. 4:10)

This short prayer for blessing contains numerous allusions to earlier canonical texts and anticipations of later prayers found in Chronicles. For instance, part of God's covenant promise to the patriarchs and Israel was that he would enlarge their borders (Exod. 34:24; Deut. 19:8); similar language is used here. The reference to God's hand recalls the exodus wrought by the strong hand of the Lord (Exod. 13:14, 16). And later in Chronicles, this expression will figure in several key prayers, including David's great penitential and intercessory prayer, where he asks that God's hand be against himself rather than the people (1 Chr. 21:17; 29:12, 16).

Perhaps we are being invited to see Jabez as an ideal or model citizen of God's kingdom. Jabez, the child of pain, may be intended to represent all the children of Eve, who became "the mother of all living" (Gen. 3:20). Born in affliction, in exile from Eden, as Jabez did so also they are to put their trust in God and seek him in prayer and worship.

At a pivotal moment in the Chronicler's narrative, David will pray that all the "families of the peoples" will "call on his name," as David himself did (1 Chr. 16:8, 28; cf. 21:26). Here in the overture to his work, the Chronicler anticipates this calling upon God by the families of the world. The episode ends with a simple statement: "And God granted what he asked" (4:10). This is the subtext of the genealogy and, indeed, the entire book of Chronicles: God hears prayers. He is found by those who seek him. God will grant the entreaties of his faithful whom he has restored in the land, if only they will trust in him (5:20).

## Christian Interpretation

The first Christian commentators, beginning in the New Testament, believed that the Chronicler's divine history reached its zenith in Christ and the church. Perhaps that is why Matthew chose to begin his Gospel as the Chronicler began his work—with a genealogy. And perhaps this is one reason why the early editors of the New Testament chose to start the Christian canon with Matthew—so that the first book of the Christian canon would begin as the final book of the rabbinic canon did—all the better to emphasize the continuity between the Old and New Testaments and the unity of the economy of salvation from Adam to Jesus.

This also seems to be the motivation behind Luke's appropriation of the Chronicler's genealogy in tracing Christ's human lineage back to "Adam, the son of God" (Luke 3:38). Textual criticism shows that the genealogies in both Matthew (1:1–17) and Luke (3:23–38) draw extensively from the Septuagint translation of Chronicles (Davies and Allison 1988: 167–88; Fitzmyer 1981: 499–504). Structurally, in establishing the Abrahamic and Davidic pedigree of Christ, both Luke and Matthew work according to the Chronicler's generational scheme, which culminates in the Babylonian exile. They also appropriate the Chronicler's underlying theological message: both follow the Chronicler in deliberately editing their lists to highlight how God's purposes continue despite human failure and sin.

Luke explicitly makes the connection between the creation of the world and the new creation that God wants to bring about, between Adam and the new Adam, Jesus Christ. Throughout his early pages, Luke seems to be deliberately writing "the continuation of biblical history" (Dahl 1966: 152–53) and even a "new Genesis" (detailed tracing of Lukan typologies in Goulder and Sanderson 1957). Matthew begins his work with a deliberate echo of the title of the Bible's first book, *biblos geneseōs*, perhaps "to draw a parallel between one beginning and another beginning, between the creation of the cosmos and Adam and Eve on the one hand and the new creation brought by the Messiah on the other" (W. Davies and Allison 1988: 150).

It is also likely that the Chronicler's truth-be-told, warts-and-all portrait of the Davidic line had an influence on Matthew's similar genealogy in the New Testament, which also highlights the moral irregularities and defects in the line of Christ, "the son of David, the son of Abraham" (1:1).

In Matthew and Luke, then, we have an important appropriation and interpretation of the Chronicler's genealogy in light of Christ. What is eschatology in Chronicles has become history in Matthew and Luke: the realization of the Chronicler's most ardent hopes for the future. And as throughout Chronicles, the text has rich possibilities for Christian understanding of the economy of salvation and the divine pedagogy. This is something that Christians have seen almost from the beginning. Jerome says:

> The book of Paralipomenon is an epitome of the Old Testament and is of such scope and quality that anyone wishing to claim knowledge of scripture without it should laugh at himself. For because of the individual names mentioned and the composition of words, both historical events omitted in the books of Kings are touched on and innumerable questions pertinent to the gospel are explained. (*Epistle* 53.8)

# 2

## Highly Exalted for the Sake of His People Israel

*The Rise of David and His Kingdom (1 Chr. 10–16)*

**Major Divisions of the Text**

1. David's predecessor, Saul (10:1–14)
   Saul's death (10:1–7)
   Fate of Saul's corpse (10:8–12)
   Transfer of the kingdom to David (10:13–14)
2. Early days of Davidic rule (11:1–12:40)
   David's covenant with all Israel (11:1–3)
   All Israel captures Jerusalem and establishes it as David's capital (11:4–9)
   David's mighty men (11:10–47)
   David consolidates his support among the twelve tribes (12:1–37)
   David is made king over all Israel (12:38–40)
3. David restores the ark to Zion (13:1–14:17)
   Decision of all Israel and the start of the ark's return (13:1–8)
   God's anger breaks forth (13:9–12)
   Blessings of the ark (13:13–14)
   God's blessings upon David and Israel (14:1–17)
4. David restores the ark to Zion (15:1–16:43)
   The liturgical procession of the Ark of the Covenant (15:1–29)
   David's priestly blessing of all Israel (16:1–3)
   All Israel's liturgy of thanksgiving (16:7–36)
   David orders the worship of the ark at Jerusalem and the tabernacle at Gibeon (16:37–43)

## Synopsis of the Text

The Chronicler moves abruptly from his genealogical survey of Israel's origins straight into an account of the last days of Israel's first king and the rise of his successor, David. His intention is clear: to show that David and his kingdom represent the summit of Israel's history and the agency through which God intends to fulfill his covenant with Abraham and bestow his blessings upon the world. David's rise is told in bold strokes: his confidence and ambition in establishing Jerusalem as his capital and the ark of the covenant as his kingdom's spiritual center, the total trust he gains from "all Israel," the conquests of his mighty men in battle, and his provisions for the liturgical life of his people. David is described throughout in royal and priestly terms as the king and shepherd chosen by God; the coming of his kingdom is presented as the sign that the Lord reigns on earth as in heaven.

## Theological Exegesis and Commentary

### The Chronicler's Davidic Hope

Chronicles could be called the book of David. It is the world's family history written in a Davidic key, beginning in the deceptively simple genealogical lists, careful compositions that progressively narrow the world's family tree into a single branch—the line of the family of David.

For the Chronicler, all human history since Adam has been straining toward its fulfillment in the man of God, David, who with his son after him reigns upon "the throne of the kingdom of the LORD over Israel" (1 Chr. 28:5). What Levenson observes about the Davidic ode, Ps. 78, is true for the Chronicler's work: "It sees David's divinely commissioned reign as the consummation of Israel's *Heilsgeschichte* [salvation history], the very *telos* [goal] of their national experience" (1979: 218). More than that, the kingdom established by David at Zion, "the city of David," and the temple built by David's son Solomon are understood to be the pinnacle of God's plan for creation. This becomes clear not only at the high points, such as Solomon's prayer dedicating the temple, but also in describing David's total preoccupation with building the temple.

In David and his son, the vocation of Adam is realized: the king as priest, prince, and son of God. Moreover, in the Davidic kingdom the promise of Sinai is realized: Israel is established as a kingdom of priests and a holy nation. The Chronicler has drunk deeply from the same well of Davidic hope and expectation that inspires so much of the writing in the late exilic and early Second Temple period. At the center of Israel's history—and the history of salvation as he understands it—is the dynastic promise made to David as a *běrît ʿôlām* ("everlasting covenant"; 1 Chr. 16:17). With the prophets and the psalmists, the Chronicler anticipates the fulfillment of that promise—that

God would establish his kingdom forever through David's son, who would also be the son of God and a "priest for ever" (1 Chr. 17:11–14; cf. Ps. 110:4).

This hope casts a poignant expectancy over all his characterizations of David and Solomon and the establishment of the kingdom and the temple. Thus much more is going on here than the literary creation of a utopia, or the ideological justification for reinstituting organizational structures and cultic practices from the monarchy in the years after the exile. The Chronicler is doing reconstructive historical apologetics. In re-creating the era of David and the rise of the kingdom, he is not only describing the golden age, the summit of salvation history; he is also laying the groundwork for the restoration of the kingdom, the rebuilding of the temple, and the return of David's son.

Runnalls rightly observes: "The interest of the Chronicler in the eternal Davidic kingship at a time when it no longer existed makes emphatic the idea that the promise awaits fulfillment" (1983: 24–25). In his portrait of the kingdom, the Chronicler "was surely thinking eschatologically of the new David and the new kingdom that would shortly or eventually arise in God's good time," agrees Stinespring (1961: 211). Thus, in deliberately detailing the institutional structures of the monarchy and in offering precise descriptions of the personnel and practices of the cultic and sacrificial system, the Chronicler is giving his readers a blueprint for their own renewal of the kingdom—much as David is said to have received from God a "plan" for all these things in the original kingdom (1 Chr. 28:11–19). Equally important to the Chronicler is preparing the heart of the people, instilling in them the zeal and desire for holiness proper to the people of God. Thus his depiction of David's rise and the building of his kingdom is intended as a template for their own rise from the humiliation of the exile, to be restored as God's kingdom on earth.

### Saul Died for His Unfaithfulness

The Chronicler's portrait of David begins with an abrupt, dark sketch of the final days of Saul's reign. He had concluded the genealogies by repeating Saul's family line, tracing his descendants for twelve generations, up until the time of the exile (1 Chr. 9:35–44; cf. 8:29–40). Then unexpectedly, he begins his narrative in the heat of Saul's last battle. Nothing else is said about his reign. Indeed, it is telling that the Chronicler does not even refer to Saul as king. Israel under Saul is introduced as a defeated people, in retreat, fleeing before attacking Philistines. The battle ends with the grim intimation that Israel has been driven out of the land. After Saul's three sons are dispatched and he falls upon his sword, "all the men of Israel . . . forsook their cities and fled" (10:7).

The Chronicler offers a summary that is also an interpretation of the material found in his source: "Thus Saul died; he and his three sons and all his house died together" (10:6). The use of *bayit* (house) is deliberate and pointed. The narrative has already been tied to the genealogy by a double reference to the "sons" of Saul (10:2). And in this concluding remark, he gives us another filial reference, but also an unmistakable dynastic allusion that looks ahead to David and his son, who will build the temple as a *bayit* for the Lord, as the Lord promises to build David a *bayit*—a royal dynasty. By contrast, Saul's house has been judged by God and met with a bloody and ignominious end.

"Saul died for his unfaithfulness [*ma'al*]; he was unfaithful [*mā'al*] to the LORD. . . . Therefore the LORD slew him," the Chronicler explains, offering another interpretation not found in his source material. Only one of Saul's numerous sins is mentioned: his consulting a seer. The Chronicler instead makes two sweeping statements meant to characterize the fatal flaws of his reign: Saul failed to "keep the command [*dābār*, lit., "word"] of the LORD," and he "did not seek guidance [*dāraš*] from the LORD" (10:13–14).

*Ma'al* is almost a technical, programmatic word for the Chronicler, used to indicate the fundamental breach of the covenant relationship with God; often he associates it with a trespass against the holiness of God or an offense against the proper worship due to God. Again and again, *ma'al* is the term used to describe the overriding failures of kings during the period of the divided monarchy (2 Chr. 26:16, 18; 28:19, 22; 29:5–8, 19; 30:7; 33:19; 36:14; Milgrom 1976); and more often than not, *ma'al* is punished by military defeat and exile (1 Chr. 5:25–26; 2 Chr. 12:3–4, 8; 28:17–19; 30:6–8; 36:14–20). Already in his genealogy, the Chronicler has rendered his opinion that Judah was exiled to Babylon "because of their unfaithfulness [*ma'al*]" (1 Chr. 9:1).

In this portrait is a sense that Saul's *ma'al* has resulted in the scattering of Israel and the loss of the land (Deut. 32:5; Ezek. 39:23–26; Lev. 26:40). There are also dark cultic overtones to Saul's unfaithfulness. This becomes clear only as the Chronicler's narrative unfolds. Following Saul's demise and David's rise to power and capture of Jerusalem, David announces his intention to bring the ark of the covenant back to the capital and pronounces this critique on the reign of his predecessor: "For we neglected [lit., "did not seek" (*dāraš*)] it in the days of Saul" (1 Chr. 13:3).

The ark of the covenant of the Lord was the great sign of God's presence, his literal abode on earth, the centerpiece of the portable sanctuary known as the tabernacle during the years of Israel's wandering in the wilderness. The ark was closely associated with the Sinai covenant and the people's conquest of the land. However, the biblical record does not indicate any direct stipulations about the ark's role in the people's life once they have entered the land. Yet the Chronicler and his historical sources agree that the ark was central to David's understanding of his kingdom and kingship.

The ark appears to be very near in the background of the Chronicler's account of Saul's posthumous humiliation at the hands of the Philistines. According to the *Vorlage* of his death in 1 Sam. 31, the triumphant Philistines cut off Saul's head and hung his body on the wall of Beth-shan; no mention is made of what they did with his head. But the Chronicler informs us that they hung Saul's head in the temple of Dagon. Here we see another example of the Chronicler's haggadic reading of the historical record.

He knows, and presumably so do his readers, that the temple of Dagon was the scene of a dramatic confrontation between the God of Israel and the idols of the Philistines (1 Sam. 5:1–5). The Philistines captured the ark and placed it as a trophy of war in their temple to the deity Dagon. But in the presence of the God of Israel in the ark, the statue of Dagon fell, and "the head of Dagon . . . [was] cut off, . . . only the trunk of Dagon was left to him." In the Chronicler, the ark is nowhere in sight, and Saul's severed head hangs in the same temple, as a sign of mockery. There probably is also an allusion here to the defeat of the Philistine giant, Goliath, whose head was carried to Jerusalem to hang in infamy (1 Sam. 17:54). The Chronicler wants us to see in Saul's death the utter reversal of fortune: the total defeat and disgrace of Israel and Israel's God.

### The Lord Turned the Kingdom Over to David

But from this disaster, the Chronicler signals once more that God is in charge. Commentators often notice how the Chronicler has eliminated from his account all reference to the intrigue, maneuvering, and machinations involved in David's accession to the throne. This is true but easily misunderstood. The Chronicler is not out to whitewash history or present an idealized or utopian portrait of David. The Chronicler is writing with older biblical traditions in view. All the gritty details are already on record in the books of Samuel. The Chronicler is not interested in covering them up, even if that were possible. What is always important for the Chronicler is to interpret the biblical record, to offer a theology of history, and he does so with powerful concision: "Therefore the Lord slew [Saul], and turned the kingdom over to David the son of Jesse" (1 Chr. 10:14).

All the specifics of the earlier history, which included some twenty-four chapters devoted to Saul's reign and the early years of David (1 Sam. 8–31), amount to so much backstory. The point for the Chronicler is always the divine initiative, the economy of salvation, the plan of God. And God's plan is that David be made king and that through his kingdom God's reign be established over all the nations. Thus in two verses the narrative moves from Saul's death to the gathering of "all Israel" at Hebron to make a covenant with David. David's rise is swift and precisely ordered. He makes a covenant with "all Israel," based on an oracle of God. He gathers to himself valiant men, forms a mighty "army of God" (12:22), in short order conquers Jerusalem, defeats the Philistines, restores the ark, and sets about the plans to build the temple. All the while, his fame spreads, and the Lord brings the fear of David over "all nations" (14:17).

All that David accomplishes he does in consultation and cooperation with the people. The word used again and again is "all" (*kōl*)—all Israel, all the assembly, all the people, all the rest of the people. Reference is made to the perfect sympathy of the people with David, their "singleness of purpose" and "single mind" (12:33, 38). Steussy detects a "pattern of camaraderie" in the narrative of David's rise to power (1999: 109). Long lists are provided of the names of those who allied themselves with David. Joab is credited with the capture of Jerusalem; David's slaying of Goliath is overlooked while Elhanan's killing of Goliath's brother is mentioned (20:5). The people are not passive investors in David's fortunes; the kingdom is more than one man. The men around David are shown as making considered decisions of allegiance and self-sacrifice and impassioned oaths of loyalty; according to the Chronicler, they offer indispensable help to the king and his kingdom. The message to the Chronicler's audience is clear: their own zeal and devotion to rebuilding the kingdom will be remembered.

Williamson observes that a theme of divine assistance (*'zr*) to the monarch runs through Chronicles as a distinctive feature of his work (2004: 116–25). The theme is stressed in the gathering of mighty men to David, where the word "help" (*'zr*) is used repeatedly (12:1, 17, 18, 19, 21, 22), culminating in a prayer of allegiance spoken in "the Spirit" by the chief Amasai:

> We are yours, O David;
>> and with you, O son of Jesse!
> Peace, peace to you,
>> and peace to your helpers!
> For your God helps you. (1 Chr. 12:18)

The Hebrew expression actually suggests that the Spirit of God "clothed itself around" or "took possession" of Amasai. The mantle of the Spirit, here and elsewhere in Chronicles, further emphasizes the divine favor that now rests upon David and his kingdom (2 Chr. 15:1; 20:14; 24:20). He becomes "greater and greater, for the LORD of hosts was with him" (1 Chr. 11:9). The Chronicler's message throughout is clear: David is God's king, and his kingdom is the kingdom of God. Indeed, the only place where the expression "kingdom of God / the LORD" is found in the Hebrew Bible is in Chronicles, and it is only in reference to the Davidic kingdom of David and his son (1 Chr. 28:5; 2 Chr. 13:8). David's kingdom is the salvation of Israel, established "according to the word of the LORD concerning Israel" and "highly exalted for the sake of [God's] people Israel" (1 Chr. 11:10; 14:2); that is, David's kingdom is the fulfillment of God's covenant promises to Abraham and to Moses on Sinai. The God of David, as he declares, is "the God of our fathers" (12:17).

David's covenant with the people is expressed in physical, familial, even nuptial terms; he is one flesh with the people, his heart knit together with theirs (11:1; 12:17). Indeed, we should pause over the covenantal formula used at Hebron ("We are your bone and flesh"). The expression hearkens back to the nuptial exclamation of Adam: "This at last is bone of my bones and flesh of my flesh" (Gen. 2:23). It is used on rare occasions elsewhere in the Bible to signify covenantal or blood kinship or physical existence (Gen. 29:14; Judg. 9:2; 2 Sam. 19:12–13; Job 2:5; Brueggemann 1970). But if an Adamic typology is at work for the Chronicler, use of this expression here may have deeper significance. Could the Chronicler be making a comparison between the union of Israel and its "head"? Do we see here an attempt to interpret the origins of the bridal imagery used by the prophets to describe Israel's relationship with God (Hos. 1–3; Jer. 2:2; 3:1–5; Ezek. 16:8–14)? Does David, as king, stand in the relationship of bridegroom to God's betrothed Israel? My sense is that the answer to each of these questions is yes, but this cannot be proved definitively.

The covenant event at Hebron is also cast in Mosaic terms. The people refer to an oracle in which God declares to David, "You shall be shepherd of my people Israel, and you shall be prince over my people Israel" (1 Chr. 11:2). "My people" recalls the exodus and the Sinai covenant (Exod. 3:7; 6:7). The shepherd image, which the Chronicler carries over from his sources, looks backward to Moses, the archetypal leader of Israel, who was a shepherd in the image of God and is called "the shepherd of Israel" (Moses in Exod. 3:1; Ps. 77:20; Isa. 63:11; God in Gen. 49:24; Ps. 80:1). But this imagery also looks forward: the prophets of the exile had foretold the coming of a new shepherd, a new Davidic king (Jer. 3:15; 23:1–4; Ezek. 34:1–24; Zech. 11:4–17).

This shepherd image will recur in the great dynastic oracle of 1 Chr. 17, where it again identifies David with God in a way that no other biblical figure is related to God. As Chae observes (2006: 26): "No specific king in Israel is described in shepherd imagery as YHWH's royal representative, with the exception of David before he assumed the throne. . . . The Old Testament tends to reserve shepherd imagery for YHWH and, significantly, extends its use only for YHWH's Davidic appointee" (Ps. 78:71; Mic. 5:2–4). The Chronicler's retention of this shepherd image may, then, be an effort to associate David's kingdom with these prophetic hopes, especially those of Ezekiel (37:24–28; cf. 34:23), who foretold the reestablishment of David as king, shepherd, and prince, by an everlasting covenant of peace and the placement of his dwelling and sanctuary among the people forever—all core elements emphasized in the Chronicler's Davidic portrait.

In this imagery may also be a more subtle connection to the exodus and the conquest of the land. The people's claim, "It was you that led out and brought in Israel" (1 Chr. 11:2), recalls the language of Moses's commissioning of Joshua to "lead out" and "bring in" the people, so that Israel would "not be as sheep which have no shepherd" (Num. 27:16–17). The image may be rooted in Israel's understanding of God's mighty work in the exodus, which on occasion was likened to that of a shepherd's leading in and bringing out

(Deut. 6:23). The rare use of shepherd imagery to describe God's kingship seems almost always to be in the context of God's leading of the people out of Egypt (Pss. 80:1, 8; 95:7–11; cf. Jer. 31:10; Isa. 5:16–17; Ps. 23; Tanner 2004).

Throughout, the Chronicler presents David as a new Moses and the Davidic kingdom as the full realization of the *qāhāl*, the liturgical assembly of Israel as a kingdom of priests and a holy nation in the years after the exodus. As Allison notes (1993: 39), though David and Moses are the two dominant figures in the Hebrew Bible, the typological association of the two is not found elsewhere in scripture and is rare in extrabiblical writings. This suggests that the Chronicler attaches considerable significance to his typological portrait.

In addition to the Mosaic shepherd imagery, David, like Moses, is presented as a warrior and cult founder and as a man who speaks with the words and authority of God. The Chronicler describes both David and Moses as "man of God" (1 Chr. 23:14; 2 Chr. 8:14; 30:16) and "servant of God" (1 Chr. 6:49; 17:4, 7; 2 Chr. 24:9). The ark of the covenant, so important to Moses, is critical as well to David. As Moses repeatedly interceded for the sins of the people, David intercedes to stop the plague caused by his ill-fated census, in a scene redolent of "the destroyer" at the first Passover (Exod. 12:23; 1 Chr. 21:1). And as sin kept Moses from entering the promised land, sin keeps David from fulfilling his dream of building the temple.

There are dramatic parallels between David's installation of Solomon as his successor (1 Chr. 22) and Moses's commissioning of Joshua. The most powerful Mosaic parallel concerns the tabernacle and the temple. As Moses was given a "pattern" (*tabnît*) for the tabernacle (Exod. 25:9, 40), David too is given a *tabnît*, not only for the temple, but also for the liturgical order of worship in the temple (1 Chr. 28:11–19). According to Allison:

> It is difficult to know what one should make of the Moses-David parallelism in 1 Chronicles 22 and 28. . . . The Chronicler seems to have believed, and then set out to show, that the Davidic covenant, not the Mosaic, was definite. If so, this would explain why his work mentions Moses only in passing, why it exalts David and Solomon, and why it models David upon Moses in chapters 22 and 29; the former was made like the latter in order to be his equal, perhaps even his superior. (1993: 39)

However, the evidence in Chronicles suggests no such supersessionist conclusion but rather a strong continuity between the Mosaic and Davidic covenants. For the Chronicler, Sinai leads to Zion by way of Moriah, a statement that will become more intelligible as we proceed. David and Solomon are exalted as the ideal kings, but their kingship and kingdom are premised on the Sinai covenant and serve to fulfill that covenant, not supersede it. This is clear in the words of Nathan's prophecy and in David's response (1 Chr. 17:5, 21).

In words attributed to God himself, the kingdom and temple at Jerusalem are said to have been envisioned "since the day that I brought my people out of the land of Egypt" (2 Chr. 6:5). As Sinai was a continuation of the covenant with Abraham, so too was the kingdom of David (20:7). "The statutes and the ordinances which the LORD commanded Moses for Israel" are the foundation of this kingdom and the basis for repeated covenant-renewal movements throughout the Chronicler's history of the divided kingdom (1 Chr. 22:13; 28:7; 2 Chr. 14:4). Even the temple liturgy, which is particularly associated with David, is only the fulfillment of "the appointed feasts of the LORD our God, as ordained for ever for Israel" (2:4).

### And All Israel with David Took the Stronghold of Zion

In the Chronicler's portrait, David emerges as the "prophet like me from among . . . your brethren" that Moses had promised (Deut. 18:15–19). As the new Moses, David completes the mission of his forerunner. He leads the final conquest of the land, establishing the capital of his liturgical empire at Jerusalem and laying the foundations for the dwelling of God. Accordingly, the first act of "David and all Israel" is the conquest of Jerusalem (1 Chr. 11:4).

Jerusalem is central to the Chronicler's work. Chronicles ends with the summons of Cyrus, who calls all of God's people to return there (2 Chr. 36:23); throughout the work, Jerusalem is presented as the true capital of "the kingdom of the LORD" (1 Chr. 28:5). By some estimates, nearly one-quarter of all the references to Jerusalem in the entire Hebrew Bible occur in Chronicles. Kalimi declares: "Jerusalem is depicted by the Chronicler . . . as an absolutely theocratic city, 'the city of God/the Lord' in the full sense of the word, more than in any other biblical work" (2003: 191).

The Jebusites, the inhabitants of Jerusalem, or Jebus (11:4), are introduced very early in the genealogy (1:14), and the lines of both David and Levi are rooted in Jerusalem (3:4; 6:10, 32). The genealogy concludes with a listing of the first returnees to Jerusalem (9:3, 34, 38). Some scholars see a deliberate focusing in the genealogies to present a *mappa mundi* (map of the world) that makes Israel into the center of the nations, as Jerusalem is the center of the world (J. Wright 2006: 74).

All of this, however, raises a historical question, one crucial also to the meaning of the Chronicler's narrative: Why Jerusalem? The canonical record is indisputable: before David's accession, Jerusalem had little or no overt significance in the history or life of the people. Later writings, including Chronicles, attest to God's election of Jerusalem, making inseparable the association of the election of David, Jerusalem, the temple, and the dynastic promise to David's son (Pss. 78:68–71; 132:13–14; Zech. 3:2; cf. 2 Chr. 6:6). But unlike the election of Abraham or Israel, or even David's own election, the Bible offers us no account of God's choosing Jerusalem: it is simply asserted or assumed after the fact.

Jerusalem was a very ancient city-state in Canaan. This we know from execration texts indicating that Jerusalem was one of Egypt's vassals as early as the nineteenth century BC. Archaeologists have discovered correspondence between the pharaoh and Jerusalem's king that dates to the fourteenth century BC (Levenson 1985: 92). But until David's appearance, Jerusalem is barely noticed in the canon. It is not mentioned by name in the Pentateuch, and in the later Historical Books it is among the cities that Israel is unable to fully conquer; it remains a "city of foreigners, who do not belong to the people of Israel" (Judg. 19:12; also 1:8, 21; Josh. 15:63).

So again the question arises: How did David know that this city had been chosen by God for the dwelling place of his name (2 Chr. 6:6)? There is no record even of David's seeking God's guidance on the question of his capital; instead, David is presented as simply understanding that his royal destiny includes the establishment of Jerusalem as his capital and the restoration of the ark of the covenant.

The answer to the puzzle lies in part in the Chronicler's reading of the Abrahamic traditions, which ultimately must have some historical foundation in David's own appropriation of those traditions. The Zion tradition, including belief in the great kingship of God and his choice of Jerusalem as his dwelling place, seems to have originated in the empire of David and Solomon (Roberts 2002: 313–30). This would not have been a casual invention of David, as Ishida concludes in his study of Israel's dynastic traditions:

> It is true that all the Yahwistic traditions of Jerusalem were created by David, who brought in the Ark of Yahweh, and by Solomon, builder of the Temple for Yahweh there. Pre-Davidic Jerusalem, it is plain, had nothing to do with Yahwism except in mysterious traditions of Abraham (Gen. 14:18–20; 22:1–4). But it is hardly plausible that David and Solomon could change Jerusalem into the holiest city in Israel solely by their own initiative and actions. In the ancient Near East, the choice of holy places was not left to human arbitrariness but was determined by a manifestation of the god's presence. (1977: 121–22)

The Chronicler tells us that David did experience such a manifestation of the divine presence—at the threshing floor of Ornan the Jebusite, hence in Jerusalem. When he takes up this episode in 1 Chr. 21, the Chronicler greatly expands on the historical record found elsewhere in the Bible, drawing a typological comparison between David's experience (2 Sam. 24) and the story of Abraham's "binding" of Isaac, or the Akedah (Gen. 22). The full sense of the typology is not disclosed until later, when Solomon is said to build the temple "in Jerusalem on Mount Moriah, where the LORD had appeared to David his father, . . . on the threshing floor of Ornan the Jebusite" (2 Chr. 3:1). Moriah, "the mount of the LORD," is mentioned in only one other place in scripture—as the site of the Akedah (Gen. 22:2, 14). But while this vision may justify the site of the temple, it does not really explain David's prior decision to seek Jerusalem as his capital. Yet this decision too is ultimately rooted in what Ishida calls the "mysterious traditions of Abraham."

The choice of Jerusalem—and David's priestly-cultic understanding of his kingship—is rooted in the mysterious figure of Melchizedek, the "king of Salem" and "priest of God Most High," who "brought out bread and wine" and blessed Abraham in the name of the "maker of heaven and earth" (Gen. 14:18–20). The identification of Melchizedek's Salem and David's Jerusalem is made in the Psalms (76:2), as is the identification of Melchizedek's priesthood and the priesthood of the Davidic kings (110:4). David understood himself as a sort of new Melchizedek, and in the canon Melchizedek represents a mysterious connection with Adam, the primal priest-king. Cassuto states: "Among the motives that led David to establish Jerusalem as the centre of his kingdom and of the service of the Lord there were, it seems, apart from political, geographical, and strategic consider-ations, also reasons based on the ancient tradition relative to the holiness of Jerusalem as a site appointed for the worship of the Lord since earliest times" (1973: 78).

The Chronicler's David understood Jerusalem in connection with God's promise to choose a place for his name to dwell. The echoes of this promise in Deut. 12 are heard throughout Chronicles: the cutting off of enemies and the establishment of peace (Deut. 12:29; 1 Chr. 17:8), burnt offerings in the house where the Lord's name dwells (Deut. 12:6, 11; 2 Chr. 2:4; 7:1–7), and eating before the Lord (Deut. 12:7, 18; 1 Chr. 29:22). Thus God will tell Solo-mon, "I have chosen Jerusalem that my name may be there and I have chosen David" (2 Chr. 6:6).

### All the Assembly Agreed to Bring Back the Ark of God

For David, Jerusalem is the place that God has chosen for his name to dwell. And he has chosen to dwell there, as he dwelled with Israel since the beginning, in the ark of the covenant. Thus, after the conquest of Jerusalem, David moves methodically to restore the ark to the center of Israel's national and religious life. David's deep concern for the ark, documented by earlier biblical historians, is greatly amplified by the Chronicler.

The ark was originally built by Moses's command, according to God's own specifications: it was a chest made out of acacia wood and overlaid with pure gold on the inside and out; on the top was a cover made of solid gold, with cherubim at each end; the ark was to be borne with special poles attached to gold rings on either side and could be carried only by members of the priestly tribe of the Levites (Exod. 25:10–22). The ark contained the stone tablets of the law given to Moses (Deut. 10:1–5, 8; 31:9, 24–26), along with the priestly rod of Aaron and an urn holding manna from Israel's days in the desert (Exod. 16:32–34; Num. 17:1–10).

Going forth behind the ark borne by the Levites, Israel set out from Sinai to conquer the land promised to their father Abraham (Num. 10:33; Josh. 3:3, 6). The ark is at the center of the fall of Jericho (Josh. 6:6–16), and the ark traditions run deep in the biblical narrative and shape the dramatic contours of Israel's memory and liturgy. An ancient fragment of a prayer or hymn speaks to its importance as a symbol of God's presence with Israel in their battles against the nations: "Whenever the ark set out, Moses said, 'Arise, O LORD, and let thy enemies be scattered; and let them that hate thee flee before thee.' And when it rested, he said, 'Return, O LORD, to the ten thousand thousands of Israel'" (Num. 10:35–36).

The biblical record of David's attention to the ark reflects historical realities. Chronicles and the earlier Historical Books agree that the ark was vital to his understanding of the kingdom that he was to build at Jerusalem. The Chronicler goes further, adding to the traditions he has received. He refers to the ark by names not found elsewhere in the tradition: "the footstool of our God" (1 Chr. 28:2) and "the holy ark" (2 Chr. 35:3). Moreover, in his account of the temple's dedication, he incorporates Ps. 132 into Solomon's solemn prayer—introducing the possibility that he sees the ark's housing in the temple as the fulfillment of God's promise of "rest" for his covenant people (2 Chr. 6:41; Ps. 132:8).

The intriguing question that must be asked is why all this attention to the ark, especially since the ark played no role in the life of Israel following the exile? This is another unique aspect of Chronicles in relation to other biblical works of the exilic and postexilic period. Begg observes that the forty-six mentions of the ark in Chronicles sharply contrast with the utter silence about the ark in Ezra, Nehemiah, the second and third portions of Isaiah, Ezekiel, Haggai, Zechariah, and Malachi (2003: 133).

The ark had apparently disappeared at the time of the desecration and destruction of the temple by Nebuchadnezzar of Babylon, or perhaps before that, during the apostasy of Israel's King Manasseh. Jeremiah had prophesied of an unspecified future day when the ark "shall not come to mind, or be remembered, or missed; it shall not be made again." Apparently according to Jeremiah's idea, in that day all of Zion, not just the ark, "shall be called the throne of the LORD, and all nations shall gather to it, to the presence of the LORD" (Jer. 3:16–17). The Chronicler was likely aware of the tradition that before the sack of Jerusalem, Jeremiah hid the ark in a cave near where Moses was buried (Deut. 32:49–52; 34:1–8), foretelling that it would not be rediscovered "until God gathers his people together again and shows his mercy" (2 Macc. 2:1–8).

Clearly, by the Chronicler's time the ark was just a memory. We know from historical and rabbinic sources that it was not among the holy vessels returned to Jerusalem after the captivity (Ezra 1:7–11; Jer. 27:16–22; Isa. 52:11–12). In Solomon's temple, the ark was laid to rest in the inner sanctum, the holy of holies. But according to Josephus, in the second temple "there was nothing at all" in the holy of holies (*Jewish War* 5.219). There is speculation about the ark in the rabbinic and pseudepigraphical writings, and it is quite possible that this speculation was not far from the Chronicler's mind. So what was the Chronicler thinking? The clue is to be found in David's first address in Chronicles: "Let us send abroad to our brethren who remain . . . that they may come together to us. Then let us bring again the ark of our God to us; for we neglected [lit., "did not seek"] it in the days of Saul" (1 Chr. 13:2–3).

Is it possible that the Chronicler believes his audience is living in days like those days of Saul—in which Israel does not seek the ark, a period of *ma'al* that risks being reckoned again by God's judgment? If so, David's opening words are a kind of realized eschatology, words that were spoken in the past but continue to resonate with the Chronicler and his audience in the present. The entire ark narrative, then, reads as an exhortation to the postexilic community—to gather the remnant of their brethren to Zion and to once more seek the ark as a central element in the restoration of the everlasting kingdom promised to David. Begg's analysis seems to be on the mark:

> The Ark was one of many "goods" . . . that, in the Chronicler's presentation, characterized the time of David and Solomon . . . but that were conspicuously absent from the people's life in the Chronicler's own time. Is it plausible, . . . in a strongly parenetic work such as Chronicles, with its insistence that right behavior is richly rewarded, that all these "goods" are presented by him only as a reminder of what Israel has irrevocably lost? Is not the Chronicler's portrayal of them more likely intended to evoke the hope that all of them—as the already restored Temple—might be recovered through further efforts by Israel to please God? . . . Is it not possible, then, that in his portrayal of David assembling all Israel to fetch the Ark, the Chronicler is calling all Israel of his own time to turn its attention to the Ark once again, in hopes that by so doing it might secure the same salutary effects that David and Solomon's care for the Ark secured for them and their people? (2003: 143–44)

In evoking the ark, the Chronicler again summons the historical memory of the exodus and the entrance into the land. The ark becomes the gathering point of God's holy people. And it is striking and significant that, beginning with the convocation of Israel to embark on the mission of returning the ark ("David said to all the assembly, . . . all the assembly agreed"; 1 Chr. 13:2, 4), the Chronicler repeatedly refers to the assembly of all Israel as the *qāhāl*. This is the term for Israel's liturgical assembly that first appears in the biblical accounts of the exodus and post-Sinaitic period. The first use of *qāhāl* in the canon is found on the night of the exodus, in the divine instructions for how "the whole assembly" (*kōl qāhāl*) is to prepare for the journey (Exod. 12:6).

The Chronicler will use that same expression, *kōl qāhāl*, at pivotal moments—here in the mission to restore the ark (1 Chr. 13:4), in Solomon's accession to the throne (29:10, 20), in the covenant renewal under Jehoiada (2 Chr. 23:3), and at the Passover of Hezekiah (30:4, 23). But *qāhāl* generally seems to be his ideal form for Israel. By some reckonings, *qāhāl* is used forty-eight times in the Pentateuch and thirty-seven times in Chronicles (Johnstone 1997: 1.168). For the Chronicler, Israel is fundamentally a *qāhāl*, a kingdom of priests, a liturgical empire. Israel is not primarily a national entity organized for military, political, or economic purposes; in Israel all those ordinary rationales for governments are to be ordered to the singular overriding reason of giving worship to God. This is what Israel exists for, and this is Israel's mission as God's firstborn among the nations.

It thus is fitting that David consults with "all the assembly" (*kōl qāhāl*) in launching his bid to return the ark (1 Chr. 13:2, 4). The kingdom under David, like the original people of God formed at Sinai, will be a people defined by their attendance to God in the ark. David devotes his first address in Chronicles to the subject of the ark and stresses the family nature of the *qāhāl* (13:2–3). He speaks of gathering all their "brethren," of "the ark of *our* God," and of "the will of the LORD *our* God." The *qāhāl* is a family of God. And the Chronicler describes this "assembled" (*qāhāl*) family of "all Israel" as occupying essentially the entire territory of the promised land—from Shihor (probably the Wadi or Brook of Egypt), which in Joshua marks the southwest corner of the land, to the entrance of Hamath, the northeasternmost point. As Japhet notes, this is "the most extreme concept of Israelite territory to be found in the Bible" (1979: 209; cf. Klein 2006: 332).

This was the land that was yet to be possessed at the end of Joshua's conquests (Josh. 13:1–5). And there are strong hints that the Chronicler intends to re-create or at least evoke the scene of original conquest throughout his ark narrative. He has already made a brief allusion to this history in his summary of the Gadites who joined David's army. As did the people led by Joshua and the priests bearing the ark (Josh. 3:11–4:1), these Gadites "passed over" the Jordan at that time of year when the Jordan "was overflowing all its banks" (1 Chr. 12:15). In the narrative of the ark's return, the Chronicler evokes the beginnings of Israel's journey from Sinai to the Jordan. As with Num. 10, the ark narrative has a summoning of the *qāhāl*, the blowing of trumpets, the interval of three days during the course of the journey, reference to glad festivals, sacrifices of burnt offerings and peace offerings, and the theme of "rest" for the ark of the covenant of the Lord.

The story of Uzzah, who is struck dead for reaching out to touch the ark, is a cautionary tale of liturgical abuse (1 Chr. 13:9–11). The *qāhāl* of Israel is called to intimacy with God—but on God's terms, not their own. We are meant to notice the sharp contrast between the spontaneous gaiety and abandon of the people's first efforts to retrieve the ark, which anger God and result in Uzzah's death, and the meticulous preparations that precede the second attempt. Perhaps we are meant also to recall the divine warning before the theophany and the giving of the law at Mount Sinai. There Moses was instructed to establish boundaries lest the people touch the mountain and cause God to "break forth" (*prṣ*) against them and they perish (Exod. 19:21–24). The same odd verb, *prṣ*, is used to describe Uzzah's fate and becomes a kind of watchword throughout the ark narrative (1 Chr. 13:2, 11; 14:11; 15:13; Williamson 1982: 114). The lesson seems to be that in the worship of God, there is no place for novelty or personal innovation. God desires to be worshiped in the way that he has "ordained" (15:13), which for the Chronicler means "as Moses had commanded according to the word of the LORD" (15:15).

The Uzzah incident frightens and chastens David. There is a humility and a sense of repentance in his question "How can I bring the ark of God home to me?" (13:12) and, apparently for the first time, a recognition that there is a proper way to seek the Lord. David's response apparently pleases God, who blesses the household of Obed-edom, where the ark remains; God also blesses David with many sons and daughters, growing renown among the nations, and a decisive routing of the Philistines. The turn of events is told with deliberate parallelisms. As God broke forth (*prṣ*) against Uzzah, he now breaks forth (*prṣ*) against David's enemies. As David commemorated his failure by naming the place Perez-uzza, literally, "the breaking forth upon Uzzah" (13:11), he celebrates the smiting of the Philistines by naming the battleground Baal-perazim, "the LORD of breaking through" (14:11).

Thus David lays out a careful plan and an order of worship before making his second attempt to return the ark. He prepares a place for the ark, pitches a tent for it, and reasserts the Mosaic regulations that only the Levites may carry it; he also institutes a liturgical order for Israel's future worship in the presence of the ark. Only then can all Israel bring the ark home to Jerusalem. The Chronicler marks the moment with a shift in vocabulary. For the first time in the narrative, the ark is called by its full and rightful name from the days of Moses and Joshua—"the ark of the covenant of the LORD," which the Chronicler repeats in rhythmic, almost litany-like fashion during the procession of the ark from Obed-edom (15:25, 26, 28, 29; Num. 10:33; Deut. 10:8; Josh. 3:3).

### David Blessed the People

In the joyous procession that marks the return of the ark, David is portrayed as both Israel's king and its chief priest. He is clad, as the Levites are, in a fine linen robe and an ephod. Elsewhere in scripture and later rabbinic tradition, this garb is associated with the vestments of Aaron the high priest (Exod. 28:4, 31, 34; Rashi [1992: 103] says David's ephod was "like the ephod of Aaron"). In another priestly move, David officiates in the sacrificial offering of seven bulls and seven rams. Although the Chronicler paints a similar picture of shouting and jubilation, it is probably just a coincidence that the only other place where this specific kind of offering is made is in conjunction with Balaam's prophetic word: "The LORD their God is with them, and the shout of a king is among them" (Num. 23:21; seven offerings in Num. 23:1, 29–30; Job 42:8). Nonetheless, David's portrayal as priest-king is unmistakable. He does things here and elsewhere in Chronicles that Israel's priests typically perform, such as making burnt offerings and peace offerings (Num. 3:6–8, 14–38; 4:47; 6:16–17; 8:14–26) and invoking God's blessing upon the people (Num. 6:22–27; Deut. 10:8; 21:5).

The Chronicler's priestly depiction of David has long been noticed, most famously by Wellhausen: "See what Chronicles has made out of David! The founder of the kingdom has become the founder of the temple and the public worship, the king and hero at the head of his companions in arms has become the singer and master of ceremonies at the head of a swarm of priests and Levites; his clearly cut figure has become a feebly holy picture, seen through a cloud of incense" (1994: 182).

Contrary to Wellhausen, the Chronicler's priest-king is not a figure of weakness but just the opposite: a figure of great power. Not only is he leading "all Israel" in the triumphal procession; God also is described as helping (ʿzr) David and the Levites in their worship (1 Chr. 15:26). Everything is seen as participation in God's own initiative, anticipating David's own theology of worship: "Everything is from you, and from your hand we have given back to you" (29:14, quoted from Knoppers 2004: 2.943).

Certainly the Chronicler is here continuing the new-Moses theme already identified. Moses too "gathered" (qāhal) the qāhāl (Num. 20:10), pitched the tent for the ark (Exod. 33:7), officiated over the sacrifices (24:7–8), and blessed the children of Israel (39:42–43; Deut. 33:1; Johnstone 1997: 1.190). And the installation of the ark at Zion, the place chosen by God for his name to dwell, marks the summation of the process begun with the completion of the tabernacle at Sinai. David's blessing of the people echoes Moses's blessing of the people because his establishment of the ark in Jerusalem marks the final conquest of the land promised to Abraham. David's extraordinary ritual feeding of "all Israel, both women and men" (1 Chr. 16:3), also associates him with the covenant banquet of Moses and the elders at Sinai and the manna in the wilderness, yet also with the promise of Deuteronomy that the people would one day eat in the presence of God in the place where God will choose to dwell (12:7, 18).

The Chronicler has also tapped into some deeper biblical tradition of royal priesthood, associated also with Jerusalem and likely established during the Davidic period of the monarchy. David's actions, read canonically in light of this biblical tradition, can be well understood as reflecting his aspirations to be a new Melchizedek. Again, as in the questions of his capture of Jerusalem and restoration of the ark, there is a question of how David formed his cultic intentions. Before this procession there is only one biblical precedent for a righteous king's performing priestly functions—the mysterious Melchizedek of Salem, who brought out bread and wine and blessed Abraham in Gen. 14. Melchizedek is the first person to be designated "priest" in the canon; according to later Jewish interpreters, he represents the divine ideal for the priesthood (Philo, *Allegorical Interpretation* 3.79; Josephus, *Jewish War* 6.438). Melchizedek appears again in the Hebrew canon only once more—in a powerful Davidic tradition. In Ps. 110:4 he is the namesake of an eternal "order" of priesthood, bestowed along with divine sonship upon the Davidic king by a divine oath: "The LORD has sworn . . . , 'You are a priest for ever after the order of Melchizedek.'"

Numerous scholars suggest that the story of Melchizedek's blessing of Abraham played a central role in the traditions of Jerusalem, helping to establish the continuity of the kingdom of Israel with the covenant promises made to Abraham. Vawter writes: "By this story Abraham, and in Abraham the seed of Israel, is brought into intimate contact with that which was destined to be the holy city of David, and accordingly Abraham receives the blessing of the Jerusalemite priesthood" (1977: 198). These scholars suggest that Melchizedek was deliberately invoked as a part of a strategy aimed at "legitimizing the national cult of David and Solomon" (Cross 1998: 41).

Later Jewish tradition attaches much symbolic significance to Melchizedek's name, which means "king of righteousness," and the name of his kingdom, Salem, which denotes "peace." For instance, both of these concepts are operative in the Chronicler's depiction of Solomon. However, the key biblical link between Melchizedek and the Davidic kingdom remains Ps. 110:4.[1] There is considerable scholarly consensus that this psalm, attributed to David, is preexilic and likely one of the oldest in the Psalter. It may have originated in the liturgical context of an enthronement ceremony for a new Davidic king, possibly even the coronation of Solomon. There are important points of contact between the themes and language of the psalm and the Chronicler's work, including the psalm's reference to the universal reign of Zion's king over the nations, the divine deliverance of the king from his enemies, and the apparent filial relation of the Davidic king to God (i.e., the Davidic covenant in 1 Chr. 17). The psalm speaks of a "footstool" (*hădōm raglayim*) for God—a rare word in the Bible used uniquely in Chronicles and the Psalter to describe the ark (1 Chr. 28:2; Ps. 110:1; cf. 99:5; 132:7; Lam. 2:1; Isa. 66:1).

Psalm 110:4 establishes the Davidic monarch as an heir to the oath sworn to Melchizedek. The significance of this is well explained by Ishida:

Melchizedek represents the prototype of the priest-king of Jerusalem in this psalm. . . . By a twist of chronology he is made an ancient priest of Yahweh who

1. On the textual issues regarding Ps. 110, see Stuhlmueller 1983: 130–31.

has dwelt on Mount Zion (Ps. 110:2). Accordingly, in the view of the psalmist, it was Yahweh who designated him as a priest-king of Jerusalem in the past, and now Yahweh will give the same position to the Davidic kings who are ruling in Jerusalem as successors to him. . . . The purpose of the psalm is twofold. On the one hand, by mentioning the "order of Melchizedek" as Yahweh's designation, it shows that the kingship and the priesthood of Jerusalem have been associated with Yahweh since the days of Melchizedek, who was contemporaneous with Abraham. On the other, it serves to justify the priestly function of the Davidic kings. . . . It appears that David tried to defend his priestly authority by claiming succession to the "order of Melchizedek," a mysterious priest-king of Jerusalem in the past. (1977: 139–40)

More was at work in the Davidic appeal to Melchizedek, however, than ancient *realpolitik* or ideological turf battles between the priestly caste and the monarchy. Recalling the royal and priestly imagery employed in the creation accounts and reading in light of the Davidic hope expressed in the Psalms and the Prophets—in the Chronicler's David we see not only a new Melchizedek, but also a new Adam; or perhaps better: in the Chronicler's David we see a new Adam by way of Melchizedek. With the ark established at Zion, the God Most High (*'ēl 'elyôn*), the maker of heaven and earth (Gen. 14:18–22), "sits enthroned" above the nations (1 Chr. 13:6), ruling through his "first-born, the highest of the kings of the earth" (Ps. 89:27), who is priest and king.

The Davidic kingdom at Zion is a partial fulfillment of the divine intention for creation. This will become clearer when we look at the terms of the Davidic covenant and the temple. In this wider lens we are able to better understand David's priestly concerns—not only his offering of blessings and sacrifices but also his institution of the temple cult—as an expression of the everlasting priestly order of Melchizedek. This priestly order cannot have meant the eclipse of the Levitical priesthood. We know that because of the central role the Levites play in Chronicles. The royal priesthood of the Davidic king evidently existed alongside the Levitical priesthood of Aaron and his descendants, which remained, even under David, the official priesthood for God's covenant people (Exod. 40:12–15; Num. 17:1–13; 18:1–7).

The biblical data leads us to see David's priesthood as evoking the pre-Levitical hereditary priesthood of the period of natural religion—that is, as a part of the religion of Abraham and the patriarchs. The association of David and Melchizedek, like the identification of the temple and Moriah, serves to plant the kingdom of God at Zion deep in the soil of the ancient, pre-Israelite history of the world. Jewish tradition overwhelmingly identified Melchizedek with Shem, the righteous firstborn of Noah, an interpretive tradition that continued in early Christianity. That makes Melchizedek a representative of this era of natural religion—when the priesthood was rooted in the patriarchal family structure.

Before the institution of the Levitical priesthood after the golden-calf incident, priesthood was not a profession or a caste: it was a natural part of the family, with fathers as the head of the family, and their heirs, the firstborn sons, performing the priestly functions of offering sacrifices, leading prayer, and imparting blessings. This natural religion seems to reflect the order of creation, which understands the human vocation in royal, priestly, and filial terms. The *qāhāl*, so stressed by the Chronicler, also hearkens to this era of natural religion. Although an Israelite institution, the *qāhāl* before the golden-calf apostasy seems to have functioned as a family of families, with "young men of the people of Israel," likely the firstborns, offering sacrifices and peace offerings (Exod. 24:5–6).

Perhaps in David we are meant to see expressed the "priestly soul" intended for all humanity in the beginning. In addition, in presenting David as the priest-king, the Chronicler also appears to be evoking the prophetic hopes for a Davidic Messiah. The ideal priest-king of the past foreshadows the one who is to come. Judaism, perhaps even in the time of the Chronicler, read Ps. 110 in messianic terms; this continued into the Christian era, most notably in the typology of Jesus Christ as a new Melchizedek in the Letter to the Hebrews. The author of Hebrews, according to Lane, finds in the Melchizedek tradition "the unmistakable implication that the Levitical priesthood will be replaced by the eternal priesthood foreshadowed and prefigured in the person of Melchizedek" (1991: 163).

Already in the exilic prophecy of Ezekiel, we sense a similar mood. Ezekiel envisioned the restoration of the exiles, the reunification of the divided kingdom, and the reestablishment of the temple under God's "servant David" (37:24–28). Levenson observes that the Davidic figure in Ezekiel is a priest-king, and the restored Israel is a kingdom of priests: "Ezekiel hoped . . . for a community so fundamentally liturgical and sacral in nature that the Davidid . . . could only be a liturgical figurehead like the High Priest. . . . Ezekiel 40–48 hopes not for a restoration of the monarchy, but for a restoration of the monarch, who is now redefined according to his deepest and truest function as the servant of God, or devoted to the divine service, to liturgy" (1976: 143).

### *Let Them Say among the Nations: "The LORD Reigns!"*

The order of Melchizedek, understood in the context of the monarchy, can be seen as the divine service of the God Most High, the Lord of creation, the Lord of history, and the Lord of the nations. The liturgy of this divine service is fundamentally a liturgy of thanksgiving. That is how we should read Melchizedek's original offering of bread and wine and Abraham's tithe—as thanksgiving to the Most High for having been delivered from the threat of death, from the hands of the enemy. As such, this liturgy is one of remembering God's mighty deeds of deliverance and of praising the name of the God who delivers and rules the nations.

This defines the contours of the liturgy that David establishes at Zion as he appoints the Levites to "remember" (*zkr*), "give thanks" (*ydh*), and "praise" (*hll*; 1 Chr. 16:4).

The Chronicler concludes his account of the ark's restoration with a long priestly psalm of remembrance, thanksgiving, and praise, attributed to the priest-king David.

The Chronicler's song of David creatively combines passages from three psalms—Ps. 105:1–15 (= 1 Chr. 16:8–22); Ps. 96 (= 1 Chr. 16:23–33); and Ps. 106:1, 47–48 (= 1 Chr. 16:34–36)—and is a profound work of biblical theology in its own right. In this priestly song of redemption, David interprets Israel's history as an economy of salvation, flowing from the covenant with Abraham to this moment, when the ark has been restored. It is a common practice among translators to "correct" the Chronicler's quotations so that they agree with the psalms he is drawing from. This is a dubious practice because, as Williamson declares (1982: 128), these psalms were no doubt familiar to the Chronicler's audience from their regular worship; therefore, even the few changes that the Chronicler has made would have been significant and noticed. As Selman says, these "small variations make it almost certain that earlier scripture has been reinterpreted and applied to the circumstances of the Chronicler's time" (1994a: 168).

Beginning with a triple call to "seek" (*dāraš*) the Lord and a repeated call for "remembrance" (*zkr*), the psalm celebrates God's "deeds" and "his wonderful works." While Ps. 105 was speaking of the *mirabilia Dei* in the exodus, David's use of the psalm associates these earlier works with the installation of the ark (1 Chr. 16:10–15). The psalm is declaring that the exodus, the conquest of Jerusalem, and the return of the ark are all of a piece—expressions of God's love for the seed of Israel, his chosen ones (*bhr*). David twice says that God's covenant with Israel is forever (*běrît 'ôlām*; 1 Chr. 16:15, 17). Central to this promise is the inheritance of the land, which was given to a people "few in number, and of little account," who first spent years of "wandering from nation to nation" (16:18–22).

Here we see the Chronicler's homiletic intent. On the one hand, in the context of his narrative, David's psalm presents the restoration of the ark as the fulfillment of the promised inheritance. On the other hand, the Chronicler's audience would no doubt hear a deliberate echo of their own situation—a people no longer in charge of their land or their destiny, with many of their brethren scattered and wandering among other nations and kingdoms (13:2). With their efforts to harmonize the Chronicler with the text of Ps. 96, translators lose an obvious meaning. In the Hebrew text, the Chronicler changes the psalm from third-person plural (they) to second-personal plural (you). This sets up a thought that does not seem to make any sense: "When *you* were few in number, insignificant and sojourners in it, *they* wandered from nation to nation, from one kingdom to another people, he allowed no one to oppress them; he rebuked kings on their account saying, 'Touch not my anointed ones, do my prophets no harm'" (1 Chr. 16:19–22).

This is an example of the Chronicler's liturgical historiography: it serves to bring his audience into contact with the common story of God's people. Riley offers a sensitive summary of what the Chronicler is up to in this passage: "In this way the Chronicler identified his contemporaries with the patriarchs, whose experience was of vulnerability as a landless minority. Like their ancestors they were aliens in their own land which was ruled by the Persians. Yet like them they were also protected by the Lord as a people with royal status and a prophetic mission" (1993: 137). That mission, as the psalm proclaims, is to bring all the nations and peoples of the world—and indeed all the cosmos, the heavens and the earth—to the worship of Israel's God (1 Chr. 16:23–33).

David's priestly song builds to an exhortation to worship the living God, followed by a denouement that declares the Lord's coming "to judge the earth" (16:33). In the context of the Chronicler's narrative, the Lord's coming to Zion in the ark is readily associated with the Lord's coming in judgment of the nations and the idols of the peoples: "Let them say among the nations, 'The LORD reigns!'" (16:31). This was the divine intention from the beginning, as Johnstone recognizes (1997: 1.194)—that all the children of Adam "acknowledge God's purpose portrayed in Israel's history, his sole deity and transcendent power declared in creation, and to 'ascribe to the LORD the glory due to his name'" (16:29).

Yet the Chronicler swiftly adds a coda that comes as a kind of non sequitur—a prayer-plea for the people to be delivered "from among the nations," followed by a prayer blessing "the LORD, the God of Israel" (16:35–36). It is a strange way to end a thanksgiving celebration. In the context of the Chronicler's narrative, the prayer has David, at his moment of triumph—the completion of the inheritance of the land, the establishment of God in the place where he has chosen for his name to dwell—foreseeing the crack-up of the kingdom and Israel's exile and begging for deliverance in advance, as it were. "Say also: 'Deliver us, O God of our salvation, and gather and save us from among the nations'" (16:35).

In one sense, this is a continuation of the Moses typology, for David is here prophesying the future punishment of the people, as Moses foretold the scattering of the people for their failure to keep the covenant (Deut. 4:25–30; 28:15, 36, 62–65; 30:1–5). The Chronicler is also reinforcing his theme that God is in charge of history. The Lord who enthroned David also knew that the kingdom would be laid low. Yet he could count on his readers' knowing the fuller context of Ps. 106, which he is quoting here: "Many times he delivered them. . . . He remembered for their sake his covenant" (Ps. 106:43, 45).

David is shown to have a prophetic foreknowledge of the future, and the Chronicler's audience knows that this prayer, which he made for them in their exile, has been answered in part by the decree of Cyrus. In making that prayer their own, the readers in the Chronicler's generation were making a confession of faith in the God of Israel, confident that he would reunite them with their brethren still scattered among the nations. The song of the priest-king is to be heard as a call for faithfulness, for renewal, for a hope grounded in the Lord's faithfulness to his covenant.

## Christian Interpretation

Paul wrote to the early Christians about Israel's experience of the exodus: "Now these things happened to them as a warning, but they were written down for our instruction, upon whom the end of the ages has come" (1 Corinthians 10:11). The Chronicler has much the same perspective: the entire tradition of scripture was written for the instruction of his audience. Indeed, the Chronicler's patterns of inner-biblical interpretation made perfect sense to Jesus and the apostolic church; Chronicles might even be read as a workshop in biblical theology for the New Testament writers: we find operative in Chronicles many of the interpretive principles that become normative for the New Testament writers' use of the Old Testament.

The Chronicler writes and interprets history typologically. For the Christian reader, Chronicles offers a rich source for understanding some of the inner-biblical roots of important types found in the New Testament. Davidic covenant typology, Zion, and the kingdom of God are discussed later in this commentary. Here three important New Testament images are illuminated by a typological reading of the Chronicler.

### The Church

The Chronicler's extensive use of *qāhāl* and the verb *qhl* to describe the sacral convocation of Israel is suggestive. The Septuagint almost always translates *qāhāl* as *ekklēsia*, which is the term that Christ and the apostolic writers adopted to describe the church as the new people of God. In the Septuagint version of Chronicles, then, we likely find the seeds of New Testament ecclesiology.

For instance, in Matthew 16:18–19, one of only two places in the Gospels where Jesus uses the word *ekklēsia* (also 18:17), the description is redolent of imagery associated with the Chronicler's depiction of David, his son Solomon, and the temple. The church, as the people of God, is described as a new temple and a new kingdom, founded upon a rock, built on the Son of God. These are all Davidic images found in Chronicles, but it is clear that the church is being portrayed in Matthew 16 as a restoration of the kingdom of David and the temple of Solomon.

Bultmann is no doubt correct that "in content, the 'Church (of God)' *ekklēsia (tou Theou)*, corresponds . . . with *qāhāl (yhwh)*" and "in understanding themselves as Congregation or Church, the disciples appropriate to themselves the title of the Old Testament Congregation of God, the *qāhāl-yhwh*" (1951–55: 1.38). This New Testament understanding owes its source, in significant measure, to the Chronicler's depiction of the Davidic *qāhāl*.

### Ark of the Covenant

Early Christian tradition, beginning within the New Testament, associated the ark of the covenant with both the church and Mary, the mother of Christ. Given the prominence of the ark in Chronicles, the Christian reader would do well to consider the possible influences this work might have had on the development of that imagery.

Scholars detect distinct parallels between the story of the ark's restoration to Jerusalem and the story of Mary's visiting her cousin Elizabeth in Luke 1. It seems that Luke wrote his scene with intentional parallels to the joyous homecoming of the ark (Ratzinger 1983: 81–82). While some of the verbal parallels are more apparent in the Greek text of the Chronicler's source, 2 Sam. 6, Luke's text nonetheless provides us with a rich resource for New Testament allusion (Hahn 2001: 63–64; Hahn and Mitch 2001: 21). For instance, when the aged Elizabeth greets Mary, she "exclaims" (*anaphōneō*; Luke 1:42). The Greek word is found only here in the New Testament and appears in the Greek Old Testament only in the Chronicler's descriptions of Levitical worship before the ark (1 Chr. 15:28; 16:4, 5, 42; 2 Chr. 5:13). In Luke, Elizabeth is identified as being of Levitical descent (Luke 1:5). Perhaps Luke means his readers to understand that Elizabeth recognizes Mary as bearing the living God within her and is thus compelled to liturgical exultation—as the Levites were charged with playing their instruments loudly and lifting up their voices before the ark.

The Chronicler was apparently aware of the Second Temple era traditions regarding the hiding of the ark and the sacred vessels before the Babylonian plunder and destruction of the temple. These traditions are also presumed in the book of Revelation's dramatic depiction of the ark of the covenant revealed in the temple of heaven—an image connected to the image that immediately follows it, that of a heavenly queen mother (11:19–12:5).

Revelation is depicting the return of the lost ark, according to the traditions associated with the prophet Jeremiah (2 Macc. 2). The ark is revealed to be a woman—an image of the mother of Christ and the mother of Christians, that is, the church, the new *qāhāl*. The vision is heavily typological and filled with Old Testament allusions. The woman, as Beale observes, is portrayed as "the continuation of true Israel in the twelve apostles and the church they represent" (1999: 629).

The author of Revelation, like Luke, is drawing on traditions of Levitical worship before the ark. In the vision, the ark is revealed after the last of seven angels sounds his trumpet, announcing the coming of God's kingdom (11:15; cf. 8:2; 10:7). This alludes to the order of worship established by David for the ark, wherein priests were appointed to "blow trumpets continually, before the ark of the covenant of God" (1 Chr. 16:6; cf. 15:24). The ark is thus associated with the coming of the kingdom and the new people of God, portrayed as a woman, bride, and mother.

### The Priest-King Melchizedek

The Chronicler depicts David as a royal high priest; in the Psalter, divine sonship and priesthood are associated with the Davidic king. This imagery was profoundly influential in the development of New Testament Christology. If David was indeed a new Melchizedek, Christ is the *definitive* new Melchizedek. Thus the Christian reader can find in the Chronicler's portrait of David, and later Solomon, much to illuminate the Melchizedek typology in the Letter to the Hebrews. There Jesus's royal-priestly primogeniture is presented as the fulfillment of the Davidic sacral kingship associated with "the order of Melchizedek." By the sworn oath of God, Jesus is both king and high priest, exercising his ministry in the heavenly Zion as the firstborn Son of God.

3

# His Throne Shall Be Established Forever

## God's Covenant with King David (1 Chr. 17)

### Major Divisions of the Text

1. David's desire to build a house for God (17:1–2)
2. Dynastic oracle (17:3–15)
    David cannot build a house for God (17:3–6)
    God's establishment and blessing of David (17:7–8a)
    Further blessings promised to David and peace to Israel (17:8b–10a)
    God's promise of an everlasting dynasty to David (17:10b–15)
3. David's covenant prayer (17:16–27)
    Praise and thanksgiving for God's greatness and blessings (17:16–22)
    Petition for God to fulfill his covenant promises (17:23–27)

### Synopsis of the Text

The dynastic oracle of the prophet Nathan is at the heart of the Chronicler's work. Everything that precedes this oracle anticipates it, as everything that follows in Chronicles flows from it. By this oracle, God makes his covenant with David, promising David a son who will build a temple and reign forever over the kingdom of Israel, which will be the kingdom of God on earth.

## Theological Exegesis and Commentary

### Good Things Promised to His Chosen Servant

God's covenant with David is the theological summit of the salvation story the Chronicler has come to tell. It is difficult to exaggerate the importance of the Davidic covenant for understanding the Chronicler's purposes. The dynastic oracle delivered to David through the prophet Nathan (1 Chr. 17:3–15) forms an *inclusio* with the divine word spoken to Solomon after the temple is dedicated (2 Chr. 7:11–22). The Chronicler's purposes unfold in the narrative space between these two speeches; at the same time, in these two speeches by God we find his understanding of the economy of salvation neatly summed up.

As a biblical theologian, the Chronicler operates with a liturgical or sacramental worldview. History is not merely the record of human endeavors and personalities intersecting with natural forces and other environmental factors. In these complex interstices he sees the hidden hand of the Lord of history—creating, choosing, and shaping destinies; rewarding those who seek him and forsaking those who do not. Now, at the center of his narrative, he reveals the goal toward which all history is directed—God's covenant with David, his dwelling at Zion, and the establishment of his kingdom on earth. History is linear for the Chronicler, yet he sees God as writing that history with a rhythmic and at times almost circular hand. He sees patterns of recurrence and repetition; what comes later often bears a certain family resemblance to what has come before. David is a figure of Moses, but there is also an Adamic typology at work. The Chronicler's genealogies trace David's line back to Adam, the image and firstborn son of God. And the Chronicler's David is the figure in whom God's purposes for creation find their fulfillment. At the summit of salvation history, in the Davidic covenant we can trace the lineage of the earlier covenants with Adam, Noah, Abraham, and Moses.

The actual message the Chronicler intended to convey is the subject of sharp scholarly dispute in the modern period. Much of the dispute reaches a crescendo over the Chronicler's depiction of the covenant with David and the subsequent monarchy and temple under Solomon. Here again, in the Chronicler's depiction of the covenant, we must see more than nostalgia for golden days gone by and more than a royalist ideology that seeks to legitimize the divine right of Davidic kings or the Levitical priesthood under postexilic conditions in Israel. In moving reasonably among the scholarly extremes, Williamson concludes with admirable caution: "Although the term 'messianic' is perhaps too strong, it must be concluded that the Chronicler still cherished the hope that one day the Davidic dynasty would be re-established over Israel" (1982: 134). Selman, whose commentary more than any other emphasizes the Davidic key, is similarly measured on this point:

The Chronicler's overall aim was to offer an interpretation of the Bible as he knew it. More precisely, his guiding principle was to demonstrate that God's promises revealed in the Davidic covenant were as trustworthy and effective as when they were first given, even though the first readers lived centuries after almost all the events he recorded. . . .

There is no evidence in Chronicles of a strong messianic hope. . . . The Chronicler does not concentrate on the future but on the continuity between the distant past and the present or recent past. The three passages where the Chronicler's account comes nearest to his own time all stress this link rather than awaken any explicit hope for the future. The post-exilic continuation of David's line (1 Chron. 3:17–24), the account of the resettlement of Jerusalem (1 Chron. 9:2–34), and the summary of Cyrus' edict (2 Chron. 36:22–23), all indicate that God is still building his house and that he invites his people to go on participating in the task. (1994a: 26, 64–65)

Chronicles points us beyond even such wise and careful conclusions. The Chronicler was well aware of the deep vein of hope for a Davidic Messiah, expectation that in the Chronicler's own day attached to the Davidide Zerubbabel, who began the work of building the second temple (Hag. 2:20–23; Zech. 6:11–13; other Davidic prophecies in Isa. 9:6–7; 37:35; 55:3; Jer. 23:5; 33:15–26; Ezek. 34:24–25; 37:24–27; Amos 9:11). The Chronicler's genealogy extends past Zerubbabel and pushes the Davidic line well into the period of the restoration. But Chronicles is not a prophecy or an apocalypse: it is history, although history written in a haggadic or homiletic key. Yet precisely because it is haggadah, the Chronicler's history presumes a faith in the God whose story he narrates.

Such faith suggests itself as an obvious hermeneutical key for his work. Unfortunately, in aspiring to a scientific reading of the text, scholars often refuse to accept at face value the Chronicler's faith as a legitimate guide to his authorial intentions; instead they seek to ascribe some ulterior motives for his work. This basic failure of scholarly sympathy is behind a number of persistent misunderstandings of Chronicles.

In the case of the Davidic covenant, much scholarly ink has been spilled over whether the Chronicler believed the dynastic oracle to have been fulfilled in Solomon or whether he instead believed that the dynasty was for all time and hence that God would one day reestablish the two houses of David: the kingdom and the temple at Jerusalem. A great deal of the prophetic hope found in scripture and extrabiblical texts anticipates precisely such a Davidic restoration. It thus seems inconceivable that the Chronicler, an obviously devout believer in the God of Israel, could give an account of God's covenant oath to David and not be looking forward to the ultimate fulfillment of that divine promise—even if the expected fulfillment might come at a much later date, perhaps not even in his or his readers' lifetimes. Indeed, for the Chronicler to believe otherwise—that Solomon was the sole subject of the dynastic oracle or that somehow God was no longer the prime mover in the life of Israel—would be an act of *ma'al*, the covenant unfaithfulness that he is sermonizing against in so much of his work.

My view is not that far from that of Selman and Williamson. But the Chronicler's trust in God's promises to David is, by its very nature, a species of eschatological hope—hope for a Messiah who would bring about the fulfillment of those promises. Chronicles may not be as fervent in expressing that hope as other works of the period: apocalyptic fervor would not be appropriate in a work of this genre. The Chronicler's intentions are catechetical. He is preparing his readers, both in Jerusalem and in the Diaspora, to recognize the signs of the times and to play their part in the anticipated fulfillment of God's promises in the eschatological restoration of the kingdom of David and the temple.

### Oracle of Divine Dynasty

There are distinct parallels between the Chronicler's accounts of the dynastic oracle and the divine speech in response to Solomon's dedication of the temple. The prophet Nathan delivers the dynastic oracle to David (1 Chr. 17:3–15), who responds with a royal prayer (17:16–27); the process is reversed at the temple dedication, with Solomon first delivering a royal prayer (2 Chr. 6), to which God responds with an oracle addressed personally to Solomon (7:11–22). The meaning of the covenant is the theme of each divine speech, with each explaining the covenant's meaning in terms of Israel's election, God's desire to dwell with his people, and the blessings that will flow from his kingdom and his house upon the nations.

The immediate context of Nathan's oracle is David's zealous desire to build a "house" for the ark of the covenant of the Lord, the climactic expression of his royal-priestly activities. The term "covenant" (*běrît*) is not used in Nathan's oracle. But the Chronicler clearly understands that God is here making a covenant with David. He says as much elsewhere (2 Chr. 7:18; 21:7). And the assumption of a Davidic covenant is attested throughout the biblical record that he draws upon. In the Psalms we hear: "I have made a covenant with my chosen one, I have sworn to David my servant: I will establish your descendants for ever, and build your throne for all generations" (Ps. 89:3–4, 20, 27–29, 35–36). The prophet Isaiah told of God's "everlasting covenant . . . [and] sure love for David" (Isa. 55:3; cf. 2 Chr. 6:42). Jeremiah compared the Davidic covenant with a primordial covenant with creation, God's "covenant with the day and . . . with the night" (Jer. 33:20–22, 25–26).

The covenant with David is a divine gift or "grant": God binds himself by divine oath, swearing unwavering fidelity and promising unconditional blessings and everlasting kingship to David and his offspring (Weinfeld 1970: 185). This covenant of grant seems to reward David's single-minded dedication to restoring Israel as a priestly kingdom and building a house for the ark of the covenant. In the account of the covenant, the term "house" (*bayit*), referring to both the royal dynasty and the temple, occurs fourteen times, while the term "servant" (*'ebed*) appears twelve times. The use of the common term *bayit* in this context nonetheless evokes the covenant drama of the house of Jacob and the house of Israel, leading up to their flight from the "house of bondage" in Egypt. David's speech, with its rhythmic repetitions of *'ebed*, also evokes the themes of the exodus. The early chapters of Exodus involve a play on the notion of "service" and "servitude." The cruel bondage of the Israelites (1:13–14; 5:18; 14:5, 12) is described with the same word, *'bd*, used of the religious worship and ritual service that God desires of them (3:12; 4:23; 7:16; 9:1, 13; 10:3, 24–26) and of the priestly liturgical service in the tabernacle (Num. 3:7–8; 4:23; 7:5; 16:9). The climactic declaration of Israel's divine primogeniture among the nations is made in terms of this divine service that God desires: "And you shall say to Pharaoh, 'Thus says the Lord, Israel is my first-born son, and I say to you, "Let my son go that he may serve me"'" (Exod. 4:22–23).

That the exodus might not be too far from David's mind is clear from his twin references to Israel's "redemption from Egypt" in his response to Nathan's oracle (1 Chr. 17:21). Indeed, there is a covenant-renewal feel to David's prayer. It is prayed while seated "before the Lord" (*lipnê yhwh*; 17:16), an expression that frequently describes ritual and liturgical prayer, often in the presence of the ark (Wilson 1995: 131–97). With its liturgical rhythms and repetitions, the prayer suggests that David is not only accepting God's covenant for himself, but also that on behalf of the people he is renewing the covenant made at Sinai: "What other nation on earth is like . . . thy people whom thou didst redeem from Egypt? And thou didst make thy people Israel to be thy people for ever; and thou, O Lord, didst become their God. And now, O Lord, . . . do as thou hast spoken; and thy name will be established and magnified for ever, saying, 'The Lord of hosts, the God of Israel, is Israel's God,' and the house of thy servant David will be established before thee" (17:21–24).

The echoes of earlier biblical covenantal language here are unmistakable, as in Nathan's oracle. Speaking through Nathan, God employs the vocabulary of the Sinaitic covenant, identifying David as his "servant" and a "shepherd," making repeated references to "my people Israel," and calling Israel's king his "son." The covenant with David, the new Moses, is a kind of renewal of the Sinai covenant, an affirmation of God's election of Israel to be his people and to be their God (Exod. 6:7; Lev. 26:12; Hos. 1:8–9; Jer. 31:33). The election of Israel is affirmed as "for ever" (an expression used eight times in 1 Chr. 17), as the son of David becomes the focus of God's paternal love for Israel (Exod. 4:22). Significantly, David begins his prayer of response with a deliberate echo of Moses's response to God's calling at Horeb. As Moses wondered: "Who am I that I should go to Pharaoh?" (Exod. 3:11), David in amazement asks: "Who am I . . . that thou hast brought me this far?" (1 Chr. 17:16; cf. 29:14).

Commentators who see the Chronicler as somehow in tension with or rejecting the Mosaic covenant need to take a fresh look at the evidence. Levenson rightly says: "In short, as Israelites, the Davidids are bound by the Sinaitic Torah or Mosaic covenant. There is no text in the Hebrew Bible that holds that the Davidic *replaces* the Sinaitic" (1985: 99). Chronicles is no exception to that biblical rule, and there is no downplaying of the Sinaitic covenant either. Indeed, in addition to the consistent new-Moses imagery associated with David, throughout Chronicles it is clear that the Davidic covenant binds the king and the nation to "the law of the LORD" given at Sinai (1 Chr. 16:40; 2 Chr. 31:3) and the cultic and other ordinances given by "the word of the LORD by Moses" (2 Chr. 35:6; 1 Chr. 15:15). The connections between the Sinai covenant and the Davidic are emphasized elsewhere in the injunctions for the kings to obey the *tôrâ* and Mosaic precepts (1 Chr. 22:13; 28:7; 2 Chr. 6:16; 7:17; 14:4; 33:8).

Again, however, we are invited to consider the importance of the Abrahamic covenant for the Chronicler's understanding of salvation history. We cannot properly understand his vision of the Davidic covenant apart from the Abrahamic covenant, which, like the Davidic covenant, is an unconditional divine grant. The original grant to Abraham consisted of three promises—to make Abraham a great nation, to make his name great, and to make him the source of divine blessing for all the families of the earth (Gen. 12:1–3). And these promises became the basis for a threefold covenant with Abraham and his descendants—promising land (15:7–21), a royal dynasty (17:1–21), and fatherhood over countless descendants who would bring about the blessing of the nations (22:16–18).

In the Davidic covenant we see fulfillment of these covenant oaths. There are close similarities between the dynastic promises and the Abrahamic promises. David too is promised a great "name" (1 Chr. 17:8) and a place, a land in which his people will be "planted" (17:9). The "house" that God promises to build for David is a family, a line of descendants who will reign forever over Israel (17:11–12; 28:4). The conquest of Jerusalem effectively capped the conquest of the land begun under Joshua, while the rise of the Davidic kingdom delivers on the promise of a royal dynasty sprung from the line of Abraham's descendant, Judah. Already the Psalter associates the supremacy of the Davidic king and the Abrahamic blessing of the nations, in a psalm linked to Solomon:

> May his name endure for ever. . . .
> May men bless themselves by him,
>     all nations call him blessed! (Ps. 72:17)

Thus we can conclude with Clements that the Davidic covenant and the kingdom it establishes—the final covenant of the Hebrew Bible—is deeply rooted in the fundamental biblical covenant with Abraham: "Through his anointed king Yahweh exercised his dominion over the nations of the earth, communicating his blessing to them through his people Israel. . . . What Yahweh had first promised to Abraham, and reaffirmed to succeeding patriarchs, had been brought to marvelous fruition with the emergence of the Israelite state under David" (1967: 59).

In the Davidic covenant we see the meaning of God's covenant plan for history. What was promised to Abraham was never meant exclusively for Abraham's sake or even the sake of his descendants, the chosen people of Israel. From the start, God's covenant purposes were universal. The initial promise to Abraham was to bring about the divine blessing of all the families of the world, implying an original divine intention to bring all people into a single family of God through Abraham's family. The later covenant with Abraham's descendants at Sinai is nowhere presented as a new covenant; it is rather, as Clements says, the "disclosure of those cultic institutions and regulations which made possible the fulfilment of the promises made to Abraham" (1967: 75).

The Chronicler's David apparently recognizes all this. In his instructions to Solomon, he charges him "to observe the statutes and the ordinances which the LORD commanded Moses for Israel" (1 Chr. 22:13). And in his final address to the *qāhāl*, he prays that the people will forever direct their hearts toward the "LORD, the God of Abraham, Isaac, and Israel, our fathers" (29:18).

### I Will Be His Father, and He Shall Be My Son

At the heart of the covenant with David, as at the heart of the covenant with Abraham, is the promise of a son:

> When your days are fulfilled to go to be with your fathers, I will raise up your offspring after you, one of your own sons, and I will establish his kingdom. He shall build a house for me, and I will establish his throne for ever. I will be his father, and he shall be my son; I will not take my steadfast love from him, as I took it from him who was before you, but I will confirm him in my house and in my kingdom for ever and his throne shall be established for ever. (1 Chr. 17:11–14)

The divine covenant plan has familial dimensions since kinship was created between God and his creatures through the covenant. Lines of family descent—especially relationships between fathers and their firstborns, and between firstborns and their siblings—are important in the biblical narrative. And the priestly prerogatives that flow from the firstborn's status in patriarchal society are transferred to the nation of Israel in the Sinai covenant, where Israel, God's firstborn son, is called to serve him as a kingdom of priests.

All this forms the context for Nathan's oracle. The promise to David is set in the terms of the Chronicler's genealogy of grace. It is not until David joins his "fathers" in the sleep of death that his own son will be established. This is emphasized in David's final speech to the *qāhāl*, which in essence contains David's own exegesis of this oracle. David explains his understanding that God has chosen him from all his father's house, which is a part of the chosen line of Judah (1 Chr. 28:4). David himself, then, according to the Chronicler, understands his covenant as a fulfillment of Jacob's patriarchal promise that the royal scepter would not depart from Judah, the "desire of the nations" (Gen. 49:10 Septuagint).

"Offspring" (*zera'*, lit., "seed") establishes another connection between the Davidic covenant and the Abrahamic promise, which was a promise to Abraham's *seed* (Gen. 12:7; 15:5, 18; 17:7–10; 22:17–18). In David's prayer celebrating the return of the ark, he addresses the people: "O offspring [*zera'*] of Abraham" (1 Chr. 16:13). In the dynastic oracle, God's promise to Abraham's seed is fastened forever to this promise to David's seed.

In Solomon's exegesis of the dynastic oracle, he also recalls Israel's redemption from Egypt (2 Chr. 6:5; cf. 1 Chr. 17:21). And there is a strong sense that the royal-priestly primogeniture granted to David's seed (1 Chr. 17:13; 2 Sam. 7:14; Pss. 110:4; 89:26–27) restores to Israel the royal priesthood that it forfeited in the apostasy of the golden-calf incident and the idolatry committed at Baal-peor (Hahn 2009b: 197–99). Through the covenant with David, Israel reclaims its status as firstborn among the nations, and along with it the responsibilities of primogeniture—fraternal responsibility to bring the blessings of God to all the families of the world.

How did the Chronicler understand the divine sonship of the Davidic king? Scholarly opinion tends to regard the language here as either hyperbolic, mythical, or metaphorical. Others detect an adoption motif, which is much closer to what is actually going on in the text. Read canonically in light of Israel's primogeniture and in light of the royal psalms and the Davidic oracles found in the Prophets, the text is best understood in sacramental or covenantal-realist terms. The divine oath here ("I will be his father, and he shall be my son") is a promise of blessings that God will bestow in the future—the promise of divine sonship. Divine sonship, then, is a reality established by God's sworn oath in the dynastic oracle.

This seems to be the best explanation for how this oath is understood in the psalms associated with the monarchy. For instance, in Ps. 2, God speaks directly to the king: "You are my son, today I have begotten you." The Septuagint version of Ps. 110 includes a similar line ("I have begotten you from the womb before the morning"). In each case, the enthronement of the king seems to include a solemn sacramental adoption, through which the king is begotten of God by his word of divine oath. Divine sonship for the Davidic king is not understood metaphorically but ontologically. It is a new state of being, brought about by the creative power of God's word. The words of the psalm, which were likely spoken during the coronation liturgy, are uttered as divine speech. As divine speech, they create the realities they speak of—in a way analogous to the way the divine word functioned in creation ("and God said, 'Let there be *x*'; and there was *x*"; e.g., Gen. 1:3; cf. Pss. 2:7; 110:4). Thus, in another royal psalm, God can declare of the Davidic king what he once declared of Israel: "I will make him the first-born"; and the "newborn" king can respond: "Thou art my Father" (Ps. 89:26–27).

### The Kingdom of God and the House of David

What happens in this divine begetting is a profound union of the people of Israel with their king. In the Davidic king, "a child is born, . . . a son is given. . . . The zeal of the LORD of hosts will do this," Isaiah declares (9:6–7). The Davidic king is also a new-Adam figure, a son of God who stands as God's vice-regent or prince over creation. In David and the kingdom of David, we see a partial or provisional restoration of God's plans for creation, as McCartney observes: "In the Davidic theocracy, a typological and imperfect human vice-regent was reinstated as partial fulfillment of the promise to Abraham. The king of Israel was anointed on Zion as the son of God (Pss. 2:7; 89:27). . . . Therefore, the throne of David can also be called the royal throne of YHWH (1 Chron. 28:5; 29:23; 2 Chron. 9:8). When the son of David rules on Zion, the reign of God is properly upon the earth" (1994: 3).

There is a profound identification of the Davidic kingdom with the divine kingship of God. The Davidic king is both the son of God and the vice-regent of God. The Chronicler makes slight but significant alterations in his source text, which have the effect of emphasizing that the kingdom is God's and not David's. The introduction to the dynastic oracle in 2 Sam. 7:1–3 reads: "Now when the king dwelt in his house, . . . the king said to Nathan the prophet . . . , and Nathan said to the king. . . ." The Chronicler drops this threefold reference to "the king" and instead substitutes his name: "David." He is not denying that David is king, but one of the points of the dynastic oracle that follows is to relativize David's kingship, or rather to subordinate it to its true end, the kingship of God.

The Chronicler's historical source records the oracle with an emphasis on the earthly kingdom of David and Solomon:

> I will establish *his* kingdom. . . .
> I will establish the throne of *his* kingdom for ever. . . .
> And *your* house and *your* kingdom shall be made sure for ever before me; *your* throne shall be established for ever. (2 Sam. 7:12, 13, 16)

The Chronicler renders this promise this way:

> I will establish *his* kingdom. . . .
> I will establish *his* throne for ever. . . .

> I will confirm *him* in *my* house and in *my* kingdom for ever and *his*
> throne shall be established for ever. (1 Chr. 17:11, 12, 14)

The Chronicler is reminding his readers: the Davidic dynasty and temple are established to fulfill God's desire to establish *his* reign on earth. The throne of the Davidic king is *God's* throne (1 Chr. 28:5); the temple is *God's* house; the Davidic king is *God's* servant (17:4, 7). All this is being done to fulfill the promise that God made to *his* people—the expression "my people Israel" being said three times at the start of Nathan's oracle (17:7, 9, 10).

Chronicles is the only book in the Hebrew canon to use the expression "kingdom of God / the Lord" (*yhwh*). With the exception of Chronicles, Daniel, and select psalms, this notion is rare in the canon. While God is sometimes described explicitly as king (Exod. 15:18; Isa. 6:5; Pss. 47:2; 99:4), his kingdom or rule is assumed but rarely referred to (Pss. 22:28; 45:6; 103:19; 145:11–13; Dan. 2:44; 4:3, 31; 6:26; 7:14, 18, 27). By contrast, Chronicles remarkably offers sixteen references to God's kingdom or his reign, indicating the importance of this concept for the Chronicler's understanding of salvation history.

Selman points out that the Chronicler deploys this concept always in relation to the Davidic kingdom and almost always at critical junctures in his narrative (1989: 167). God "turned the kingdom over to David" in deposing Saul (1 Chr. 10:14). David's celebration of the ark's return includes the prayerful exclamation "The Lord reigns" (16:31). The promise of the kingdom is central to the covenant with David (17:11, 14) and the temple (2 Chr. 7:18). The kingdom is the reason for the promise to David and his descendants (9:8; 13:5, 8).

The Chronicler deems the Davidic kingdom to be sacramental, making manifest the kingdom of God, as seen in David's understanding of the dynastic promise. For David, the promise means that God "has chosen Solomon my son to sit upon the throne of the kingdom of the Lord over Israel" (1 Chr. 28:5). In his narrative, the Chronicler picks up on this use of the throne as a symbol for the kingdom. He describes Solomon's coronation: "Then Solomon sat on the throne of the Lord as king instead of David his father" (29:23). Later in Solomon's reign, when the Queen of Sheba comes to pay him tribute, the scene is meant to illustrate the nations' realization that God is reigning on earth through the kingdom of Israel. She says: "Blessed be the Lord your God, who has delighted in you and set you on *his* throne as king for the Lord your God!" (2 Chr. 9:8).

In David's hymnlike prayer at Solomon's coronation, he parallels God's creation of the world with the establishment of his kingdom: "Blessed art thou, O Lord, the God of Israel our father, for ever and ever. Thine, O Lord, is the greatness and the power, and the glory, and the victory, and the majesty; for all that is in the heavens and in the earth is thine; thine is the kingdom, O Lord, and thou art exalted above all" (1 Chr. 29:10–11).

As important as the Davidic kingdom is in the life and history of the people of Israel, the kingdom has even greater, cosmic significance as well. The reader must always keep in mind the larger story of salvation history that the Chronicler wants to tell. In the beginning, God created the world to be his temple and kingdom. In establishing the kingdom of David, God is finishing his creation. The building of the temple is described in terms suggesting that it is the microcosm of a new creation. Here, in the dynastic oracle, God declares again that he is building a "house"—a human house, a line of flesh and blood through whom his rule and blessings will be expressed in the world.

Johnstone is among the few who notice the wider significance of the oracle in terms of the canonical narrative. He recognizes that David's question to God, "Who am I?" while certainly evoking Moses's query at Horeb, also has existential overtones. The king seems to be grasping the immensity of his role in the divine economy and salvation history. David, seated before the Lord, is granted an intimacy with God reserved only for rare figures. As Johnstone says, "In David, the prototype order for Adam, humankind, is tending towards fulfillment" (1997: 1.206–7).

### A New Law for the Uplifting of Humankind

This perhaps explains the suggestive occurrence of what appear to be allusions to the primeval creation narrative in Genesis. In the Genesis creation story, God promises that a righteous "seed" (*zera'*) will triumph over the seed of sin and failure, setting the narrative stage for the rest of Genesis (3:15). Perhaps David's seed is understood as the fulfillment of that primordial divine promise. One significant allusion in the Chronicler is the repetition of the divine address—"O Lord God" (*yhwh 'ĕlōhîm*)—at the start of David's prayer (1 Chr. 17:16–17). Japhet, among others, observes that throughout his work the Chronicler makes deliberate substitutions and changes in the forms of address for God that he finds in his source material. Notably, he never uses the form of address *'ădōnāy* (Lord). This change becomes striking in David's prayer, where the source in 2 Sam. 7:18–19 addresses *'ădōnāy yhwh* six times. Japhet believes that "theological considerations" are at work here and that in general the Chronicler deliberately avoids the use of *'ădōnāy* (lit., "my lords") because it might have blasphemous, polytheistic connotations with his audience (discussion in Japhet 1997: 20–23; 1993: 337–38).

This explanation, however, does not fully account for the Chronicler's use of *yhwh 'ĕlōhîm*, here in David's prayer or elsewhere. This particular divine title originates, canonically speaking, in the creation narrative, where it is used about twenty times. *Yhwh 'ĕlōhîm* is "exceedingly rare in the rest of the Bible," according to Sarna, who adds: "Admittedly . . . the remarkable concentration of the combination of these divine names in this narrative [Gen. 2:4–3:24] and their virtual absence hereafter have not been satisfactorily explained" (1989: 17).

In the creation account, *yhwh 'ĕlōhîm* is the creator of heaven and earth and of man and woman. The only other use of the title in the Pentateuch comes in the confrontation between Moses and Pharaoh (Exod. 9:30). Elsewhere in the Hebrew Bible, *yhwh 'ĕlōhîm* appears infrequently as part of longer titles, such as "the LORD God of Israel" (e.g., Josh. 7:13, 19, 20; 10:40, 42; 13:14, 33; 1 Sam. 14:41; 1 Kgs. 8:23, 25; 16:13), "the LORD God of hosts" (Ps. 59:5), or "the LORD God of heaven" (Neh. 1:5). But *yhwh 'ĕlōhîm* as a stand-alone title is found only ten times in Chronicles—all of them in connection with the Davidic covenant or the temple (1 Chr. 22:1, 19; 29:1; 2 Chr. 1:9; 6:41, 42; 26:18; 32:16). This is intriguing if not altogether explicable. The title is used twice in the Chronicler's source for David's prayer (2 Sam. 7:22, 25). But the Chronicler does not use the title in the places that his source does. Instead he uses *yhwh 'ĕlōhîm* to form a kind of *inclusio* in the introduction of David's prayer:

> Who am I, *yhwh 'ĕlōhîm* . . . ?
> You are showing me a law for the uplifting of humankind, *yhwh*
> *'ĕlōhîm*. (1 Chr. 17:16–17, my trans.)

So what are we to make of the Chronicler's use of this title in his work? Perhaps inspired by his source, the Chronicler sees *yhwh 'ĕlōhîm* as a way of expressing the special connection between God's purposes in the Davidic covenant and his purposes in creation. This practice is supported by the use of *yhwh 'ĕlōhîm yiśrā'ēl* in Chronicles and elsewhere to identify the God of creation with the God of Israel.

All this may also help explain the meaning of the mysterious passage that I translated "you are showing me a law for the uplifting of humankind" (*ûrĕ'îtanî kĕtôr hā'ādām hamm'ālâ*). The Hebrew is obscure in both Chronicles and the source. Various translations are based on proposed emendations of the text.[1] In light of the creation allusion in the title *yhwh 'ĕlōhîm* and the exodus imagery elsewhere in David's prayer, the exegete and interpreter must try to

---

1. Among the proposed translations of 1 Chr. 17:17 are these:
   "You regard me as a man of distinction, O LORD God." (New Jewish Publication Society Version)
   "Thou . . . hast shown me future generations, O LORD God!" (Revised Standard Version [RSV])
   "You have looked on me as henceforth the most notable of men, O LORD God." (New American Bible)
   "Thou . . . hast regarded me according to the estate of a man of high degree, O LORD God." (King James Version)
   "And you have caused me, someone of human stature, to see into the future, O YHWH God." (Knoppers 2004: 2.677)
   "You have let me look upon the generation of humankind to come, O Yahweh God." (Klein 2006: 371)

hear the likely allusions to creation and the exodus in the references in this obscure phrase to the "law" (*kětôr*, lit., "a law") and to "humanity" (*hā'ādām*, lit., "the man"); a more literal reading also serves better to capture the overall sense of wonder felt in David's prayer. Whatever murkiness there may be in the text, it is clear that David is marveling at this covenant and its implications for the human race.

Kaiser, who has studied the verse here and in the Chronicler's source (2 Sam. 7:19), suggests a similar reading (1974: 315), following the work of Beecher: "And thou are regarding me according to the upbringing [or uplifting] *tôrâ* of mankind, O Lord God." The sense of the text is well explained by Beecher:

> What is this "*tôrâ* of mankind?". . . The most natural understanding is that David recognizes in the promise just made to him a renewal of the ancient promise of blessing for mankind. . . . There is no escaping the conclusion that . . . David recognized in the promise made to him a renewal of the promise made of old that all the nations should be blessed in Abraham and his seed. (1975: 238)

As the Sinaitic covenant gave God's *tôrâ* to Israel, David envisions his covenant as imparting the gift of divine *tôrâ* to all humanity. Recalling God's oath to Abraham—that all families of the world will be blessed through his seed (Gen. 22:16–18)—Kaiser is certainly correct in seeing that "the 'blessing' of Abraham is continued in this 'blessing' of David" (1974: 310).

### A New and Everlasting Covenant and Kingdom

As was the covenant with Abraham, the covenant with David is an "everlasting covenant" (*bĕrît 'ôlām*; Gen. 17:7; 1 Chr. 16:17). This precise expression is not used by the Chronicler, but this is the clear sense. In the Chronicler's telling, David understands that the promise of covenant blessings for all humankind will be channeled through his kingdom, which is to exist "forever." The dynastic oracle and David's response are punctuated by the adverbial expression "forever" (*'ad-'ôlām*). Twice Nathan explicitly promises that the throne of David's seed will be established forever and that he will be confirmed in God's house and in God's kingdom forever (1 Chr. 17:12, 14). In his prayer, David recalls that God made Israel to be his people forever and interprets Nathan's oracle as meaning that David's "house" would be established forever and that in "blessing" David's house, God's name would be magnified forever (17:22, 23, 24, 27). David explains God's promise to Solomon this way: "The word of the Lord came to me, saying, . . . 'Behold, a son shall be born to you; . . . his name shall be Solomon. . . . I will establish his royal throne in Israel *for ever*'" (22:8–10).

This has become an interpretive crux in Chronicles research. At the time of the Chronicler's writing, the Davidic throne was empty, the dynasty promised to David's line a distant and fading memory. It seems odd that under these circumstances the Chronicler would nonetheless be so insistent that the covenant and the kingdom are *'ad-'ôlām*. The question then becomes, What does "forever" mean for the Chronicler?

There is a measure of conditionality in the dynastic promise. The king may lose his throne if he fails to keep the Lord's commandment, but nonetheless God's covenant promise remains forever. He will not withdraw his "steadfast love" (*ḥesed*) from the king as he took it from David's predecessor, who remains nameless in the oracle (1 Chr. 17:13; 22:12–13; 28:6–7). In David's final instructions to Solomon, he warns him that if Solomon forsakes God, God "will cast you off for ever" (28:8–9). This is a personal warning to Solomon. It does not contemplate any rejection by God of the dynasty he promised to David.

In the Chronicler's account of the divided kingdom, the promise of a dynasty to David's line continues to be presented as unbreakable, even under the reign of unrighteous Davidic kings who forsake God's covenant. For instance, there is the curious case of Abijah, Solomon's grandson. In the Chronicler's source (1 Kgs. 15:1–8), Abijah is an apostate whose scandalous reign is dealt with in only eight verses. The Chronicler, on the other hand, makes no mention of his idolatry. Instead he puts in Abijah's mouth perhaps the most far-reaching affirmation of the intimate relationship between the kingdom of God and the sons of David: "Ought you not to know that the LORD God of Israel gave the kingship over Israel for ever to David and his sons by a covenant of salt? . . . And now you think to withstand the kingdom of the LORD in the hand of the sons of David" (2 Chr. 13:5, 8).

This is the only other place in the Hebrew canon where the expression "kingdom of God / the LORD" (*malkût yhwh*) appears (besides 1 Chr. 28:5). God's kingdom is in the hands of David's sons, a grant that is "forever" (*'ad-'ôlām*) by means of a "covenant of salt" (*běrît melaḥ*; 2 Chr. 13:5). This latter image has sacrificial and offertory overtones. Salt was added to sacrifices as a sign of permanence and appears to have been an important element in ritual meals celebrated to seal covenants (Lev. 2:13; Num. 18:19; Ezra 6:9; 7:22; Ezek. 43:24).

For the Chronicler the Davidic kingdom is a divine institution, the manifestation of the kingdom of God on earth. Selman is correct that the notion of God's kingdom is rooted in the Sinai covenant, which is where the word "kingdom" first appears with reference to Israel (1989: 181–82). This further emphasizes the intimate connection between the Davidic kingdom and Israel's vocation as a "kingdom of priests." Selman observes:

> It is likely that the later associations of the Kingdom of Yahweh with Zion, the Davidic line, and the son of man, are part of the means by which this ideal [the kingdom of priests] was being restored, or rather, properly instituted. Indeed, one of the major reasons why the Kingdom of God was spoken of so cautiously in much of the Old Testament may be precisely because of Israel's failure to measure up to its ideals.

The kingdom of God has come on earth in the Davidic kingdom. And God's covenant is forever, a covenant of salt. Thus the promise of the dynasty is stronger than the virtue or sin of any individual king. God's covenant oath is sworn to David—and through David is given to Israel *'ad-'ôlām*, for the whole of time. Thus when Isaiah reenacts the Davidic covenant, he renders "you" in the plural—the promise spoken to David is meant for Israel: "I will make with you [plural] an everlasting covenant [*běrît 'ôlām*], my steadfast, sure love for David" (Isa. 55:3).

According to the Chronicler, David understood all this. "The LORD God of Israel chose me . . . to be king over Israel for ever [*'ad-'ôlām*]" (1 Chr. 28:4). Every king of Israel is David, in some sense. That is why the prophet Ezekiel can prophesy what amounts to a second coming of David, in which the "servant" (*'ebed*) David will be established as the one shepherd and king "for ever" (*'ad-'ôlām*) by a new "everlasting covenant" (*běrît 'ôlām*), in which God's sanctuary will be established "for evermore" (*lě 'ôlām*) among his people (37:24–27; cf. 34:23). Given this widespread expectation of a restoration and fulfillment of the kingdom of David, it seems highly unlikely that the Chronicler did not harbor similar hopes.

## Christian Interpretation

The Davidic covenant functions for the Chronicler in a way similar to the role that the death and resurrection of Jesus Christ play in the New Testament. What the cross is for the apostolic writers, the Davidic covenant is for Chronicles—the summit toward which all history was set in motion, the peak from which the meaning of the past is to be grasped, and the way forward into the future made clear. Since Christ's death and resurrection form a single salvation-historical event, when we talk of the Davidic covenant in Chronicles, we are talking not only about the dynastic oracle given to David, but also of the temple at Zion and the promise that the throne of David's seed shall be established forever.

The dynastic oracle of salvation in 1 Chr. 17 is partially fulfilled in the figure of David's son Solomon. In Solomon, the promise of a son to rule on David's throne and to build the house of God is fulfilled, at least provisionally. By building his temple on Moriah, the site of the Akedah and Abraham's offering of Isaac, and by disseminating wisdom and knowledge of God to the ends of the earth, Solomon becomes, at least for a while, the promised "seed of Abraham," through whom the nations of the earth are blessed (Gen. 22:15–18). For the Christian reader of Chronicles, however, the definitive fulfillment of both the Davidic covenant (an eternal heir on David's throne) and the Abrahamic covenant (blessing to all the nations) must await the new covenant to be established in Christ.

And the Chronicler's account of the Davidic covenant helps us to understand the pervasive Davidic covenant typology that runs like a bright line through the New Testament. For instance, Matthew's Gospel opens the New Testament by identifying Jesus as "son of Abraham" and "son of David" (Matthew 1:1), as the one who fulfills the Davidic and the Abrahamic covenants. The New Testament ends on a Davidic note, with Jesus identifying himself as "the root and the offspring of David" (Revelation 22:16).

The Davidic typology is most apparent in Luke. There Jesus is presented as the Christ, son of David and Son of God, whose birthplace, ministry, resurrection, and enthronement are all depicted in terms drawn from the Davidic covenant. The angel Gabriel's description of Jesus to Mary is taken directly from the dynastic covenant oracle in 2 Sam. 7 and 1 Chr. 17. Also in fulfillment of the dynastic promise to David, Jesus is described throughout Luke as the "Son of God," and his royal mission is inextricably bound to Jerusalem and the temple; the kingdom he envisions is to embrace all twelve tribes of Israel and all the nations, and it is to be eternal. All of these are features of the Davidic covenant as expressed in Chronicles and elsewhere in the Old Testament (for a more complete discussion, see Hahn 2009b: 217–32).

# 4

---

## God Gives Rest to His People

---

*The Beginnings of the Temple-Kingdom Age (1 Chr. 18–29)*

### Major Divisions of the Text

1. David establishes the kingdom in the land (18:1–20:8)
   David defeats the Philistines, Moabites, Zobah, and Edomites (18:1–13)
   David's cabinet (18:14–17)
   David defeats the Ammonites and Philistines (19:1–20:8)
2. David's census (21:1–22:1)
   David orders the census (21:1–6)
   David's repentance and Israel's punishment (21:7–14)
   David's intercession and God's mercy (21:15–17)
   David purchases the altar from Ornan (21:18–25)
   David's sacrifices are accepted by God (21:26–27)
   David declares the site of the house of God (21:28–22:1)
3. David prepares for the building of the temple (22:2–23:1)
   Provisions for workers and materials (22:2–5)
   Private commissioning of Solomon (22:6–16)
   Exhorting Israel's leaders (22:17–19)
   Solomon is appointed king (23:1)
4. David establishes the liturgical hierarchy of the Levites (23:2–26:32)
   Levitical census (23:2–6)
   Levite clan (23:7–23)
   Other Levite groups (23:24–26:32)

5. David establishes his imperial government (27:1–34)
   Divisions of the army (27:1–15)
   Tribal officers (27:16–24)
   The king's officials (27:25–34)
6. David's farewell address to all Israel (28:1–29:25)
   David explains the divine oracle of dynasty (28:1–8)
   David's public commissioning of Solomon (28:9–10)
   David reveals the plan for the temple and the liturgy (28:11–19)
   David's commissioning of Solomon (concluded; 28:20–21)
   David appeals for the consecration of Israel (29:1–5)
   Gifts for the temple (29:6–9)
   David's final prayer (29:10–20)
   Solomon is appointed king (29:21–25)
7. David's reign summarized (29:26–30)

## Synopsis of the Text

The dynastic oracle of 1 Chr. 17 is the hinge of the Chronicler's work. The chapters that follow show the initial fulfillments of that oracle. God gives David victory over the surrounding nations, and David establishes the regional tranquility and rest necessary to build the house where God has chosen for his name to dwell. In these chapters, David consolidates his kingdom and makes preparation for his successor, Solomon, who will complete the task of building the temple and establishing the kingdom of God on earth. Like Moses, however, David will be prevented from seeing the accomplishment of his dreams and his mission because of a grievous failure of leadership. This failure, which disqualifies him from building the temple, becomes a defining drama in these final chapters of 1 Chronicles.

## Theological Exegesis and Commentary

### Cities of Our God: The Kingdom Enters into Its Rest

In Nathan's dynastic oracle and the Davidic covenant, God's purposes were revealed—the kingdom of God, the divine sonship of his servant on the throne of Israel, the temple, and the blessing of the nations through the knowledge of the God of Israel. The episodes that follow in the Chronicler's history show the immediate blessings of God's covenant with David. His military battles are depicted as the fulfillment of the initial promises of the dynastic oracle. David "subdues" (*hiknîa'*) the Philistines as God had promised: "I will subdue all your enemies" (1 Chr. 17:10; 18:1; 20:4).

Throughout these chapters we hear echoes of the earlier conquest of the land under Moses and Joshua. Joab's exhortation before the battle with the Ammonites—"Be of good courage [*ḥzq*]" (1 Chr. 19:13)—is the same as that given by God and Moses to Joshua before his entrance into the promised land (Deut. 31:7, 23; Josh. 1:6, 7, 9). Like Joshua and the people (Josh. 1:11, 14), David and all Israel cross over the Jordan (1 Chr. 19:17–18). And again like Joshua (Josh. 6:24), David dedicates the spoils of his military victory—silver, gold, and bronze—"to the LORD" (1 Chr. 18:8, 10–11). Selman observes that by depicting David's triumphs in the south (Philistines, Edom, Amalek), east (Moab, Ammon), and north (Aramean states), the Chronicler shows David as coming "nearer than any other Israelite leader to completing the task first given to Moses and Joshua" (1994a: 187; cf. 198).

Through his wars, David is bringing about the rest that God promised for his people as a precondition for building God's house. Moses had foretold that when the people crossed over the Jordan, God would give them "rest" (*hēnîaḥ/měnûḥâ*) from their enemies and would establish a central sacred "place" (*māqôm*), where they could come to offer burnt offerings and sacrifices (Deut. 12:8–11; cf. 3:20; 25:19). In the Bible's Historical Books, the conquests of Joshua were said to have accomplished this rest for the people (Josh. 1:13, 15; 21:43–45; 22:4; 23:1). But this rest did not result in the promised establishment of a central sanctuary. There remained, as von Rad says, "a latent element of expectation" of the promised rest in the canonical history from which the Chronicler is drawing (1966: 95).

The Chronicler is interacting with this ancient tradition of expectation. He appears to be conscious that David has fulfilled the conditions set forth in Deut. 12 for the establishment of the central sanctuary:

> But when you go over the Jordan, and live in the land which the LORD your God gives you to inherit, and when he gives you rest from all your enemies round about, so that you live in safety, then to the place which the LORD your God will choose, to make his name dwell there, thither you shall bring all that I command you: your burnt offerings and your sacrifices, your tithes and the offering that you present, and all your votive offerings which you vow to the LORD. And you shall rejoice before the LORD your God, you and your sons and your daughters, your menservants and your maidservants, and the Levite that is within your towns. (12:10–12)

In the Chronicler's source material, the dynastic oracle includes God's promise to give to David, and by extension to all the people, "rest [*hēnîaḥ*] from all your enemies" (2 Sam. 7:11)—the same language found in Deuteronomy and elsewhere in the canonical history. In this source material, David's desire to build the temple is premised on his belief that Deuteronomy's promise had been fulfilled, that "the LORD had given him rest [*hēnîaḥ*] from all his enemies round about" (2 Sam. 7:1). Significantly, the Chronicler excises both of these references to David's rest from his account and makes Solomon the beneficiary of that covenant rest. But David is the agent or catalyst for that rest.

In Chronicles, David is not granted rest, but by his holy warfare Israel is given rest. David himself characterizes his accomplishments in those terms. Preparing to turn the reins of the kingdom over to Solomon, he declares to Israel's leaders: "Is not the LORD your God with you? And has he not given you rest[1] [*hēnîaḥ*] on every side? For he has delivered the inhabitants of the land into my hand; and the land is subdued [*kābōš*] before the LORD and his people" (1 Chr. 22:18). In drawing up the order of worship for the temple that Solomon would build, David again affirms that "the LORD, God of Israel, has given rest [*hēnîaḥ*] to his people; and he dwells in Jerusalem for ever" (23:25). In both of these statements the language hearkens to earlier divine promises concerning the land (Exod. 23:31; Num. 32:22; Josh. 18:1), in addition to Deuteronomy's promise of rest and a dwelling place for the name of God.

We also hear a deeper sounding of the biblical tradition. The word "subdue" that David uses stems from the Adamic tradition and may suggest that in his conquests the mandate given to Adam to subdue the earth has been fulfilled (Gen. 1:28; Cohen 1989). Following the delivery of the dynastic oracle and a series of victories won with the help of God, David and all Israel have brought peace to the earth; they have made the world safe for the dwelling of God's name. Even the curious and unique expression used by Joab, "cities of our God" (*'ārê 'ĕlōhênû*) in 1 Chr. 19:13, evokes an era in which human society is ordered to the divine purposes.[2]

### David's Fall and the Covenant Testing of Israel

At this moment when the land could be said to be in a state of Sabbath rest like that of the first week of creation, God puts Israel to the test. The scene in 1 Chr. 21, a unique literary construct of the Chronicler, is layered with allusions to earlier Old Testament history and is one of the most visually drawn and intensely dramatic in all the canon.

The Chronicler's canonical source in 2 Sam. 24 also records David's illicit census, but without any of the cosmic drama found in the Chronicler. In the source the story is inserted as almost an addendum following David's final speeches to the people and before the long account of his final days. The source also poses religious and theological difficulties in that it describes the census as the consequence of God's becoming angry with Israel and inciting David against the people. The reason for God's anger is never explained in the text, although it is presented as a *second* instance of God's anger: "Again the anger of the LORD was kindled against Israel" (2 Sam. 24:1).[3]

1. The RSV's "peace" is replaced with the more literal "rest" here and in the next quotation.
2. Jerusalem is characterized as "city of God" in Pss. 46:4; 48:1, 8; 87:3; 101:8; Isa. 60:14.
3. The word "again" likely refers to 2 Sam. 21; see Williamson 1982: 142.

The Chronicler recasts the entire event as a covenant "testing," similar to the earlier testings of Abraham and the children of Israel in the wilderness. This explains the underlying imagery of the Akedah and the exodus found in the account. And this is apparently how David interprets the event. In his great final prayer in Chronicles, he seems to refer to the census: "I know, my God, that thou triest [*bḥn*] the heart" (1 Chr. 29:17). The word that David uses here, *bḥn*, is a synonym of *nsh*, the biblical term used elsewhere to describe God's testing of his covenant family. God "tested" (*nsh*) Abraham in asking for the sacrifice of his only son, and again sought to "prove" (*nsh*) his firstborn Israel in the wilderness (Gerleman 1997).[4] In the final pages of this work, the Chronicler will use *nsh* to describe the testing of the new David, Hezekiah (2 Chr. 32:31).

Gerhardsson notes that *nsh* is "normally used within the covenant relationship—interpreted in the widest sense to cover all covenants between God and his worshippers whether the latter are a nation, tribe, family, or . . . individual (patriarch or king). In these contexts the word seems to imply primarily a testing of the partner in the covenant to see whether he is keeping his side of the agreement" (1966: 26–27).

The Chronicler is describing just such a test, though he does not use the word. Our clues to his intent are not only the inner-biblical allusions in the text, but also the appearance of the figure of Satan. This is one of only three places where the name "Satan" is used in the Hebrew canon, and the Chronicler is obviously drawing from these other rare portraits in composing his drama. *Śṭn* implies opposition or hostility and is used to describe adversaries and adversarial situations (Gen. 27:41; 49:23; Num. 22:22, 32; Pss. 38:20; 109:4; Wanke 1997). But here, and in Job and Zechariah, two other early postexilic works, the term is used as a name, *Śāṭān*.

In each of these works, *Śāṭān* is described as a supernatural figure, under the control of God, but granted a quasilegal authority to accuse or test the bonds of the covenant and the faithfulness of the believer (Day 1988). Thus there is a strong legal sense to Satan's "standing up" (*'md*) against Israel, as there is when the same formal term for legal accusation is used in relation to the *Śāṭān* in Zech. 3:1. Satan incites (*swt*) David, a term used also in Job's discussion of Satan (Job 2:3, where God is "incited" by Satan). The Targum on 1 Chr. 21:1 gives an accurate interpretation of what the Chronicler intends, envisioning a scene similar to that in Job—with God's permitting the temptation of Israel as he permitted the temptation of Job: "The Lord raised up Satan against Israel, and he incited David to number Israel."

Satan is being permitted to test the faithfulness of David to his covenant. But it is not David whom Satan stands up to accuse—it is Israel. David is

---

4. For *nsh* see Gen. 22:1; Exod. 16:4; 20:20; Deut. 8:2, 16. For *bḥn* see Pss. 17:3; 66:10; 81:7; Job 23:10; 34:36; Jer. 12:3; 20:12; Ezek. 21:13; Zech. 13:9. *Bḥn* and *nsh* are parallel in Pss. 26:2; 95:9.

tempted as Israel's representative. Indeed, the entire scene reminds us of the close bond between David and the people. He is of one bone and flesh with them; he is their shepherd. As a consequence, his personal decision brings "guilt" or "retribution" (*'ašmâ*) upon all Israel, as Joab warns (1 Chr. 21:3).

There is nothing intrinsically wrong with taking a military census, which is what David calls for, a "numbering of . . . men who drew the sword" (21:5). Other listing and censuses are taken in Chronicles (1 Chr. 23:3; 2 Chr. 2:17; 17:13–19; 25:5; 26:11–13), and the Mosaic law sets out the requirements for the kind of census that David is apparently taking here—although it does warn of a deadly penalty if the proper procedures are not followed (Exod. 30:11–16). Similar to the case of the initial attempt to return the ark (1 Chr. 13), David does not follow the letter of the law—and again the result is that innocents will pay with their blood. An allusion to the law may be intended here, as the penalty prescribed by Moses in Exod. 30:12, a "plague" (*negep*), is related to the word for punishment visited upon the people for David's census (*maggēpâ*; 1 Chr. 21:17, 22).

However, God's displeasure seems to stem less from David's failure to pay the half-shekel tax required by Moses than from a deeper violation of the spirit of Israel's covenant. We hear this in Joab's warning: "May the LORD add to his people a hundred times as many as they are" (21:3). This is an obvious reference to God's covenant promise to multiply Abraham's descendants so greatly that they could not be numbered. This reading is confirmed by a later reference to David's census, in which it is said that "wrath came upon Israel" because "the LORD had promised to make Israel as many as the stars of heaven" (1 Chr. 27:23–24; cf. Gen. 15:5; 22:17; also 13:16).

David's covenant faith—and by extension the covenant faith of the people—is being put to the test. Even though the Lord was with them, giving them victory over their enemies (1 Chr. 18:6, 13), David still wants to "know [the] number" of battle-ready men available to him (21:2). Johnstone, who detects a subtle but consistent Adamic typology running through Chronicles, sees here a connection with the primordial sin of Adam: "It is not enough for [David] to trust the promise of God about the uncountability of Israel as the people of God; as in the story of the tree of knowledge in Gen. 2–3, he seeks humanly to know, in order to supplement, if not supplant, unquestioning reliance upon God (contrast 1 Chron. 14:2)" (1997: 1.227).

As in the cases of Adam, Abraham, and Israel in the wilderness, God permits a testing of David and his fledgling kingdom. But why? The answer is related to the deep biblical theme of primogeniture. The covenant establishes a father-son kinship between God and Israel (Fensham 1971: 128–33). The covenant has a paternal and filial shape: Adam and Israel are portrayed as firstborn sons of God, while firstborn sons figure prominently in the covenant promises to Abraham and David.

For the first time the Davidic covenant establishes a direct filial tie between God and his chosen ruler for Israel. From this point forward God's filial relationship with his chosen people must pass through the Davidic king. This suggests a new kind of relationship between the people and God. Moses understood himself at times in maternal relationship with Israel, but he would never speak of God as *'ābî* ("my Father"; Num. 11:10–12; cf. Ps. 89:26). In the kingdom of David, the king is God's own son, "begotten" by God. This suggests a previously unimaginable intimacy between God and his chosen king. The king must truly be a man after the heart of God. And for that he requires a divine pedagogy that includes testing the strength of his faith. As Gerhardsson notes:

> The covenant relationship was seen in terms of the father-son relationship, and so it became natural to regard temptation as the paternal act of discipline and a part of the son's upbringing. The development in this direction began early. . . . The verb *nsh* is sometimes placed in parallelism with *bhn* "to test by trial," or *srp* "to test by fire, purge," and found with verbs like *ysr*, *hwkyh*, and *'nh*, "to mortify," "to discipline," "to bring up." . . . Since the covenant relationship is defined in family terms these aspects are naturally taken up into the picture. In the Book of Proverbs there are many sayings from the ancient patriarchal pedagogic about the hard discipline which a man has to impose on his son. (Gerhardsson 1966: 32; also J. Sanders 1955)

Through the temptation of the census, the son of God, Israel, and Israel's king are being trained and disciplined in God's fatherly ways. Moses had described Israel's testing in the wilderness in such terms: "Know then in your heart that, as a man disciplines [*ysr*] his son, the LORD your God disciplines [*ysr*] you" (Deut. 8:5). In the typological writing of his account, the Chronicler clearly has the wilderness years in view, in addition to the testing of Abraham. David's sin, like Israel's in the wilderness, threatens God's firstborn with extinction. There is a deadly irony here in that God sends "the angel of the LORD destroying" (1 Chr. 21:12)—the same expression used to describe the angel of death sent to destroy the Egyptians' firstborn in the exodus (Exod. 12:13, 23). The angel that once destroyed Israel's enemy is now sent to destroy Israel. The irony continues as the sword of the angel is mentioned repeatedly—as if to say that no matter how many swordsmen David can muster, Israel will never be any match for "the sword of the LORD" (1 Chr. 21:12, 16, 27, 30; cf. 21:5).

The Chronicler draws his dramatic picture with allusions to two episodes from the late wilderness era. The first allusion is to the blessing of Israel by Balaam, who had been hired by the Moabite king to curse Israel. The Chronicler's earlier reference to David's sacrificial offering of seven bulls and seven rams may have been an allusion to the only other place where that exact offering was made—by Balaam before his prophecy of "the shout of a king" in Israel (1 Chr. 15:26; Num. 23:1, 21, 29–30). Here an allusion is unquestionable. In Num. 22:22, 31, God places an angel as "adversary" (*śṭn*) to "stand against" (*'md*) Balaam and block his way, just as he sends *Śāṭān* against (*'md*) David and Israel (1 Chr. 21:1, 15, 16). Balaam's eyes are opened to see an angel with a drawn sword in his hand (Num. 22:23, 29, 31), as David's are opened to see the destroying angel, also with a drawn sword in his hand (1 Chr. 21:16). Balaam falls on his face at the sight (Num. 22:31), as David and the elders do (1 Chr. 21:16). And as Balaam confesses, "I have sinned" (Num. 22:34), David too uses these exact words (1 Chr. 21:7, 17).

The Chronicler also seems to be drawing from an episode in Josh. 5:13–15. Joshua like David lifts up his eyes to see a man standing against ('md) him, with a drawn sword in his hand (Josh. 5:13; 1 Chr. 21:16, 20). And Joshua too falls on his face when the "man" identifies himself as the commander of the Lord's army and tells him that he is standing on holy ground.

There appears to be more than literary artistry at work in the Chronicler's use of these allusions. The episodes in both Joshua and Numbers take place when Israel is encamped across the Jordan from Jericho, on the threshold of the promised land (Num. 22:1; Josh. 5:13). As the fragmentary story in Joshua ends with his recognizing that he is in a holy "place" (māqôm), Balaam's encounter with the angel in Num. 22 leads to his erecting altars and offering sacrifices in Num. 23. And in addition to prophesying a king for Israel, Balaam refers to the very covenant promise that David is guilty of forgetting in 1 Chr. 21—"Who can count the dust of Jacob, or number the fourth part of Israel?" (Num. 23:10). What these earlier stories anticipated is being fulfilled here in Chronicles. Joshua's conquest of the land has been completed by David, and David's encounter with the sword-bearing angel will now lead to the revealing of the definitive holy place (māqôm; 1 Chr. 21:22, 25) and altar.

### What David Saw on the Threshing Floor of Moriah

The meaning of this place, altar, and the sacrifices that David will offer depends on still another inner-biblical typology played out on the threshing floor of a certain Ornan, a Jebusite, a resident of Jerusalem. This is the second instance of a threshing floor in Chronicles. And as in the case of the threshing floor of Chidon, where Uzzah is struck down for touching the ark, there are strong cultic overtones to the threshing floor of Ornan. The threshing floor at Chidon was referred to as a māqôm ("place"; 1 Chr. 13:11), and here again the threshing floor will repeatedly be called māqôm, a term with cultic associations that originated in the theology of the Deuteronomist.

The Chronicler places Jerusalem and this mysterious threshing floor at the center of the cosmos, at the intersection of heaven and earth. The angel who is to destroy Jerusalem is depicted as "standing by the threshing floor" and "standing between earth and heaven" (21:15–16). At this crossroads the fate of the covenant people is to be decided, not to mention the future of the nations. The "pestilence . . . fell[ed] seventy thousand men of Israel" before the angel was sent to destroy Jerusalem (21:14). As the Chronicler describes the threat to Jerusalem and Israel in imagery drawn from the killing of the firstborn in the exodus, he depicts their deliverance from the destroying angel in typological language drawn from Abraham's offering of his firstborn in Gen. 22.

The scenes have marked similarities. Both David and Abraham are said to "lift up their eyes to see" visions of divine import. In Chronicles, the angel stands between heaven and earth, his sword unsheathed and raised above Jerusalem, as Abraham put forth his hand and raised his knife above Isaac. By divine command, the hands of both the killer angel and Abraham are stayed. In place of both the firstborn people of Israel and the beloved firstborn Isaac, burnt offerings are made instead. Both stories end with an apparent allusion to the temple: David recognizes that this is to be the site of the house of God and Israel's altar of burnt offering; Abraham names the site "the LORD will provide/see" because, as he had hoped, God had seen to it to provide the lamb for the sacrifice instead of Isaac. Thus the Genesis account concludes with an apparent anticipation of the temple: "As it is said to this day, 'On the mount of the LORD it/he shall be provided/seen" (22:14).

As Levenson points out, in both Gen. 22 and 1 Chr. 21 "there is a play on [the word] Moriah and the verb *rā'â*, 'to see,' and its derivative nouns *mar'â* and *mare'ê*, meaning 'sight, spectacle, vision.' The visionary experiences of Abraham and of David here serve as authorization for the inauguration of the Temple on Mount Zion/Moriah. The theophany authenticates the sanctuary" (1985: 94–95).

The Chronicler sees the establishment of the temple as the fulfillment of the Abraham story. "The mount of the LORD," elsewhere identified with Sinai (Exod. 4:27; Num. 10:33), is now identified with Zion, Jerusalem (Pss. 24:3; 48:1; 99:9; Isa. 2:3; 13:4; 18:7; 30:29). Later the Chronicler's typological understanding is explained more fully, as he reports that "Solomon began to build" the temple "on Mount Moriah where the LORD had appeared to David his father, at the place that David had appointed, on the threshing floor of Ornan the Jebusite" (2 Chr. 3:1). Moriah (*môrîyâ*), which according to popular etymology means "the vision of the LORD," is mentioned in only one other place in scripture—as the site of the binding of Isaac.

Nowhere else in scripture is it recorded that the temple was built on the place where Abraham offered Isaac. The Chronicler, however, wants his readers to see the temple in profound continuity with this foundational moment in salvation history—when God swore an oath to Abraham to bless all the nations through his seed. God's oath to Abraham resembles the promise made to David regarding his seed, which David received as a new law for the uplifting of the human family.

In Chronicles the holy "place" (*māqôm*) where God provided the sacrifice that spared Abraham's firstborn and triggered the swearing of his oath of blessing has now become the holy ground where sacrifice will be offered to spare the lives of the children of Abraham. As God accepted the burnt offerings of Abraham in this place, on this same site, God in the future will accept the offerings of his people and grant them his mercy. Dillard observes:

> The Chronicler not only adds the material designating Ornan's threshing floor as the Temple site, but he also makes an identification of this location with Mount Moriah, an identification unique to 2 Chronicles 3:1. The imagery is pregnant: at the same site where Abraham once held a knife over his son (Gen. 22:1–19), David sees the angel of the LORD with sword ready to plunge into Jerusalem. In both cases death is averted by sacrifice. The Temple is established there as the place where Israel was perpetually reminded that without the shedding of blood there is no remission of sin (Heb. 9:22). (1985: 107)

What is going on here in Chronicles is a beautiful and compelling justification and explanation of the sacrificial liturgy of the temple. The temple liturgy is explored in greater detail later, but here are the outlines of the Chronicler's liturgical theology. It is a liturgy of reconciliation and atonement, of making a substitutionary offering for sin. But it is also a liturgy of joyous thanksgiving, for Israel realizes that it is saved by the faithfulness of God to his covenant oath to Abraham. The divine oath, sworn in recognition of Abraham's fidelity in his covenant test, is what spares Israel in this moment of David's infidelity—an interpretation found in the Targum on 1 Chr. 21:15:

> When he [God] was destroying it [Jerusalem], he observed the ashes of the binding of Isaac which were at the base of the altar, and he remembered his covenant with Abraham which he had set up with him on the mountain of worship; [he observed] the sanctuary-house which was above, where the souls of the righteous are, and the image of Jacob which was engraved on the throne of glory, and he repented in himself of the evil which he had planned.

In this episode David is portrayed as both a repentant sinner seeking forgiveness and as a royal high priest interceding on behalf of his people with petitionary prayer, burnt offerings, and peace offerings. The intersection of these two portraits is highly significant for the Chronicler's theology of liturgy. David fails his covenant test, but from this disaster God brings about the establishment of the central sanctuary promised in Deut. 12. More than that, through this incident, God teaches his covenant son, the king, an essential lesson about what it means to be the shepherd of God's people. A true shepherd, David comes to learn, must intercede for and even be willing to lay down his life for his flock. Text criticism helps to reconstruct the crucial text in David's conversion: "It is I, the shepherd, who did wrong. But these sheep, what have they done? Let thy hand, I pray thee, O LORD my God, be against me and against my father's house; but let not the plague be upon thy people"

(1 Chr. 21:17).[5] The shepherd offers his own life for his sheep, recognizing that the people are not his own but God's. This is a dramatic turning point in Chronicles. The king performs public penance so that all can see the subordination of the earthly realm to the heavenly, the kingship to the priesthood, the leader of armies to the Lord of hosts—providing here a choice specimen of right political theology.

Selman, Knoppers, and others correctly believe that there was a strong pedagogic intent in the Chronicler's portrait of David as repentant sinner. The Chronicler understood Israel's history as one of *ma'al* (1 Chr. 9:1; 10:13–14; 2 Chr. 36:14). And other contemporary writings show that Israel's sinfulness continued even after the humiliating chastisement of the exile (Ezra 9–10; Neh. 9:1–37; Zech. 1:1–16; Mal. 1:6–3:15). In this story of David's repentance and the acceptance of his offering for his sin, the Chronicler wants to show his audience that God's blessings continue to be available in the temple—that, as the refrain of the liturgy has it, "His steadfast love endures for ever" (1 Chr. 16:34, 41; 5:13; 2 Chr. 7:3, 6). Selman observes: "The Chronicler's aim is not to heighten Israel's condemnation. . . . Indeed, the very opposite is true, for the Chronicler saw that in the grace of God complete atonement was always available. The temple existed as the place *par excellence* where all sinners could receive forgiveness and bring their offerings again in worship" (1994a: 202; cf. Mal. 3:10; Neh. 10:32–39).

For Knoppers, the interpretive key of the census episode is the divine blessing that flows from David's act of public repentance. More than an exemplary king, David becomes a kind of paradigm for the postexilic people, who must reclaim their vocation as a kingdom of priests and a light to the nations. For this covenant people, David becomes a model for their private prayer and the moral standards to which they must hold their public leaders. Knoppers writes:

> The image of David as the model of a repentant sinner is a constituent element in the Chronicler's depiction of David. The David of the census story is a person of confession and supplication *par excellence*, a human sinner who repents, seeks forgiveness, intercedes on behalf of his people, and ultimately secures the site of the future Temple. Precisely because David is a pivotal figure in the Chronicler's history of Israel, David's repentance and intercession are paradigmatic. The Chronicler's conviction that errant Israelites have both the opportunity to reform and the potential to make new contributions to their nation is evident in the reigns of Rehoboam (2 Chron. 12:5–12), Jehoshaphat (2 Chron. 19:1–11), Amaziah (2 Chron. 25:5–13), and even Manasseh (2 Chron. 13:10–17). But this principle is formatively and preeminently at work in the career of David. In the context of a national disaster of his own making, David is

5. The RSV and most English translations render the first sentence as "It is I who have sinned and done very wickedly." But based on the manuscript evidence, we prefer the translation "It is I, the shepherd, who did wrong." See discussions in Japhet 1993: 384; Williamson 1982: 147–48; and Selman 1994a: 208.

able to turn that catastrophe into the occasion for a permanent divine blessing upon Israel. (1995: 469)

David's confession leads to the command that he build an altar; when the sacrifices he offers are accepted by God, he takes this as a sign that the temple should be built on this site (1 Chr. 22:1). His public repentance, accompanied by sacrifice, triggers the mercy of God, who commands the angel to sheath his sword. Thus this new *māqôm* on "the mount of the LORD" will become the seat of mercy for the kingdom.

The account of David's procurement of the threshing floor for the altar carries forward the Chronicler's Abrahamic typology. The scene deliberately recalls Abraham's purchase of the Cave of Machpelah from Ephron as a burial site for his wife, Sarah. In Genesis, this purchase comes almost immediately after the Akedah, as Sarah's death becomes the prelude to the finding of a wife for Isaac, the chosen firstborn in whom God's blessing is to be extended to the nations. The encounter between David and Ornan follows the pattern of Abraham's negotiations with Ephron and also includes several literary associations, such as the term "full price," a phrase found only twice in the Bible—here and in the story of the Cave of Machpelah (Gen. 23:9; 1 Chr. 21:22).

In Gen. 23, the story of Abraham's purchase of the burial tomb for Sarah is "extraordinarily detailed, indicating the importance that the episode had assumed in the consciousness of Israel," Sarna says (1989: 156). The cave was the only property in the promised land that was purchased by the patriarchs: all the rest was gained through military conquest. The hereditary burial grounds where Abraham, Isaac, Jacob, and their respective wives were laid to rest (25:9; 49:29–32; 50:13), the cave was a kind of "firstfruit . . . of the land of promise," as Williamson observes (1991: 20–25, at 22). The Chronicler seems to be suggesting that this firstfruit is about to yield the riches of its harvest. As Abraham purchased the tomb from a Gentile who acknowledged him as "my lord" (23:11), so now David will purchase the site of the temple from a Gentile who recognizes him as "my lord the king" (1 Chr. 21:23). The Gentiles are thus shown as cooperating, however unknowingly, in the events that will bring about their own salvation and blessing. David pays an exorbitant amount for the threshing floor—the equivalent of fifty shekels for each of the twelve tribes—a figure that again stresses the unity of "all Israel" and the immense value of the temple.

Ancient extrabiblical tradition identifies the Cave of Machpelah as the place where Adam and Eve were buried. It is likely that the Chronicler knows this tradition, as well as the traditions that say the temple was built on the site of the garden of Eden, which is also the site of Mount Moriah (numerous citations from tradition in Beale 2004: 67n90, 99n36, 100n39, 108n60). Chronicles conceives of the temple as a new creation or, better, as the goal of God's original creation. This is emphasized here in David's priestly offering upon the altar.

In a scene deliberately crafted to evoke the first sacrifices in the tabernacle in the wilderness, David the king is again shown in the image of a priest. He calls upon the Lord and offers burnt offerings and peace offerings, the same offerings made by Moses and Aaron in the tabernacle. And as fire descended from heaven and consumed the offerings on the altar of the tabernacle (Lev. 9:22–24), so too David's offering is accepted by "fire from heaven" (1 Chr. 21:26). As this divine fire looks back to the tabernacle in the wilderness, it also looks ahead to the dedication of the temple, in which King Solomon's priestly offerings will also be consumed by fire from heaven (2 Chr. 7:1).

The days of the worship of false gods are coming to an end. Perhaps that is the meaning of the Chronicler's unmistakable allusion to still another story from Israel's past—that of Gideon, the mighty judge who while threshing wheat was commanded by an angel to deliver Israel from its enemies and to replace the altar of Baal with an altar to the living God. Gideon too built an altar, and his sacrifice upon it was consumed by divine fire (Judg. 6:11–14, 21–24). And whereas David conducted a military census out of his lack of faith, Gideon did something like the opposite. He performed an act of faith by allowing God to reduce the size of his army drastically, trusting God to bring him victory over the multitudes of Midianites and Amalekites with just a few hundred men (Judg. 7).

The Chronicler is signaling that at the threshing floor of Ornan we have reached a decisive transition point in Israel's worship and in salvation history. It is no coincidence that the Chronicler refers to the "tabernacle . . . which Moses had made in the wilderness" and "the altar of burnt offering . . . at Gibeon" (1 Chr. 21:29). The days of the separate sanctuary are clearly numbered. Solomon will worship at Gibeon to inaugurate his reign (2 Chr. 1:3–13), but Gibeon will not be mentioned again after the temple is built upon the site of Ornan's threshing floor and the Mosaic tent of meeting is brought to Jerusalem (5:5).

Making a pointed contrast between Moses's tabernacle and its altar of burnt offering, and the new house of God and its altar of burnt offering for Israel, David clearly has in view the single central sanctuary promised in Deut. 12. His cry of recognition, "Here shall be the house of the LORD" (1 Chr. 22:1), is the summation of a careful literary effort by the Chronicler. With an intricate series of allusions to every stage of Israel's history of worship—from the patriarchs Abraham and Isaac at Moriah, to the tabernacle of Moses in the wilderness, to Joshua's conquest of the land and the period of the judges—the Chronicler illustrates the continuity of the temple with God's purposes and suggests that his saving plan has reached its pinnacle. This interpretation is found in the Targum on 2 Chr. 3:1, which describes Moriah as the site where "all the generations worship before the Lord"—not only Abraham, Isaac, and David, but also Jacob, whose vision of the heavenly temple is said to have occurred there as well (Gen. 28:16–17).

### He Has Chosen Solomon My Son to Sit upon the Throne

The remainder of 1 Chronicles will be spent in detailing David's plans for the temple and the kingdom—for Solomon's accession to the throne, for the building of the temple, for the establishment of the religious and political hierarchy of the kingdom of God on earth. The final eight chapters (1 Chr. 22–29) are unique to the Chronicler, with no parallel elsewhere in the biblical record. This material includes several valedictory-style addresses and prayers of David as well as details of his organizational plans and polices to guide the royal government and the conduct of the liturgy, which focuses on the transition of power to Solomon and the Chronicler's portrait of King David's final days.

David's final speech to the sacral assembly, the *qāhāl* (1 Chr. 28:2–10, 20–21; 29:1–5, 10–19), is a masterful summary of the Chronicler's themes, focused on the temple and the dynasty. Beginning with his unique address—"Hear me, my brethren and my people" (28:2; cf. Lev. 25:46; Deut. 3:18; 24:7; Judg. 20:13)—David's speech is cast in the familial and filial context of the covenant with which the Chronicler began his work. Thus 1 Chronicles ends as it begins, with the tracing of the genealogy of election. David uses the term of "election" (*bāḥar*) four times, establishing the divine chain that connects Solomon to God's plan for Israel. There is a steady intensification of filial language as David reminds the people (1) that God "chose Judah" (1 Chr. 28:4); (2) that from the house of Judah, he chose "my father's house"; (3) that from "among my father's sons," he chose David "from all my father's house to be king over Israel for ever"; and finally (4) that "of all my sons, . . . he has chosen Solomon my son to sit upon the throne of the kingdom of the LORD over Israel" (28:5).

The natural familial lines of descent are then elevated to the supernatural level as David reveals the dynastic promise to his brethren: God "said to me, 'It is Solomon your son who shall build my house, . . . for I have chosen him to be my son, and I will be his father'" (28:6). On the basis of this divine oath, David exhorts both Solomon and the people to "seek" or worship (*dāraš*) God and to obey his commandments "that you may possess this good land, and leave it for an inheritance to your children after for ever" (28:8).

The genealogy of blessing and grace is thus to extend into the future—beyond the generation of David and Solomon and into the generation of the Chronicler's audience. David concludes his address—after providing personal instructions to Solomon and giving him a written plan for building the temple and shaping the liturgy and worship—with a long prayer of blessing, praise, and thanksgiving addressed to the "LORD, the God of Abraham, Isaac, and Israel, our fathers" (29:18).

David's last public act in Chronicles is to lead "all the assembly" (*kōl-haqqāhāl*; 29:1, 10, 20) in an extravagant liturgy of sacrifice, offering a thousand bulls, a thousand rams, and a thousand lambs, along with accompanying drink offerings. Indeed, with the exception of the sacrifices that will be offered when Solomon dedicates the temple, no greater sacrificial offering is recorded in the Bible. Dramatically, "the *kōl-haqqāhāl* blessed the LORD, the God of their fathers, and bowed their heads, and worshiped the LORD, and did obeisance to the king" (29:20). This is an extraordinary and unprecedented acknowledgment of the remarkable closeness between God and his earthly representative, the king. Surely here is the heart of the Chronicler's theocratic vision, that the kingdom of Israel under David and Solomon is the kingdom of God on earth. David had begun his final prayer with the affirmation "All that is in the heavens and in the earth is thine; thine is the kingdom, O LORD" (29:11). Here again, the righteous king is shown to be a man of prayer, who devotes all the wealth and resources of his kingdom to worship.

The account ends with the people eating and drinking before the Lord with great joy, an image associated with the sharing of a sacrificial meal to seal the covenant with God. Eating before the Lord in joy is one of the divine promises associated with the rest of the chosen people and the building of the central sanctuary—in language very close to that used in the Mosaic promise (1 Chr. 29:22; Deut. 12:7, 18). The covenant meal at Mount Zion contains an echo of the covenant meal celebrated by Moses and the elders at Mount Sinai (Exod. 24:11). Throughout the Chronicler's royal succession narrative in these chapters, the Abrahamic typology recedes and the Mosaic typology reemerges. The most striking evidence of this is David's delivery to Solomon of a "plan" (*tabnît*) for the temple and the liturgy (1 Chr. 28:11, 12, 18, 19)—just as Moses was given the *tabnît* for the tabernacle (Exod. 25:9, 40). David, the new Moses, is turning over authority to Solomon, the new Joshua. McCarthy observes that this material "almost gives the impression that the Chronicler has studied Deuteronomy–Joshua with great care, but it may be that his overloaded texts reflect an actual tradition. The sequence between 1 Chronicles 22 and 1 Chronicles 28 is like that between Deuteronomy 31 and Joshua 1 and 13" (1971: 36).

McCarthy, Williamson, and others clearly establish the influence of Joshua's accession on the Chronicler's account of Solomon's accession (e.g., Williamson 2004: 141–45). First, there is the installation speech, which includes three parts—encouragement ("Be strong and of good courage"), a description of the divine mission ("You shall bring the children of Israel into the land which I swore to give them"), and assurance of divine assistance ("I will be with you"; Deut. 31:23). This same pattern and much of the same language can be seen in David's commissioning of Solomon: he is encouraged ("Be strong and of good courage"), his mission to build the temple is described, and he is promised God's help ("The LORD be with you"; 1 Chr. 22:11–13, 16; 28:10, 20). As in the transfer of power to Joshua, the transition in Chronicles is a two-stage affair, with David first commissioning Solomon in private (Deut. 31:23; 1 Chr. 22:6–16) and then before the entire *qāhāl* ("in the sight of all Israel"; Deut. 31:7; 1 Chr. 28:8). In both cases, the obedience of Israel is noted in strikingly similar language (Deut. 34:9; 1 Chr. 29:23), and both Joshua and Solomon are "exalt[ed] . . . in the sight of all Israel" (Josh. 3:7; 4:14; 1 Chr. 29:25).

Again, more than literary styling is at work here. The Chronicler seems to be drawing this parallel because he sees a final typological correspondence between the careers of David and Moses: each was disqualified by sin from completing the task for which God raised him up, and the task of each was completed by divinely appointed successors. God did not permit Moses to enter the promised land because of his failure of leadership at Meribah in the wilderness (Num. 20:1–13, 24; 27:12–14; Deut. 3:23–27; 32:48–52; Ps. 106:32–33). The precise sin of Moses is the subject of centuries of debate in the rabbinic literature (Milgrom 1989: 448–56). Possibly the Chronicler detected some similarity between Moses's lack of trust (*lō'-he'ĕmantem*; Num. 20:12) in God's promises and the lack of trust shown by David in ordering his military census.

Whatever the connection, the Chronicler definitely depicts Solomon's succession, and indeed his entire reign, as the completion of David's mission. Allen rightly observes, "The combined reigns of David and Solomon are regarded as the inauguration of a temple age which persisted to the Chronicler's day" (1988: 24). The continuity is accentuated more in Chronicles than in the earlier canonical history; there David in his final years is depicted as a diminished and ultimately incapacitated figure, while Solomon's rise to power is painted in dark hues of intrigue and turpitude. For the Chronicler, Solomon is the destined temple builder, and his destiny is inextricably linked to David's disqualification from the task. Far from a weak figure, David is vigorous and engaged, overseeing even the minutiae of the transfer of power in Chronicles.

### The Shedding of Blood and the Building of the Temple

In the earlier canonical history, it is Solomon who explains why he is building the temple and David is not. The explanation is pragmatic, although it does reflect the theology of "rest" in Deut. 12. David could not build "because of the warfare with which his enemies surrounded him"—in other words, because he was burdened with the practical work of planting the kingdom in the land and providing for its defense. The temple can be built under Solomon because God granted Solomon "rest on every side"—the exact language of the Deuteronomic promise (1 Kgs. 5:3–4; Deut. 12:10).

The importance of the theme of the chosen people's rest continues in Chronicles, but here it is David who explains his disqualification twice, first in a private audience with Solomon, and later in a speech to the *qāhāl*:

> My son, I had it in my heart to build a house to the name of the LORD my God. But the word of the LORD came to me, saying, "You have shed much blood [*šāpak dām*] and have waged great wars; you shall not build a house to my name, because you have shed so much blood [*šāpak dām*] before me upon the earth.

Behold, a son shall be born to you; he shall be a man of rest[6] [ '*iš mĕnûḥâ*]. I will give him rest [*wahănîḥôtî*] from all his enemies round about; for his name shall be Solomon [*šĕlōmōh*], and I will give peace [*šālôm*] and quiet [*seqeṭ*] to Israel in his days. He shall build a house for my name." (1 Chr. 22:7–10)

I had it in my heart to build a house of rest for the ark of the covenant of the LORD, and for the footstool of our God; and I made preparations for building. But God said to me, "You may not build a house for my name, for you are a warrior [ '*iš milḥāmôt*] and have shed blood [*šāpak dām*]." (1 Chr. 28:2–3)

In each of these explanations, David claims to have received direct revelation from God concerning the reasons for his disqualification, using direct citations of the Deuteronomic promise: the "rest from enemies" theme, and the temple is for "the name" of God. The contrast between Solomon and David is made quite explicit: David is literally "man of war" ('*iš milḥāmâ*), while Solomon's very name (*šĕlōmōh*) is made the subject of a wordplay on "peace" (*šālôm*).

As in the case of Moses, David's exact offense is ambiguous. The interpretive options are many (for good reviews, see Knoppers 2004: 2.772–75; Riley 1993: 79–82; for the Jewish interpretive tradition, see Japhet 1997: 476–77). Some scholarly consensus seems to have been reached around the broad idea that, because of the blood spilled by his wars, David has rendered himself cultically impure. But there are real problems with this interpretation. The first is that David's wars are all carried out with God's backing and his assistance and that the Chronicler generally has a favorable attitude toward holy warfare.

More problematic is establishing the relationship between the description of David as a man of war and his "shedding of blood" (*šāpak dām*). Most commentators, no matter what conclusions they draw, assume that these are two parts of the same condemnation, meaning that *because* David is a man of war, he is guilty of shedding blood. The problem, as Kelly brings out so well, is that elsewhere the accusation *šāpak dām*, while definitely implying acts of killing for which one is held morally accountable, is never used in reference to the chosen people engaged in warfare (1998: 57–58).

Reading canonically, the expression seems to be rooted in the covenant with Noah: in the new world after the flood, it is stipulated that innocent blood cannot be shed because the human person is made in the image of God (Gen. 9:6). The language here looks back to the garden at Eden, to the time before brother first shed the blood of brother and caused the earth (*'ereṣ*) to cry out with the voice of innocent blood (4:10–11; cf. 37:22). And when the prohibition appears again in later legislative texts, the context is Israel's dwelling in the promised land, which is depicted as a new creation. This is the imagery found in Num. 35:33–34, where the blood shed by the murderer is said to "pollute the land [*'ereṣ*]" and to "defile the land [*'ereṣ*]" where God

---

6. The RSV's "peace" is replaced with the more literal "rest."

himself has chosen to dwell. In Deut. 19:10, provision is made "lest innocent blood be shed in your land [*'ereṣ*] which the LORD your God gives you for an inheritance" (cf. 19:7–13; 21:7).

In the prophetic writings, the accusation *šāpak dām* occurs almost always in the context of listings of the immorality of the people in Jerusalem (Ezek. 16:38; 22:3, 4, 6, 9, 12, 27; 24:7; Isa. 59:7; Jer. 7:6; 22:3) or in the land (Ezek. 33:25; 36:18). The shedding of innocent blood in the holy precincts of Zion or more generally in the land marks a fundamental breach of the believer's covenant relationship with God. Murray's review concludes: "The biblical evidence is clear that *šāpak dām* is the most heinous offense one human can commit against another, on par with idolatrous worship as an offense against God" (2001: 466, citing Gen. 9:6; Deut. 19:10; 1 Sam. 25:31; Num. 35:33–34; Jer. 7:6; 22:17; Ezek. 22:4; 33:25; 36:18; Ps. 106:38). David, according to the biblical evidence, deserves to be put to death for the shedding of blood. This suggests something of extraordinary magnitude in the accusation being leveled against David in Chronicles (2001: 463n18). His offense, as expressed in the divine censure he quotes, is this: "You shall not build a house to my name, because you have shed so much blood before me upon the earth" (1 Chr. 22:8).

Thus David is doubly disqualified to build the temple, being both a man of war and one who shed innocent blood. But if David's wars might not be the source of his shedding innocent blood, what is? Medieval Rabbi David Kimchi believed it to be the blood of all the innocents whom David deliberately killed, especially Uriah the Hittite, the cuckolded husband of Bathsheba (Berger 2007: 159–60). This seems to make sense. The earlier canonical history records not only the outrageous slaying of Uriah (2 Sam. 11:14–17), but also, as Kimchi points out, implicates David in other killings of innocent people (Kimchi also cites 1 Sam. 22:22; 27:9).

The problem with this interpretive line is that in the Chronicler's account no mention is made of Uriah or David's adultery. The only innocent blood that David appears to be responsible for is that of the seventy thousand or more who died as a result of his sinful census (1 Chr. 21:14). The seventy thousand were killed in the pestilence visited upon Israel as a direct consequence of David's sin. But much in the Chronicler's census account evokes the account of the shedding of Uriah's blood, found elsewhere in the biblical record.

In both, the dramatic action is initiated by a command of David to Joab (1 Chr. 21:2; 2 Sam. 11:14). In each case David's actions are rebuked by repetition of the prophetic word "thus says the LORD" (1 Chr. 21:10, 11; 2 Sam. 12:7, 11). Because of David's sin, Uriah and other innocents "fell," as seventy thousand "fell" because of the census (2 Chr. 21:14; 2 Sam. 11:7). In both cases God's displeasure is expressed in terms of evil having been done in his sight (1 Chr. 21:7; 2 Sam. 11:27; 12:9). The "sword" figures prominently in both episodes, as the sign of both David's sin and God's judgment (1 Chr. 21:5, 12, 16, 27, 30; 2 Sam. 11:25; 12:9–10). David's penance is expressed by his prostrating himself on the ground, and he is accompanied in his penance by the elders (1 Chr. 21:16; 2 Sam. 12:15–17). And in both accounts he intercedes to spare the lives of those endangered by his sin (1 Chr. 21:17; 2 Sam. 12:16). The most telling detail of comparison is David's simple confession, "I have sinned" (ḥāṭā'tî), found in both episodes (2 Chr. 21:8; 2 Sam. 12:13).

Though David hears the words of divine forgiveness in 2 Sam. 12:13, he receives no assurance in Chronicles that his sin will not result in the death he deserves. Yet the effect of the narrative in 1 Chr. 21 is to communicate that very point—not just to David, but to all Israel. David is saved by God's covenant love, through his repentance, his trust in God's mercy, and his offering of sacrifices on the site designated by God. The message for David's readers is the same. Having returned from the oppression and indignity of the exile, they know, as David does, that it is far better to fall into the hand of the Lord than to fall into human hands (21:13). And it is hard not to hear an urgent contemporary ring to David's command to "arise and build the sanctuary of the LORD God" (22:19).

### Christian Interpretation

The Chronicler's focus on the Davidic dynasty continues in 1 Chr. 18–29, as initial provisions are made for the practical implementation of the liturgical empire that God wants to establish on earth. The Chronicler's hopes for David, Solomon, and the kingdom are fulfilled finally and perfectly only in the incarnation of Christ and his church.

The dramatic image of the angel of the Lord standing on the site of the future altar of the future temple (21:16), an image that recalls Jacob's dream of the temple ladder (Gen. 28:12), evokes for Christians something of the true nature of the church, the liturgy, and the kingdom. It reminds us that the kingdom of God is sacramental, as the Lord's own prayer tells us: "Thy kingdom come, . . . on earth as it is in heaven."

The church, as the temple and kingdom of God on earth, the extension of Christ's own body, is a sacramental family that unites heaven and earth. In David's consolidation of his empire and his preparations for the temple, we see the proper relation of the spiritual and temporal orders. The temporal is to be ordered to the spiritual, for the purpose of the sanctification of the people through worship and prayer. In the sacraments of the church, the temporal order is sanctified: the natural child is given supernatural life in baptism, the natural family is rendered holy through matrimony, the fruits of the earth and human labor are transformed in the Eucharist, and so forth.

The kingdom of David, as organized in these chapters, is a kingdom of priests ordered to worship under the authority of the priestly king and the hierarchical priesthood of the Levites. In a similar way, the pilgrim church on earth is united to the kingdom of heaven, as a royal priesthood, especially through the sacramental ministry of the bishop and prebyters, "after the order of Melchizedek" (Hebrews 5:5–7:17; 1 Peter 2:9; Revelation 1:6; see Hahn 2009b: 292–305). The church, then, as the fulfillment of the Davidic kingdom, is not a nation-state or an empire. The church is a convenantal family, a eucharistic kingdom, that exists to sanctify its members and to enlarge its borders to embrace all the peoples of the world.

These chapters in Chronicles also give us beautiful insights into the meaning of worship and the liturgy. Early Christians adapted the beginnings of David's final prayer (1 Chr. 29:11) for their eucharistic liturgy: "Thine, O Lord, is the . . . power and the glory . . . ; thine is the kingdom" (*Didache* 8.2). The Christian liturgy, like the worship of the temple, is the cult of heaven and earth. It is the remembrance of salvation through the divine mercy shown to us in Christ. The forgiveness received by David, whose sin of shedding innocent blood warranted death under the law, is the forgiveness that the Christian receives from the sacrifice of Christ. God's mercy is the theme of the pivotal episode in 1 Chr. 21. This is fitting because the liturgy of Israel will be a liturgy of penitential self-offering and thanksgiving for salvation, as is the Christian liturgy, which is the fulfillment of the temple liturgy.

# 2 Chronicles

# 5

## Liturgy and Empire

### *Theocracy in the Temple Age (2 Chr. 1–9)*

**Major Divisions of the Text**

1. Kingdom of Solomon (1:1–17)
   Solomon worships at the tent in Gibeon with all Israel (1:2–6)
   Solomon's wisdom and wealth (1:7–17)
2. Building the house of God (2:1–5:1)
   Solomon prepares to build the temple (2:1–18)
   The Jerusalem site on Mount Moriah at Ornan's threshing floor (3:1)
   The temple's ground plan and exterior (3:3–13)
   Temple furnishings (3:14–4:22)
   Work on the temple is completed (5:1)
3. Temple dedication and inauguration of the liturgy (5:2–7:22)
   Ark and tent are installed (5:2–14)
   Solomon's great prayer of dedication (6:1–42)
   God accepts Solomon's prayer and Israel's sacrifices (7:1–10)
   God's promises regarding the temple (7:11–22)
4. Solomon's empire (8:1–9:31)
   Solomon's building work (8:1–6)
   Worship order is established in the temple (8:12–15)
   Queen of Sheba's pilgrimage to Solomon's kingdom (9:1–9, 12)
   Solomon is recognized above all the kings of the earth (9:13–28)
   Solomon's death and succession (9:29–31)

## Synopsis of the Text

Solomon is established in his kingdom and builds the temple. Using a rich array of typology and inner-biblical allusion, Chronicles portrays this as the culmination of biblical history, a recapitulation not only of the tabernacle built by Moses in the wilderness but also of creation itself. The kingdom of Solomon is the new people of God, a liturgical empire called to bring the blessings of God to all nations through its temple and its law. The Chronicler envisions the kingdom of Israel as a liturgical empire—an empire that will exercise its dominion, not through military might or economic supremacy, but through the blessings of the liturgy celebrated in the temple and through the wisdom taught by its kings. In the vision of worship unfolded in these chapters, the Chronicler sees Israel as leading the nations and indeed all creation in the offering of a great thanksgiving (*tôdâ*) to the Creator.

## Theological Exegesis and Commentary

### The Son of David, Established in His Kingdom

Chronicles was originally written as a single book. Nonetheless, the traditional division of the book comes at a natural point in the narrative, with the transition of the monarchy from David to Solomon. The nine chapters that begin 2 Chronicles are filled with reminders that the kingdom of David is the kingdom of Solomon and that this kingdom is the earthly manifestation of God's reign over creation. Allen observes: "The combined reigns of David and Solomon are regarded as the inauguration of the Temple age which persisted to the Chronicler's day" (1988: 24). The promise of the temple is made jointly to both David and Solomon, and Israel's liturgy is established under their direction (33:7; 35:4). The Chronicler even speaks of "the way of David and Solomon" (11:17).

For the Chronicler the focus is on covenant, theocracy, temple, and liturgy. The singular focus on Solomon's covenant role explains why the Chronicler omits prominent aspects of Solomon's reign found in 1 Kings—his multiple foreign wives, his forays into idolatry, his military blunders (1 Kgs. 11:1–40). Nor is need found to repeat staples of Solomonic lore, such as the bloody familial drama of his accession (1 Kgs. 1–2) or his legendary decision between two women who were disputing the custody of a child (3:16–28).

As David's first royal act was to rally Israel to recover the ark of the covenant, so Solomon's first action as king is to lead Israel in a pilgrimage to offer sacrifices to God. The scenes are told in similar language and include similar details: both mention Israel's leaders, the ark, and the key theological term for "seeking" God; in addition, both mention "all Israel" and "all the assembly" (*qāhāl/ekklēsia*; 1 Chr. 13:1–6; 2 Chr. 1:2–6). The Chronicler's explanation of this pilgrimage (1:3–6) is crucial to his overarching concerns. The parallel narrative in 1 Kgs. 3 explains that at the time of Solomon's accession, the people were offering their sacrifices at various "high places" (*bāmôt*) because "no house had yet been built for the name of the LORD." From that account, it seems that Solomon made the trip to Gibeon more than once and that when he would go there, "he used to offer a thousand burnt offerings upon that altar" (3:2–4).

By contrast, the Chronicler describes a single dramatic royal pilgrimage to Gibeon by Solomon as the head of the *qāhāl/ekklēsia* of "all Israel" (2 Chr. 1:3–6; Brooks 2005). It is a pilgrimage of rededication and covenant renewal in a time of transition in the monarchy. According to the Chronicler, king and people journey to the high place because "the tent of meeting of God" (*'ōhel mô'ēd hā'ĕlōhîm*) is there. In case his readers do not grasp the significance of this, he explains that this is the tent that "Moses the servant of the LORD had made in the wilderness." He also refers to the tent by the other name used for it in the Bible: "the tabernacle of the LORD" (*miškan yhwh*; Exod. 39:32–33, 40; 40:2, 6, 29; cf. 25:9; 27:21; 28:43). At Gibeon, Solomon leads the people as both king and priest, offering a thousand burnt offerings (*'ōlôt*) upon the "bronze altar that Bezalel . . . had made" (2 Chr. 1:5). Again the Chronicler reminds his readers of the ancient Mosaic roots of the tabernacle, referring to the craftsmen whom God appointed to build the tent-tabernacle, ark, altar, and furnishings of the tent (Exod. 31:1–11; 35:30–36:1; 37:1). He also reminds them that David had earlier established the ark, once housed in the tabernacle, in a temporary tent at Jerusalem (2 Chr. 1:4).

### The Tent before the Temple

All of this is curious and significant. Only the Chronicler gives us the tradition that the tabernacle of the Lord and the altar of burnt offering were located in the high place at Gibeon. He alludes to this tradition at three strategic moments in his narrative: following David's restoration of the ark to Jerusalem (1 Chr. 16:39); following the cosmic drama at the threshing floor of Ornan, site of the future temple (21:29); and here at the start of Solomon's reign and in preparation for his building the temple. Most scholars surmise that the Chronicler made up this tradition to serve two narrative goals: to justify Solomon's sacrificing at one of the "high places," which elsewhere in scripture are described as notorious sites of idolatry, and to stress the continuity of Israel's temple liturgy with the order of sacrifice and worship set up by Moses.

The biblical evidence is admittedly murky. Leviticus prohibits offering sacrifices anywhere but at the tent of meeting (Lev. 17:8–9). From at least Joshua's day and continuing through the period of the judges, the tent, ark, and their attendant priests apparently resided at Shiloh (Josh. 18:1; 19:51; Judg. 18:31; 20:27; 21:19; 1 Sam. 1:3, 9; 3:3; Klein 1983: 6–7); the tent had perhaps evolved by that time into a more permanent structure, for it is occasionally referred to in this period as "the house of God" (*bêt-hā'ĕlōhîm*; Judg. 18:31) and "the temple of the LORD" (*hêkal yhwh*; 1 Sam. 1:9; 3:3). At some point the sanctuary at Shiloh was destroyed, perhaps when the Philistines captured the ark of the covenant (1 Sam. 4). The destruction is not recorded in the Bible's Historical Books, but the trauma of the event fixed itself in the Israelite mind. In Jeremiah, God speaks of the desolation of "Shiloh, where I made my name dwell at first" (Jer. 7:12–14; 26:6; cf. Ps. 78:60).

Why is the Chronicler so uniquely concerned and so deliberate in accounting for the restoration of both the ark and the tent? This is an important question. David's initial political-military act is to retrieve the ark from Kiriath-jearim, where it has come to rest after plaguing its Philistine captors (1 Sam. 5:1–7:2). That much tracks the history of David found in earlier biblical sources. It is at this point that the Chronicler introduces details about the tabernacle that have no parallel in his source materials. Simultaneous with David's installation of the ark on Zion, he stimulates anew the tabernacle cult at Gibeon. David installs the ark at Jerusalem in a specially made tent or booth and makes provision for worship there (on the significance of David's tent, see Leithart 2003). The Levites under Asaph are assigned "to invoke, to thank, and to praise the LORD, the God of Israel" and "to minister continually before the ark as each day required" (1 Chr. 16:4, 37). David in turn appoints the high priest Zadok and his brother priests to minister "before the tabernacle of the LORD in the high place that was at Gibeon, to offer burnt offerings to the LORD upon the altar of burnt offering continually morning and evening, according to all that is written in the law of the LORD which he commanded Israel" (16:39–40).

Scholars mostly think that this is a narrative fiction deployed for theological reasons (Klein 2006: 369n69; Japhet 1993: 527–29; also Williamson 1982: 130–31 and Knoppers 2004: 2.652, who believe the tabernacle tradition may represent historical realities). But there is no reason to posit a tension between history and theology in the Chronicler's narrative. What is reflected here is the Chronicler's belief that God's plan for Israel and the blessing of the nations includes a plan for Israel's covenant worship. In the background is an integral understanding of the role of the ark and the tent in Israel's history, and the Chronicler interprets that history in light of Deuteronomy's promise of a single sanctuary (Deut. 12:5–6). He is interpreting data from the canonical record that some might see as an irregularity in Israel's worship in the years immediately prior to the temple. His interpretation is that these years marked a transitional period in which indeed there were two cultic centers in the kingdom: the ark at Jerusalem and the tabernacle at Gibeon. But he wants his readers to know that this bifurcated order of worship was established by none other than God's servant David and that worship in both sites was in strict accord with "all that is written in the law of the LORD" (1 Chr. 16:40; also 16:4–6, 37; cf. Exod. 29:38–42; Lev. 1:3–9; 4:1–5:19; Num.

4:5–15; 28:2–8; Pss. 33:2; 75:1; 79:13; 92:1; 100:4; 105:1–2; 136; Knoppers 2004: 2.642). With the coming of Solomon and the temple, the days of this parallel worship structure are numbered. The Deuteronomic promise is to be realized in the temple that Solomon will build. In the temple, the ark and the tent of Moses will be reunited to serve as the locus of the royal cultus (2 Chr. 5:5; cf. 1 Kgs. 8:4).

Solomon's accession is described in quick strokes as he establishes his royal priorities and priestly prerogatives. The elect son of David, heir to the covenant promises, is the Chronicler's paradigm of the faithful king, one who subordinates all the power and wealth at his disposal to the worship of God and the fulfillment of God's covenant purposes. As it was said of David, it now is said of Solomon: the God of Israel is "his God" and is "with him" and exalts him (2 Chr. 1:1). "God imparts to Solomon sacramentally the quality of his own kingship," as Johnstone declares (1997: 1.298).

As he leads Israel in public worship, Solomon is also depicted as seeking God privately in prayer. The scene is reminiscent of Moses, who first talked to God as a friend in the tent of meeting (Exod. 33:11):

> And Solomon said to God, "Thou hast shown great and steadfast love to David my father, and hast made me king in his stead. O Lord God [*yhwh 'ĕlōhîm*], let thy promise to David my father be now fulfilled, for thou hast made me king over a people as many as the dust of the earth. Give me now wisdom and knowledge to go out and come in before this people, for who can rule this thy people, that is so great?" (2 Chr. 1:8–9)

Solomon's prayer envisions the sweep of salvation history—understood in terms of the sequence of the covenants that God has made with his people. Using the rare form of divine address (*yhwh 'ĕlōhîm*) that David used in his covenant prayer (1 Chr. 17:16–17), Solomon connects God's purposes to creation and the garden of Eden.[1] His address also refers to the Abrahamic covenant. The kingdom established by God's covenant with David is the earthly political expression that fulfills God's promise to make Abraham's descendants more numerous than "the dust of the earth" and the source of blessing for all the families of the earth (Gen. 13:16; 28:14). Solomon also acknowledges Israel's special election by using vocabulary drawn from the exodus and Sinai traditions; as Moses did so often (Exod. 3:7, 10; 5:1; 6:7; 22:25; cf. Lev. 26:12), Solomon reminds the Lord that this is the people whom the Lord called "my people" (2 Chr. 1:10).

The kingdom is the fulfillment of God's covenant purposes, beginning in creation. Because Solomon seeks not power or wealth but "wisdom and knowledge," these other things are added unto him. He is said to be the richest

---

1. As noted in the discussion of 1 Chr. 17, this form of address is limited almost exclusively to the creation narrative of Gen. 2:4–3:24.

and most powerful of kings (1:11–12, 14–17). Gold and silver are said to be as plentiful as stones, export and trade are booming, and Solomon controls a vast military might in the form of horsemen and chariots. Solomon's wealth and power are not for his or for Israel's aggrandizement but are the means for bringing about the peace and rest prerequisite to building a house for Israel's God.

### The House and City He Chose for His Name to Dwell

Elsewhere in the biblical record it is testified that Solomon began to build the temple in the fourth year of his reign, "the four hundred and eightieth year after the people of Israel came out of the land of Egypt." Based on this, scholars tend to date the temple to about 966 BC (1 Kgs. 6:1, 37–38). None of these details are found in Chronicles even though the building of the temple marks the climax of his narrative. Instead the Chronicler roots the temple in Israel's sacred geography, linking it to the chosen people's history of sacrifice, which he will trace through typology and other forms of inner-biblical allusion back to creation.

The Chronicler's typological vision of history and his international and universalist preoccupations have been on display from his initial genealogies. These concerns intensify in his account of the temple. From Solomon's first letter to King Huram of Tyre, the construction project is framed by a contrast between the God of Israel, who is the God of creation, and the gods of the nations. Solomon explains his purposes: "to build a house[2] for the name of the LORD," whom he identifies as both his personal God ("my God") and Israel's national deity ("our God"; 2 Chr. 2:1, 4, 5). Evoking "the name of the LORD," the Chronicler once more points the reader back to Deuteronomy's promise of the central sanctuary. Solomon will pray at the dedication of the temple: "This house [is] the place where thou hast promised to set thy name" (2 Chr. 6:20; also 1 Chr. 22:8–10; 2 Chr. 6:10; cf. Deut. 12:5, 11, 21; 14:23, 24; 16:2, 6, 11; 18:6–7; 26:2; Schniedewind 2003: 230).

Solomon's dedication prayer, in which he refers fourteen times to the divine name, reflects the highest development, in a canonical reading, of what scholars call "name theology" (2 Chr. 6:1–11, 14–42; cf. 1 Kgs. 8:15–53; Wilson 1995). In the canonical narrative, men and women first began to call on the name of God in the time of Adam's descendant Seth (Gen. 4:26). In the patriarchal period the building of altars is related to God's appearances and the patriarchs' calling upon his divine name (Gen. 12:7–8; 26:23–25; Exod. 20:22–24). The promise of Deuteronomy was that God's people would finally one day offer their sacrifices at a place where God would choose for his name to dwell. And in a private revelation to Solomon following the temple

---

2. The RSV's "temple" is replaced with the more literal "house."

dedication, God reveals this fulfillment: "I . . . have chosen this place for myself" (2 Chr. 7:12), using an expression found only in Deut. 12:18; 14:25; 15:20; 16:2.

With the temple we have come to the summit of the history of sacrifice. After years of journeying with Israel, going "from tent to tent and from dwelling to dwelling" (1 Chr. 17:5–6), God will rest in his house on Mount Zion. Jerusalem (or Zion) and the temple are inseparable and interchangeable in this conception of God's dwelling (2 Chr. 33:4, 7; also Isa. 18:7; Jer. 7:10–12, 14, 30; 25:29; 32:34; 34:15; Ps. 102:21; Joel 2:32). The house and the holy city have been chosen by God. From there his divine blessings will flow out to the peoples of the earth. For there his name will be established and magnified forever among all the nations (1 Chr. 17:24).

The house for his name is not a literal house or dwelling place of the Lord. Solomon recognizes this: "Who is able to build him a house, since heaven, even highest heaven, cannot contain him?" (2 Chr. 2:6; 6:18). God's throne is in heaven, and his footstool is in his temple on earth (1 Chr. 28:2; Pss. 99:5; 132:7; Isa. 66:1). Heaven remains the dwelling place of God, but in a mysterious way he will dwell with his people on earth in the sanctuary where he will cause his name or divine presence to be. In this place God will "hear from heaven" (2 Chr. 7:12, 14–16; 20:9).

God's name *is* God. Where his name abides, there is God. The temple will be the seat of his government over the earth. Thus the Chronicler says that Solomon desired to "build a house[3] for the name of the LORD and a house for his kingdom [*ûbayit lĕmalkûtô*]" (2:1, 12). The establishment of the temple will finally reveal to the world that Israel's God is the one true God. Solomon announces this in his initial letter to Huram: "The house which I am to build will be great, for our God is greater than all gods. . . . Heaven, even the highest heaven, cannot contain him" (2:5–6).

The triple use of "heavens" (lit., "the heavens, and the heavens of heavens") recalls the psalmist's portrayal of Israel's God as the creator of the heavens and the earth (Ps. 148:4; Sir. 16:18). The Chronicler never explicitly makes such a statement of faith; nor does David, Solomon, or any Israelite quoted in his account (but cf. 1 Chr. 16:26). The one affirmation comes from a *non-Israelite*. King Huram calls Israel's God by name (*yhwh*) and acknowledges God's special election of Israel and his sovereignty over the universe: "Because the LORD [*yhwh*] loves his people he has made you king over them. . . . Blessed be the LORD God of Israel, who made heaven and earth" (2 Chr. 2:11–12). It is no doubt symbolic for the Chronicler that this confession of God's universal dominion is made by a foreign king. In this confession we see the beginning of God's blessing of the nations through the children of Abraham, as promised.

---

3. The RSV's "temple" is replaced with the more literal "house" twice in this quotation.

## The Ashes of Moriah and the Legacy of David

Williamson detects in Huram's confession an allusion to the priest-king Melchizedek's blessing of Abraham in Gen. 14:18–20 (1982: 200). This is likely, given the Chronicler's interest in Abraham and the inner-biblical analogies found elsewhere between Salem and Jerusalem (Ps. 76:2) and between Melchizedek and the Davidic royal priesthood (110:4). A mysterious king comes on the stage at the dawn of salvation history to bless Abraham's God and to recognize this God as creator of heaven and earth. Now, at the summit of salvation history, a foreign king again appears to bless Abraham's God and to acknowledge God's dominion over heaven and earth.

The Abrahamic motif is prominent in the Chronicler's telling of the temple's location (2 Chr. 3:1). He actually gives his readers three markers: one geographic (Jerusalem), another salvation-historical (Mount Moriah), and the third Davidic (the threshing floor of Ornan, where God had appeared to David). David's name is used twice, and the temple site is said to have been that "appointed" (*hēkîn*) by David. The Chronicler is here recalling the cosmic drama that led God to reveal the temple site to David (1 Chr. 22:1). This Davidic emphasis is yet another example of the Chronicler's concern to show Solomon as "the faithful accomplisher" of the divine charge given to David (Riley 1993: 85–87). But more is going on here. The Chronicler's intention is clearly to point backward from David's experience at Ornan's threshing floor to what happened many centuries earlier on that same site, here identified as Mount Moriah.

The detail that the temple was built on Mount Moriah ties the temple to the most important sacrifice in Israel's sacred history, Abraham's binding of Isaac, the Akedah, which occurred on an unspecified mount in the land of Moriah (Gen. 22:2). The Chronicler is the only biblical writer to make this connection. In later Jewish literature this tradition is a commonplace and is connected with another tradition—that the ashes of the ram sacrificed in place of Isaac remained at Moriah for many generations (Grossfeld 1977; Kalimi 2002: 18–19n26). The Targum on 1 Chr. 21:15 presumes this tradition when it states that as God was about to destroy Israel to punish David's imprudent and impious census, he "gazed at the ashes of Isaac's Aqedah which were at the base of the altar, and he recalled the covenant with Abraham which he established on the mountain of worship, and the heavenly temple [lit., "the temple that is above"], . . . and he retracted his decree" (cf. Targum on 2 Chr. 3:1).

It seems unlikely that the Chronicler himself is the source of traditions about Moriah and the ashes; more likely he was aware of some ancient form of these traditions in drafting his account. This may explain why the "burnt offering" (*ʿōlâ*) plays such an important part in his telling of the threshing-floor drama and in his summaries of the purposes of the temple and the priesthood (1 Chr. 22:1; 23:31; 2 Chr. 2:4; 7:1, 7; 8:12; 13:11; 23:18; 29:7; 35:16). Is this an intentional inner-biblical echo? God sent Abraham to Moriah and told him to make Isaac a "burnt offering." The term is used six times in the Akedah, culminating with Abraham's sacrificing the ram "as a burnt offering instead of his son" (Gen. 22:13). The term is also repeated several times in the Chronicler's threshing-floor episode; that episode culminated in a burnt offering, as God answered David with "fire from heaven upon the altar of burnt offering" (1 Chr. 21:26; cf. 21:23, 24, 26 [twice], 29).

Abraham's offering of the ram instead of his son is "the first burnt offering in the history of Israel," according to Cassuto (1973: 76–77).[4] This offering was the culmination of a series of encounters in the Abrahamic narrative that prefigured aspects of the sacrificial system of the temple. The meeting with Melchizedek ended with Abraham's giving "a tenth of everything" to the Jerusalemite priest, probably an allusion to the tithes Israel would pay for the Levitical priesthood (Gen. 14:20; cf. Num. 18:21–32; Cassuto 1973: 73).[5] In the "covenant of the pieces," each of the animals that Abraham was instructed to cleave in two was associated with sacrifices later enjoined upon Israel. The promise that God made with the smoking fire pot and the flaming torch passing between the pieces included the conquest of the land and its peoples—the last of the peoples listed being the inhabitants of Jerusalem (Gen. 15:9, 21; Cassuto 1973: 74).[6]

The Chronicler appears to be tapping into an ancient tradition of Jerusalem/Moriah as a holy place of sacrifice. The Targum on 2 Chr. 3:1 states: "And Solomon began to build the temple of the Lord in Jerusalem on Mount Moriah, on the site where he had worshiped and prayed in the name of the Lord; that is the place of worship where all generations worship before the Lord, and it was there that Abraham offered his son, Isaac, as a sacrifice. But the *Memra* [word] of the Lord saved him, and a ram was designated in his stead."

In the Akedah itself, Moriah is referred to as "the mount of the Lord," an expression used elsewhere in the Bible to speak of the Temple Mount in Jerusalem (Gen. 22:14; cf. Isa. 2:3; 30:29; Mic. 4:2; Ps. 24:3). Significantly, the Chronicler refers to the altar that David built on Ornan's threshing floor as "the altar of burnt offering for Israel" (1 Chr. 22:1; cf. 2 Chr. 4:1, 19; 5:12; 6:12, 22; 7:7, 9; 8:12; 15:8; 23:10; 29:18–21; 32:12; 35:16). This detail is found only in his account and provides another link with Israel's history of sacrifice. The altar of burnt offering was a part of the tabernacle in the wilderness and was associated with the perpetual priesthood of Aaron and his sons (Exod. 30:28; 38:1; 40:10–15; Lev. 4:7–10). What does the Chronicler's use of this

---

4. Noah's burnt offering (Gen. 8:20) is the first in the biblical canon prior to this sacrifice by Israel's forefather Abraham.

5. A tithe is also mentioned in association with Jacob's vision of "God's house," perhaps referring to Moses's promise that Israel would pay its tithes to "the place which the Lord your God will choose, to make his name dwell" (Gen. 28:22; Deut. 12:5, 11, 18; cf. Amos 4:4).

6. Cassuto notes that in other lists of the peoples in the Pentateuch, the Jebusites are the final people mentioned (Exod. 3:8, 17; 13:5; 23:23; 33:2; 34:11).

expression mean? That with the temple a new tabernacle and a new altar are about to be revealed. Thus, as heavenly fire consumed the first offerings Moses and Aaron made at the altar in the wilderness, so the offering at David's altar was accepted with divine fire (Lev. 9:22–24; cf. 4:7–10). The symbol will be completed when Solomon's first offering in the temple is likewise greeted with fire (2 Chr. 7:1).

This language of the burnt offering again points us back to the promise of Deut. 12:13–14: "Take heed that you do not offer your burnt offerings [*ōlôt*] at every place that you see; but at the place [*māqôm*] which the LORD will choose in one of your tribes, there you shall offer your burnt offerings [*ōlôt*], and there you shall do all that I am commanding you" (see further 12:6, 11, 27; cf. 33:10).

The Chronicler summons all of this background as he begins his account of the temple. This site at Moriah—"where all generations worship before the Lord" (Targum on 2 Chr. 3:1), where God tested the faith of both his servants Abraham and David and accepted their sacrifices—is the place he has chosen for his name to dwell. Only the Chronicler tells us of God's revelation to Solomon that the temple is his "chosen . . . place" (*bāhar māqôm*) to be "a house of sacrifice" (*bêt zebah*; 2 Chr. 7:12). The expression *bêt zebah* occurs nowhere else in the Bible. It characterizes Israel's relationship to God in terms of the liturgy of sacrifice. Israel will worship God with sacrifice and will teach the nations that this is how they must serve the Lord and receive his blessing.

### Typology of the Temple: The New Tabernacle

The description of the temple construction in Chronicles is about half that found in 1 Kings. But behind the Chronicler's apparent pro forma listing of contractors' considerations is a rich layering of typology and biblical allusion. The primary symbolism of Chronicles depicts the temple as a new tabernacle and a new creation. The beginnings of the tabernacle typology are found in David's reception of a divine "pattern" (*tabnît*) for the temple and its liturgy (1 Chr. 28:11, 12, 18, 19), just as Moses had received a *tabnît* for the tabernacle (Exod. 25:9, 40). As the tablets of the covenant given to Moses were said to be "written with the finger of God" (Exod. 31:18), the Chronicler says the temple plan given to David was put in "writing from the hand of the LORD" (*biktāb miyyad yhwh*; 1 Chr. 28:19).

The typology continues in the master craftsman that the king of Tyre sends to assist Solomon. Huram-abi, like Bezalel the builder of the tabernacle (Exod. 35:31–35), is an expert in metals, woods, and fine linens (2 Chr. 2:13–14). The Chronicler has already alerted his reader to this typology in describing Solomon's pilgrimage to the bronze altar at Gibeon (1:5). Here he gives Huram-abi's descent; his father is a man of Tyre, and his mother is from the Israelite tribe of Dan. This detail seems intended to recall that Bezalel's assistant, Oholiab, was from Dan (Exod. 31:6; 35:34). We see again the internationalism of the temple, which is built by representatives of the nations under the direction of God's firstborn son, the children of Israel. We also see again the emphasis on the unity and continuity of the divine plan. "As the temple was associated with the patriarchs by its site, so it was associated by its design with Moses," says Williamson (1991: 27).

The temple building and its furnishings are modeled on those of the tabernacle, as if to say that the purposes of these articles is fulfilled in the temple. As there was in the tabernacle, so we find in the new temple an altar of bronze (2 Chr. 4:1; Exod. 27:1–8), large lavers for priestly purification and sacrificial washing (2 Chr. 4:2, 6; Exod. 30:19–21), golden lampstands and tables (2 Chr. 4:7–8; Exod. 25:23–40), tables for the bread of the presence (2 Chr. 4:19; Exod. 25:30; 35:13; 39:36), and a veil to partition off the holy of holies (2 Chr. 3:14; Exod. 26:31–35; 36:35–36).

The Chronicler's mention of the veil is one of several signs that the temple symbolism perhaps runs deeper than an analogy to the tabernacle; he intends his depiction of the temple to pick up and continue a latent new-creation symbolism found in traditional understandings of the temple's construction. But first we must trace the relationship between the tabernacle and creation. Jewish and Christian interpreters have long noticed the intertextual relation between the accounts of creation and the building of the tabernacle. Fishbane observes "a series of key verbal parallels" between the two accounts (1979: 12). There is also a mutual interplay between the two, with creation being understood as the building of a cosmic temple, and the tabernacle being depicted as a recapitulation of the cosmos. Each provides a space in which God will dwell with his people. This symbolism, in turn, underlies the Chronicler's account of the temple.

The creation of the world in Gen. 1–2 is recounted in liturgical terms and ritual rhythms, unfolding in a heptadic pattern, with a series of repeated sevens—beginning with the first verse, which contains exactly seven words in Hebrew, and proceeding with seven clearly defined creative speech-acts of God ("and God said, 'Let . . .'"), seven statements of divine approval ("It was good"), and culminating in the divine rest of the seventh day (*yôm haššebî'î*; Balentine 1999: 82–95, 136–41; also Hahn 2005d). This same heptadic pattern is found in the account of the tabernacle. Moses's time on the mountain can be seen as a kind of new creation. The cloud of divine presence covers the mountain for six days; on the seventh day Moses is called into the cloud to receive the divine blueprint (*tabnît*) for the tabernacle (Exod. 24:15–16; 25:8–9). The instructions that God gives him are delivered in seven speeches (introduced by "the LORD said" or "the LORD spoke"; 25:1; 30:11, 17, 22, 34; 31:1, 12; Beale 2004: 61), the last of which commands the observance of the Sabbath as a "perpetual covenant" and a "sign . . . that in six days the LORD made heaven and earth, and on the seventh day he rested" (31:16–17;

Blenkinsopp 1976; Kearney 1977; Sarna 1986: 213–15; Gorman 1990: 47; cf. Balentine 1999: 138n41). On a closer reading, the creation-tabernacle connections are even more apparent (Balentine 1999: 139; cf. Levenson 1985: 142–44):

> And God saw everything that he had made, and behold, it was very good. (Gen. 1:31)
> And Moses saw all the work, and behold, they had done it. (Exod. 39:43)
>
> Thus the heavens and the earth were finished. (Gen. 2:1)
> Thus all the work of the tabernacle of the tent of meeting was finished. (Exod. 39:32)
>
> On the seventh day God finished his work which he had done. (Gen. 2:2)
> So Moses finished the work. (Exod. 40:33)
>
> So God blessed the seventh day. (Gen. 2:3)
> And Moses blessed them. (Exod. 39:43)

Many of the details of the creation-tabernacle typology are picked up in the Chronicler's description of the temple building (2 Chr. 3:2–5:1): similar vocabulary, similar liturgical cadences, and the pattern of sevens. The Chronicler's narrative is structured around fourteen paragraphs that begin with the phrase "and he made" (*wayya'aś*; 2 Chr. 3:8, 10, 14, 15, 16; 4:1, 2, 6, 7, 8, 9, 11, 18, 19). If seven is the number of creation, the doubling of seven, or fourteen, is perhaps to be understood as the perfection or completion of creation.

Solomon is depicted as building the temple from the inside out—from the inner sanctuary, the holy of holies, to the outer courts—and then furnishing it. First he makes the holy of holies, then the cherubim for the ark and the veil that separates the sanctuary from the nave. Next, he makes the two pillars for the entrance to the temple and the chains and pomegranates to adorn the pillars. The bronze altar is built next, followed by the molten sea and the ten basins for sacrificial washing. He makes ten golden lampstands, ten tables, and one hundred golden basins. Then he makes the court for the priests and the outer courtyard. With Huram, he is depicted as making the cast-bronze utensils, and finally Solomon is said to have made "all the things that were in the house of God" (4:19).

### Typology of the Temple: The New Creation

The Chronicler's intent is clearly to evoke the tabernacle narrative (Exod. 36:8–39:32), which similarly turns on the repetition (nearly forty times) of the same verb, *'āśâ* ("to make"; Williamson 1982: 208). The two accounts conclude in the same way, with both Moses and Solomon said to have finished all of their work (2 Chr. 5:1; Exod. 39:32). But again we sense a deeper level of inner-biblical allusion at work. The words that conclude the Chronicler's description are our clue: "Thus all the work that Solomon did for the house of the LORD was finished" (2 Chr. 5:1). Not only do these words recall Moses's finishing the tabernacle (Exod. 40:33), but the same words describe how God finished the work of creation—"make" (*'āśâ*) and "work" (*mělā'kâ*; Gen. 2:1–3).

The temple is a new tabernacle. But more than that, the temple is a new work of divine creation. Here the Chronicler is tapping into a deep stratum of the biblical worldview that sees the temple as a microcosm of heaven and earth. Although the theme is most fully developed in the extrabiblical literature, we hear echoes of this thinking in the Pentateuch, Psalms, Prophets, and Chronicles. God, the psalmist says, "built his sanctuary like the high heavens, like the earth, which he has founded for ever" (Ps. 78:69; cf. Jer. 17:12). This connection between sanctuary and creation explains much of the architectural symbolism in the temple. Although the fullest explanation of this symbolism again comes in the extrabiblical Jewish tradition, this tradition is firmly rooted here in Chronicles and elsewhere in the Bible. Levenson's methodological considerations are helpful as we explore the implicit or incipient symbolism of the temple:

> It is . . . not surprising that the text of the Hebrew Bible is so taciturn about the theology of the Temple. It does not tell us the meanings of the iconography; we have to reconstruct them. It does not specify the prayers that must have accompanied the sacrifices; we have to reconstruct them, mostly from the psalms, as best we can. . . . But to take this taciturnity at face value, to take it as an indication that . . . the decorations in Solomon's Temple held no symbolic significance, or that the sacrifices were a dumb show because Leviticus supplies no words, is to miss the social dynamics at work. It seems more probable that it was precisely the vitality of the Temple mythos which accounts for the fragmentary character of the references to it. It was too well-known, too much part of the common cultural landscape, to be allowed free and independent expression. (1985: 120–21)

Our understanding of the temple symbolism is aided by comparisons with the iconography of other sanctuaries in the ancient Near East and by the elaborations of later rabbinic tradition. Thus, in Solomon's temple the curiously named basin for washing the sacrificial gifts, called the "sea" (*yām*), is thought to recall the primordial division of the waters (Gen. 1:6; Ps. 74:12–17; Isa. 51:9–11) and perhaps evokes the four rivers that flowed out of Eden to water the earth (Gen. 2:10–11). Elsewhere in scripture, the temple is frequently associated with life-giving water; one psalm speaks of the temple as "the fountain of life" and refers to "the river of thy delights" (*naḥal 'ădānêkā*, lit., "the river of your *Edens*"; Ps. 36:8–9; cf. Jer. 17:7–8, 12–13). In his vision, the prophet Ezekiel sees water flowing from the right side of the temple, south of the altar—in the vicinity where the Chronicler says the *yām* is located (Ezek.

47:1; Joel 3:18; 1 Kgs. 7:39; Gen. 2:10; Hurowitz 2005: 81). Confirming this association of the temple with the springs of life, the Chronicler describes the *yām* and its accoutrements with traditional images of abundance and fertility: it is shaped like a lily and seated atop a pedestal made of twelve bulls, three of which face each of the four corners of the earth.

As the sea evokes the primordial waters, so the great altar that Solomon builds is a symbol for the foundations of the earth, a symbolic association found throughout the biblical record, beginning with the "altar of earth" that Moses is commanded to build (Exod. 20:24–25; 29:12; Lev. 4:7, 18, 25, 30, 34; Ezek. 43:14, 16; Beale 2004: 33). The altar of the temple, as the prophet Ezekiel said, stands, literally, at "the bosom of the earth" (*ḥêq hā'āreṣ*; Ezek. 43:13–17, esp. 14). Some scholars believe the "bronze platform" (*kîyôr*) that Solomon built to pray upon in the temple court is another symbol of the earth (2 Chr. 6:13; Levenson 1986: 52). The pillars that Solomon erects at the north and south points of the temple entrance are also symbolic. Throughout scripture we find it asserted that God established the earth on a foundation of "pillars" (Pss. 75:3; 18:15; 82:5; 102:25; 104:5; Isa. 48:13; 51:13; Job 9:6; 26:11). Only Chronicles has Solomon naming these pillars, and the Hebrew names he gives them, "Jachin and Boaz" (2 Chr. 3:17), connote stability and strength. Boaz, perhaps not coincidentally, is also the name of David's great-grandfather (Ruth 2–4), already mentioned in the Chronicler's genealogy (1 Chr. 2:11–12). Johnstone is probably correct in seeing a deliberate Davidic point being made here: "The stability imparted by God at creation to the whole earth is maintained by the activities of David's house, God's representative and agent on earth" (1997: 1.321).

The temple building is adorned with gold, onyx, and "all sorts of precious stones" found also in Eden (1 Chr. 29:1–2; 2 Chr. 3:6; cf. Gen. 2:12). The Chronicler calls the gold used in the temple "fine" (*ṭôb*; 2 Chr. 3:5, 8), the same word used to describe the gold in the land of Havilah, near Eden (Gen. 2:12). These stones are also associated with the robe of the high priest of the temple (Exod. 28:4–43; Beale 2004: 41–42). As the holy garments of Aaron were made "for glory [*kābôd*] and for beauty [*tip'eret*]" (Exod. 28:2, 40), the stones inlaid in the temple are likewise for "beauty," to reflect the divine glory (*tip'eret*; 2 Chr. 3:6).[7] The abundant floral imagery associated with the temple—flowers, lilies, pomegranates, cypress, palms—also evokes the sacred garden of creation. The lampstands and possibly the pillars are stylized to represent the tree of life in the garden (Exod. 25:31–40; 30:27; 37:17–24; 1 Kgs. 7:49). The "lampstand" (*měnōrâ*; 2 Chr. 13:11) is associated with the light of creation. In later Jewish tradition, the veil of blue and purple and crimson embroidered

7. *Tip'eret* is also associated with the precious stones in 1 Chr. 22:5 and 29:11. Curiously, this purpose ("beauty") has dropped out of such modern translations as the RSV and the New American Bible.

with cherubim is said to represent elements of the cosmos (3:14). Finally, the cherubim variously engraved on the walls and carved to accompany the ark are an obvious symbol of the cherubim—found in the garden (Gen. 3:24) and the holy of holies (Exod. 25:20–21; 26:1, 31; Num. 7:89)—stationed by God as sentinels before the tree of life.

Solomon's temple is, then, an architectural recapitulation of the cosmic temple of creation. Ezekiel identified "Eden, the garden of God," with the temple site (God's "holy mountain") in his lament over the king of Tyre, a highly typological passage that compares the king's sin with that of Adam's in the garden (Ezek. 28:13–14; Hahn 2005d: 107–8). These inner-biblical interpretations and their fleshing out in later Jewish tradition help us to comprehend the significance of the temple for the Chronicler's worldview. In speaking of Moriah and "the mountain of the house of the LORD" (2 Chr. 3:1; 33:15), the Chronicler understood the temple to be on "the cosmic mountain" (Clifford 1972), Zion, at "the center of the nations" (Ezek. 5:5), elevated high above all the earth (Ps. 48:1–3), and indeed at the "very navel [*tabbûr*] of the earth" (Ezek. 38:12).[8] From this "navel," according to Jewish tradition, God created the world. *Midrash Tanḥuma, Kedoshim* 10, likely the oldest commentary on the whole Pentateuch (AD 800), shows this temple connection:

> Just as the belly-button is positioned in the center of a man, thus is the land of Israel positioned in the center of the world, as the Bible says, "dwelling at the very navel of the earth" (Ezek. 38:12), and from it the foundation of the world proceeds. . . . And Jerusalem is in the center of the land of Israel, and the Temple is in the center of Jerusalem, and the Great Hall is in the center of the Temple, and the Ark is in the center of the Great Hall, and the Foundation Stone is in front of the Ark; and beginning with it, the world was put on its foundation. (quoted from Levenson 1985: 118, 139)

Many scholars believe that in the temple's "great hall" or holy of holies is the "rock of foundation" that Jewish tradition believed was affixed with the name of God and sealed above the long shaft leading to the abyss of the netherworld (Isa. 28:16; Ps. 118:22; *Targum Pseudo-Jonathan* on Exod. 28:30; in Levenson 1985: 134). This was a sign of God's lordship over creation and the elemental forces of chaos. Another sign of his divine rule was the tabernacle veil, which, according to first-century Jewish historian Josephus, was the model for the temple veil and was embroidered with "a kind of image [*eikōn*] of the universe" (*Jewish War* 5.212). The ark of the covenant was the ultimate sign, considered to be variously the throne or the footstool of God, a sign of his divine presence and his sovereignty over all his creation (1 Chr. 28:2; Pss. 99:5; 132:7–8; Isa. 66:1). Indeed, Josephus points to a kind of sacramental idea of

---

8. The reading *tabbûr* is disputed, but Levenson 1985: 115–17 is correct in reading this passage in light of the later rabbinic tradition.

the temple, in which the reality of God's presence in creation was symbolized and made manifest in the things of the tabernacle and, by extension, the temple: "For if anyone do without prejudice and with judgment look upon these things, he will find that they were every one made in way of imitation and representation of the universe" (*Jewish Antiquities* 3.179).

### Glory Filled the House: Sabbath Rest in the New Creation

If the temple is a new creation, it means that the temple recapitulates God's purposes for creation; this is seen powerfully in Chronicles. To understand the symbolism, however, and the meaning of the temple in the biblical imagination, we need to keep in mind the broader outlines of the biblical theology of creation. In a canonical reading, the meaning of the creation in Genesis is made clear in the Sabbath ordinances of Exodus, which explain the Sabbath as a sign of the eternal covenant of creation (31:12–17; 35:1–3; Timmer 2009). Creation is ordered to the Sabbath—to the covenant "rest" of the seventh day, in which God dwells with his people in communion and love.

A canonical reading of Hebrew scripture indicates that God's purposes in creating the world are liturgical. The world is made for worship. The covenant made in creation establishes the world as the temple and the kingdom of God. This interpretation of Hebrew scripture is reflected in the Chronicler's typology of the temple as the new Eden. The Sabbath, as the goal of creation, establishes a relationship in which God's blessings flow to his creatures in the liturgy of sacrifice. This "sabbatical" understanding is underscored vividly at Solomon's liturgy dedicating the temple. The priests bring up the tent of meeting from Gibeon and the ark of the covenant from its place in Jerusalem and install them in the temple. All Israel is engaged in the sacrificial offering of countless sheep and oxen, to the accompaniment of joyous strains of the Levitical songs, and "the house, the house of the LORD, was filled with a cloud [*ānān*], so that the priests could not stand to minister because of the cloud [*ānān*]; for the glory of the LORD [*kābôd-yhwh*] filled the house of God" (2 Chr. 5:13–14).

This is a deliberate analogy to the dedication of the tent in the wilderness. There, on the occasion of the offering of the first sacrifices, "the cloud [*ānān*] covered the tent of meeting, and the glory of the LORD [*kābôd-yhwh*] filled the tabernacle. And Moses was not able to enter the tent of meeting, because the cloud [*ānān*] abode upon it, and the glory of the LORD [*kābôd-yhwh*] filled the tabernacle" (Exod. 40:34–35; cf. Lev. 9:23–24).

The tent of meeting is incorporated into the new temple because in the temple the purposes of the tent are fulfilled: there God's presence will abide, and he will meet and speak with his people; there he will bless and sanctify the people through the ministry of his priests; and there they will renew their covenant with him (Exod. 29:42–46). The Chronicler's understanding is attested in various psalms where the temple and the tent are placed in parallelism, indicating that they were understood synonymously or interchangeably (Pss. 26:8; 27:4–5; 74:7–8; Levenson 1986: 33–34; Friedman 1980).

Both the "cloud" (*'ānān*) and the "glory" (*kābôd*) are signs of the divine presence, of God's permanent dwelling in the midst of his people (Pss. 132; 84; 23:6; 27:4–5; Isa. 6:1; Ezek. 43:1–3; 44:4; Zech. 2:4–5; 8:3; cf. Exod. 25:8; 29:33–44; Lev. 9:4, 6, 22–23; Num. 7:89). In Isaiah's vision he witnessed the Lord seated high on a throne, with the train of his garment filling the temple and the seraphim singing, "Holy, holy, holy is the Lord of hosts; the whole earth is full of his glory" (6:1–3). This is also the meaning of the temple in Chronicles: that God, the creator of heaven and earth, the king of the universe and the Lord of history, fills his creation; that the glory of God fills all the whole earth and all the heavens (Pss. 24:1; 50:12; 72:19; 139:7–13; Jer. 23:23–24; Amos 9:1–6; Prov. 15:3; Wis. 1:7; 8:1).

In his temple, heaven and earth meet and are made one. Though God dwells in the highest heavens, he also dwells now on Zion. Hence the psalmist can sing: "The Lord is in his holy temple, the Lord's throne is in heaven" (Ps. 11:4).

This is a constant theme in scripture: God dwells in heaven but also in his temple at Zion. Congar suggests (1962: 84) that the term "Zion" was used in a special way to refer to Jerusalem and the temple as the dwelling of God (Pss. 74:2; 76:2; 78:68–69; 132:13–14; Isa: 2:3; 4:5; 8:18; Jer. 31:6). Chronicles uses the term "Zion" only twice—when David returns the ark to Jerusalem (1 Chr. 11:5) and here, when Solomon installs the ark in the completed temple (2 Chr. 5:2); both times Zion is identified as the "city of David." In the temple, men and women can touch heaven. It is the recapitulation of creation, when God walked in harmony and spoke with familiarity with his people. The temple is the symbol of God's divine humility and condescension. In his gracious humility the Creator of the cosmos, whom the highest heavens cannot contain, has condescended to dwell in this place where he has placed his name.

These themes of universality and personal intimacy are emphasized in Solomon's prayer for the dedication of the temple. Throughout he uses the rare term for the God of creation, *yhwh 'ĕlōhîm*. He names *yhwh 'ĕlōhîm* as the God of Israel, the God who made his covenant with the "children of Israel" (2 Chr. 6:11, 14; cf. Exod. 10:20; Deut. 4:44). Yet *yhwh 'ĕlōhîm* is no nationalistic deity. He is also the Lord of "all the peoples of the earth" (2 Chr. 6:33; cf. Deut. 28:10; Josh. 4:24), who has come to dwell with all "humankind" (*'ādām*; 2 Chr. 6:18). The temple is the seat of God's reign over the nations, but also the throne from which he will reign over all nations and over every human heart. This God of the highest heavens, though he dwells in "thick darkness" (2 Chr. 6:1, 18; cf. Exod. 20:21), is an intimate and personal god. He "knowest the hearts of the children of men" (2 Chr. 6:30), and in the temple he will make himself accessible to hear their prayers, forgive their sins, and judge their thoughts and works.

The temple-dedication ceremony is described in terms designed to make us think of an almost cosmic completion or recapitulation. Israel's celebration has an all-encompassing nature. There is the rhythmic repetition of the word "all" (*kōl*): the ceremony includes *all* the heads of the tribes, *all* the men of Israel, *all* the elders, *all* the holy vessels, *all* the congregation, *all* the Levitical singers (2 Chr. 5:2–12). Again, there are unmistakable references to the Sabbath. In the beginning, "God finished his work [*mĕlā'kâ*] which he had done [*'āśâ*]" (Gen. 2:2); in the building of the temple, Solomon finished "the work [*mĕlā'kâ*] that [he] made [*'āśâ*]" (2 Chr. 5:1; also 7:11). The conclusion of the creation story too is punctuated by images of totality and repetitions of the word *kōl*: God finishes the heavens and the earth and *all* their hosts; he rests from *all* his work. And as God "blessed" (*brk*) the seventh day (Gen. 2:3), Solomon his king "blesses" (*brk*) all the congregation of Israel (2 Chr. 6:3).

The Chronicler sees the temple's completion as completing creation and inaugurating a new age, a new Sabbath. This is the meaning of the accumulation of "seven" imagery, which is also redolent of the creation narrative. Solomon dedicates the temple in the seventh year, in the seventh month, during the Feast of Booths or Tabernacles, a feast that lasts seven days (2 Chr. 5:3; 7:8–10; cf. Lev. 23:33–43; Deut. 16:13–15). Solomon delivers a solemn dedicatory prayer built around seven petitions (2 Chr. 6:12–42). It is a prayer of submission, which he prays on his knees before the temple, hands spread wide and uplifted toward heaven "in the presence of all the assembly of Israel [*kōl-qĕhāl yiśrā'ēl*]" (6:12–13).

Solomon's prayer culminates in a threefold invocation for God to enter into his "rest" in the temple:

> And now arise, O Lord God [*yhwh 'ĕlōhîm*], and go to thy resting
>     place,
>   thou and the ark of thy might.
> Let thy priests, O Lord God [*yhwh 'ĕlōhîm*], be clothed with salvation,
>   and let thy saints rejoice in thy goodness.
> O Lord God [*yhwh 'ĕlōhîm*], do not turn away the face of thy
>     anointed one!
> Remember thy steadfast love for David thy servant. (2 Chr. 6:41–42)

These lines are thought to be an adaptation of Ps. 132:8–10, a liturgical prayer that celebrates the ark and the Davidic covenant. Earlier David had called the temple "a house of rest for the ark . . . of the Lord" (1 Chr. 28:2). The rest envisioned is an "eschatological rest" (Williamson 1982: 220), secured in fulfillment of God's covenant with his beloved servant David (Isa. 55:3). That the Chronicler understands this rest in an eschatological way is emphasized by his altering the psalm to insert the triple reference to the name of God used in the creation account, *yhwh 'ĕlōhîm*. The temple of creation is intended to be the place of rest for *yhwh 'ĕlōhîm*. Now the temple at Zion will fulfill God's original purposes in creation. In the dedication liturgy of the temple, the God of creation is assuming his throne, coming to rest on the new Sabbath of the new creation.

The Chronicler's account, then, is more than the completion of an earthly sanctuary; this temple on earth is a recapitulation of the sanctuary of creation. At the start of his great prayer, Solomon affirms: "I have built thee an exalted house [*bêt-zĕbul*], a place for thee to dwell in for ever" (2 Chr. 6:2). The rare word *zĕbul* (lofty), used in only three other places in scripture, is always associated with the heavens and God's heavenly habitation (Hab. 3:11; Isa. 63:15; 1 Kgs. 8:13; Beale 2004: 37–38, 46n36). Thus the Targum on 2 Chr. 6:2 interprets this verse in light of an ancient tradition that the temple is built on the pattern of God's heavenly dwelling: the temple is "a sanctuary house . . . corresponding to the throne of the house where you dwell, which is forever in the heavens."

What we see in the Chronicler is spelled out in a later midrash, which makes still another interpretation of Solomon's name:

> "When all the work . . . was completed" (2 Chron. 5:1)—not "the work," but "all the work"; that is, on the day the work on the Temple was finished, God declared the work of the six days of creation as finished. For the text in Genesis, "He rested . . . from all his work which God created to make" (Gen. 2:3), does not as one would expect say, "and made" but "to make"; that is, another work remained to be made (for creation to be considered as finished). Only when Solomon came and built the Temple would the Holy One, blessed be he, say: Now the work of creating heaven and earth is completed. "Now all the work . . . is completed." This is why he [Solomon] is called *šlmh* ("he who is destined to finish") because it was through the work of his hands that the Holy One, blessed be he, completed the work of the six days of creation. (*Pesiqta Rabbati* 6; quoted from Weinfeld 1981: 503n4)

This midrash reflects the Chronicler's interpretation of the biblical record. The telos of biblical history has been accomplished. The "rest" promised to the people of God in Deuteronomy is revealed to be a return to the repose of Eden, which has been replicated in the temple. For the Chronicler, the temple at Zion is the center of the new heavens and the new earth. At Zion, the God of creation will bestow his blessings on the world that he created (Ps. 134:3; Isa. 65:17).

Now we see the full meaning of the imagery of the temple. The world is once more filled with the presence of God. The earth has again become the sanctuary it was intended to be in creation. The temple represents the way the world was created to be. Indeed, later Jewish tradition makes explicit a wide strand of belief that the temple was built on the site of the garden of Eden (*Jubilees* 8.19; also *Testament of Levi* 18.6, 10; *1 Enoch* 24–27). As the world was made to be a temple, humanity was created to serve and worship God in that temple (Levenson 1984). Adam, the first human named in scripture and the first word in Chronicles, was intended to be a cosmic priest in creation, offering to God the fruits of creation in a sacrifice of thanksgiving (*Numbers Rabbah* 4.8; *Genesis Rabbah* 20.12; 34.9; Hayward 1996: 44–47, 88–95; Beale 2004: 78n118). Later rabbinic texts declare that Adam was created of "dust from the site of the sanctuary," identified with Mount Moriah (*Targum Pseudo-Jonathan* on Gen. 2:7; also on 3:23; Beale 2004: 67n90). Adam was created to be the king of God's creation, ruling in God's stead as his very image on earth, as seen in various royal first-man allegories and images found elsewhere in scripture (Ezek. 28:1–19; Ps. 8:3–8; May 1962; Van Seters 1989).

The wisdom and wealth associated with the first man (Ezek. 28:3–5) is ascribed now to Solomon (2 Chr. 1:10–12; 9:1–7), who in contrast to Adam does not abuse these gifts but subordinates them to the discernment and performance of God's will (Ezek. 28:5–6, 17). Solomon represents man as he was created to be—a man in service to God. Solomon is the new Adam, the covenant king of the new creation. His name (*šĕlōmōh*) is associated by the Chronicler with both "rest" (*mĕnûḥâ*) and "peace" (*šālôm*). He is the "man of rest" (*'îš mĕnûḥâ*; 1 Chr. 22:9), the man made for the Sabbath holiness that God intended (Kreitzer 2007; cf. Braun 1976: 585–86).

This casts Solomon's priestly and royal actions in a new light. He is leading the people of God as Adam was meant to lead the human family in serving and giving praise to their Creator. In the Chronicler's depiction of the children of Israel, we see the image of redeemed humanity, humanity as it was intended to be in the beginning. Without ever quoting the covenant vocation given to Israel at Sinai, the Chronicler portrays Israel as "a kingdom of priests and a holy nation" (Exod. 19:5–6). In her fine study of this covenant language, Wells notes that to be a kingdom of priests and a holy nation was "the purpose of the covenant [and] the goal of Israel's future" (2000: 34–35). That future is exemplified in the kingdom established under Solomon, which, as Riley notes, is a nation in the service of God, the nation as *qāhāl/ekklēsia*:

> The Israel over which the Davidic kings rule is at base a liturgical *qāhāl*; although the *qāhāl* of Israel exists before the monarchy, the Chronicler underscores the connection between the king and the *qāhāl* by portraying the Davidic king as the convener of the *qāhāl* and by showing the role of the *qāhāl* in accompanying the king as the Jerusalem cultus progresses in the Chronistic history; in this way, the development of the cultus becomes a component in the history of the liturgical *qāhāl* of the nation. (Riley 1993: 166–67)[9]

This is Israel's mission, the purpose of the kingdom and the children of the kingdom: to be the holy *qāhāl/ekklēsia* of God, a national *qāhāl*, a people

9. Compare 1 Chr. 13:1–5; 15:3–11; 23:2; 28:1; 29:1–2; 2 Chr. 1:3; 5:2–4; 6:3, 12; 20:4–13, 23.

called together to offer worship and sacrifice to the Creator of heaven and earth and to bring all nations the blessings of this God.

### Cultic Dimensions of Liturgical Empire

The Chronicler envisions the kingdom of Israel as a liturgical empire—an empire that will exercise its dominion, not through military might or economic supremacy, but through the blessings of the liturgy celebrated in the temple and through the wisdom taught by its kings. This is why the Chronicler devotes eight of his nine chapters on the reign of Solomon to the building of the temple and the organization and celebration of the liturgy.

For the Chronicler, the vocation of the monarch is preeminently cultic. Thus Chronicles tells us nothing about the economy or division of labor in the kingdom under Solomon and David and relatively little about the administration of the imperial government and its military. By contrast, five full chapters (1 Chr. 23–27) and significant portions of at least four more (1 Chr. 15, 16, 28, 29) are devoted to detailing David's establishment of the kingdom's liturgical worship. The administration and organization of the liturgy is portrayed as "the royal task *par excellence*," as Riley puts it (1993: 167).

In the Chronicler's account, David's last testament is to lay out the organization of the temple worship according to the divine blueprint (*tabnît*) he has received from the hand of God. Similarly, Solomon's crowning work is to faithfully implement David's liturgical agenda. He institutes the Davidic order of worship for the daily, weekly, and annual temple sacrifices (2 Chr. 8:12–13); he appoints the divisions of priests, Levites, gatekeepers, and treasurers. Solomon carries out his mandate perfectly: "for so David the man of God had commanded" (8:14–15).

To be king in the kingdom of Israel is to be a priest. Both David and Solomon lead the people in worship and are depicted as performing priestly acts such as offering sacrifices and blessing the people. And their priestly prerogatives are bestowed upon them in their enthronement, using priestly appointment language found in the coronation psalm: "The LORD has sworn and will not change his mind, 'You are a priest for ever after the order of Melchizedek'" (Ps. 110).

Unlike the ordinary priesthood and high priesthood, the royal priesthood is not based on heredity. "Rather," as Rooke notes, "the two distinctive features of the royal priesthood are its bestowal by divine oath ('the Lord has sworn') and its eternity ('you are a priest for ever')" (1998: 195–96; cf. Rooke 2000: 184–218; Schweitzer 2003). The king is a priest above all priests by virtue of this special relationship instituted by God. Yet the king is not depicted as exercising his priestly prerogatives except on extraordinary occasions, and the king in Chronicles is closely associated with his chief priest or high priest. This union of cult and crown begins with David and his special relationship with Zadok. Zadok is a key adviser to David, whom he appoints to oversee the worship at the tabernacle at Gibeon (1 Chr. 15:11; 16:39; 18:16; 24:3). Upon Solomon's succession to the throne, Solomon is anointed by the people "as prince [*nāgîd*] for the LORD," along with Zadok, who is anointed "priest" (*kōhēn*; 29:22). This dual anointing highlights the close and reciprocal relationship in the kingdom between the king as the heir of the house of David, and the high priest as the heir of the house of Aaron (Zech. 6:9–13; Japhet 1993: 513–14; Klein 2006: 541; cf. Schniedewind 1994: 77; Knoppers 2003a).

Day-to-day responsibility for the holiness of the people and the worship of the kingdom is the responsibility of the ordinary clergy—the sons of Aaron and the Levites. In accordance with the plan that he received from God, David established twenty-four priestly "courses," rotating terms of service (Schniedewind 1994; Williamson 2004). Each course apparently lasted a week, meaning that in a forty-eight-week lunar year each priest would serve two tours of duty. The priests' work was primarily to offer sacrifices in the temple and to be teaching the law to the people. In broad outlines, the priests were set apart to "consecrate," "burn incense," offer sacrifices, "minister" to God, and "pronounce blessings in his name" (1 Chr. 23:13).

In addition to the priests, David established the Levites as "overseers" (*nṣḥ*) of the work of the temple, with specific offices of offering thanks and praise and special responsibility for assisting the priests in all aspects of "the service [*ʿăbōdâ*] of the house of God" (23:28; also 23:4, 26–32; 2 Chr. 8:14; cf. Deut. 10:8; 18:5, 7; Knoppers 1999). The most distinctive of the Levitical duties was that of liturgical song and musical accompaniment. In addition to singers were musicians—players of harps, lyres, and cymbals—as well as the priests who blew the trumpets before the ark (1 Chr. 15:16–24). There also were gatekeepers, positioned at all four sides of the temple, to protect the holiness of the sanctuary by ensuring that its sacred precincts were not breached (26:1–19); treasurers were responsible for the temple treasury and the treasury of dedicated gifts, spoil from battles that was dedicated for the maintenance of the temple (26:20–28).

The Chronicler presents the Davidic temple liturgy as an authentic development of the tradition of worship established by Moses at Sinai. The principal symbols of Mosaic worship, the ark and the tent, are incorporated in the temple, and the authority of Moses is invoked frequently (1 Chr. 6:49; 15:15; 2 Chr. 8:12–13; 23:18; 24:6, 9; 35:6; De Vries 1988: 633; Leithart 2003: 26). Solomon describes the temple worship as "ordained for ever for Israel." The basic elements of the daily liturgy that he identifies were all introduced by Moses (Exod. 20:7–8; 25:6, 30; 40:23; Lev. 4:7; 16:12; see Johnstone 1997: 1.308): "Behold, I am about to build a house for the name of the LORD my God and dedicate it to him for the burning of incense of sweet spices before him, and for the continual offering of the showbread, and for burnt offerings morning and evening, on the sabbaths and the new moons and the appointed feasts of the LORD our God, as ordained for ever for Israel" (2 Chr. 2:4).

This description forms a shorthand for the Chronicler to describe the daily worship of the temple (1 Chr. 16:40; 2 Chr. 13:10–11; 31:3). In addition to the daily cycle of sacrifices, the Chronicler mentions other occasional sacrifices such as peace offerings (1 Chr. 16:2; 21:26; 2 Chr. 29:35), thank offerings (2 Chr. 29:31), and sacrifices for atonement (1 Chr. 6:49; 2 Chr. 29:24).

A key liturgical word is *tāmîd* ("continually, unceasingly, regularly"; 1 Chr. 16:6, 11, 37, 40; 2 Chr. 2:4). For the Chronicler, life is for perpetual worship. The liturgy of the kingdom is for the sanctification of time. Days begin and end with sacrifices and offerings; weeks are ordered to the Sabbath. The passing of months is marked by the liturgy of the new moon; and the annual calendar is divided according to the great feasts appointed by God: Unleavened Bread, Weeks, Tabernacles, and Passover (2 Chr. 8:13; cf. Exod. 29:38–42; Num. 28:3–7). In this order of worship, Israel renews its covenant with God and makes atonement for the sins that separate the people from communion with God, for as Solomon observes, "There is no man who does not sin" (2 Chr. 6:36; Endres 2007: 12). What the Chronicler calls "the duty of each day" is the duty to offer back to God sacrifices in praise and thanksgiving for all that he has given and continues to give to the people (8:13–14; 31:16).

Although the temple worship is firmly grounded in the worship of the tabernacle, there was something radically new about the Davidic liturgy. The most obvious difference was his introduction of liturgical music and the singing of psalms. The Mosaic order of sacrifice basically involved priests offering sacrifices for the people in silence, except for the blowing of trumpets before the ark (Num. 10:8–10). David established a new ministry of praise and thanksgiving in song and entrusted this ministry to the Levites. For the first time in Israel's history, psalms of thanksgiving were sung in the sanctuary, with horns, cymbals, harps, and lyres (1 Chr. 16:4, 7–36; 23:2–6; 25:1–30).

Chronicles, in a way unmatched elsewhere in the Bible, depicts the worship of God as a joyous, heartfelt affair. This was by design. The liturgy was established and organized for Israel to offer to God joyful praise, thanksgiving, and rejoicing. Israel in its worship was to "raise sounds of joy"; its offerings were to be made with "rejoicing, . . . according to the order of David" (1 Chr. 15:16; 2 Chr. 23:18; 29:30). The "joy" (*śimḥâ*) so characteristic of the portrait of worship in Chronicles is another sign that Davidic worship is to fulfill the promises of Deuteronomy. It begins with David's coronation, when "there was joy in Israel," and continues throughout the work (1 Chr. 12:39–41; cf. 15:16, 25; 16:10, 31; 29:9, 17, 22; 2 Chr. 6:41; 7:10; 15:15; 20:27; 23:18, 21; 24:10; 29:30, 36; 30:21, 23, 25, 26; Klein 2006: 326; Endres 2007: 16). We may detect here an allusion to Deuteronomy's promise of a central sanctuary. Moses had foretold that Israel's worship would be characterized by rejoicing when the people finally achieved rest from their enemies and were able to offer sacrifices in the place that God had chosen for his name to dwell (Deut. 12:6–7, 11–12, 18; 16:10–11; 26:11; 27:6–7). The Chronicler depicts that promise as being fulfilled.

### The Tôdâ *Spirituality of the Temple Liturgy*

"And they shall stand every morning, thanking and praising the LORD, and likewise at evening" (1 Chr. 23:30). This description of the ministerial office that David gave to the Levites opens a window into the Chronicler's liturgical theology. The image of all Israel at prayer, from the first celebrations of David to the liturgy of renewal celebrated by Hezekiah, is an image of the people as giving thanks and praise to the God of their fathers (1 Chr. 16:4, 7–8, 34–35, 41; 25:3; 29:13; 2 Chr. 5:13; 7:3, 6; 20:21; 29:31; 30:22; 31:2; 33:16). The spirituality of the temple liturgy reflected in Chronicles is deeply rooted in the spirituality of the Psalter and in particular in the spirituality of the *tôdâ* (sacrifice of thankgiving).

The *zebaḥ tôdâ* (sacrifice of thanksgiving) is among the peace offerings prescribed in the Mosaic law (Lev. 7:11–15), and scholars believe that many of the songs in the Psalter were originally composed to accompany the *zebaḥ tôdâ* in the temple. More than that, however, the *tôdâ*, in joining praise, thanksgiving, and sacrifice in the context of the temple liturgy, opens up to us the deep structure of Israel's liturgical imagination and becomes an interpretive key for understanding the telos and trajectory of Old Testament prayer and worship. Gese says: "The Psalter shows that in post-exilic worship, the thank offering played a role that can hardly be overestimated. . . . It can be said that the thank offering constituted the cultic basis for the main bulk of the psalms" (1981: 131).

Attempts to categorize the psalms are tricky. In Psalms studies, the *tôdâ* psalms are classified as individual songs that have a distinct thematic content and follow a basic pattern. The theme is thanksgiving for having been delivered from some life-threatening circumstance. Structurally, the songs begin with the believer's confessing faith in God and vowing to praise him and offer sacrifice; next the believer laments in frank detail the suffering he underwent; and finally he describes his deliverance and how his redemption brought him to the temple to sing God's praises in thanksgiving (Gunkel 1998; Guthrie 1981; Pao 2002; Westermann 1981).

For purposes of understanding the Chronicler, the *tôdâ* reflects a spirituality, an attitude toward life and the divine-human relationship. The spirituality of the *tôdâ* suffuses the Psalter and is found in many psalms that scholars do not technically classify as *tôdâ* psalms. The critical elements of this spirituality are the priority of praise and the essential connection between the offering of sacrifice and the offering of verbal praise and thanksgiving:

> O give thanks [*ydh*] to the LORD, for he is good [*ṭôb*];
>> for his steadfast love [*ḥesed*] endures for ever. . . .
> Let them thank [*ydh*] the LORD for his steadfast love [*ḥesed*],
>> for his wonderful works to the sons of men!
> And let them offer sacrifices of thanksgiving [*zibḥê tôdâ*],
>> and tell of his deeds in songs of joy! (Ps. 107:1, 21–22)

> I will offer to thee the sacrifice of thanksgiving [*zebaḥ tôdâ*]
>> and call on the name of the LORD. (Ps. 116:17)

> I will sacrifice to thee;
>> I will give thanks [*ydh*] to thy name, O LORD, for it is good [*ṭôb*].
>> (Ps. 54:6)

> I will praise the name of God with a song;
>> I will magnify him with thanksgiving [*tôdâ*].
> This will please the Lord more than an ox
>> or a bull with horns and hoofs. (Ps. 69:30–31)

This essentially liturgical and sacrificial vocabulary recurs throughout Chronicles. And only in Chronicles do we find depicted the actual performance of a *zebaḥ tôdâ*, both times in the context of national repentance and renewal (2 Chr. 29:31; 33:16; Mayer 1986: 437). The *tôdâ* spirituality that suffuses the Psalms pervades the Chronicler's portrayal of individual and corporate worship in the kingdom. This spirit is distinctly Davidic and is bound up with the Chronicler's understanding of the Davidic covenant. The worship that David introduces is ritual thanksgiving accompanied by sacrifice. The songs he introduces into Israel's worship are called "thanksgiving" (*hôdâ*), and the Chronicler makes a point of noting the day when David "first appointed that thanksgiving be sung to the LORD" (1 Chr. 16:4, 7). The *tôdâ* spirit is expressed neatly in David's division of liturgical labors in the kingdom: he assigns the priests to offer burnt offerings while the Levites are "chosen and expressly named to give thanks [*ydh*] to the LORD, for his steadfast love [*ḥesed*] endures for ever" (16:39–41; cf. 23:13, 30; Barber 2001: 76–80).

The book of Psalms was not a form of private devotional poetry or the literary products of spontaneous religious enthusiasm. There is never anything ad hoc or improvisational about the worship of the living God; no substantive element of the liturgy is left to the subjective creativity of individual worshipers or the community. The God of the Chronicler, like the God of Exodus, is a God who demands to be worshiped in the manner that he prescribes. This is why so much of Chronicles, again like Exodus, is given over to technical and organizational details of worship (Kleinig 1993: 31). In his fine study of praise in the Psalter, Anderson reminds us: "Prayer in the Bible was not always a spontaneous and effervescent outpouring of one's feeling toward God but could be—and perhaps more often was—a carefully prescribed cultic act" (1991: 15).

The various psalms, then, were composed for specific cultic purposes and were intended to be sung in precise liturgical settings. According to postbiblical tradition, David, the cult founder of the temple, was the principal source of the Psalter (Kugel 1986). This tradition is reflected in the book's final canonical form, with seventy-three of the one hundred fifty psalms bearing the inscription *lĕdāwid* (of David). While the Chronicler is not the initiator of this tradition (2 Sam. 23:1), he undoubtedly played a decisive role in establishing the Davidic pedigree for the singing of psalms of thanksgiving (*hôdâ/tôdâ*) and praise (*hillēl*) in the temple liturgy (1 Chr. 6:16–18; 15:16; 16:4–7; 23:5; 25:1; 2 Chr. 7:6; 8:14; 23:18; 29:25; 35:15).

This raises interesting questions about the relationship of the psalms to the temple liturgy in Chronicles. Kugel suggests that claims of Davidic authorship were important in establishing that the psalms were divinely inspired sacred scripture (1986: 134–35). This hypothesis affords insight into the Chronicler's description of the Levitical singers' work as "prophetic," a description that has long puzzled interpreters. David set apart the sons of three Levitical singers—Asaph, Heman, and Jeduthun—to "prophesy" (*nibbā'*) with lyres, harps, and cymbals under the king's direction (1 Chr. 25:1–7; cf. 2 Chr. 20:14). But the basic nature of the singers' prophetic work remains obscure. However, if the Chronicler believed that these singers were in charge of singing David's divinely inspired compositions—if their particular duty was the recitation of the psalms in the liturgy—then their ministry indeed could be called prophetic; in singing the psalms they would be proclaiming the word of the Lord to the *qāhāl/ekklēsia* and mediating the divine presence expressed in the inspired word (Klein 2006: 480–81; Kleinig 1993: 154–56).

Such an understanding seems to be behind Hezekiah's command for "the Levites to sing praises to the LORD with the words of David and of Asaph the seer" (2 Chr. 29:30). This is a clear reference to the singing of the psalms and again suggests a belief that these words were inspired or prophetic and composed for liturgical purposes. Such an interpretation is bolstered when we consider that almost half of the canonical psalms are ascribed to David, another dozen to Asaph (Pss. 50, 73–83), eleven to the sons of Korah (Pss. 42, 44–49, 84–85, 87–88)—who are probably Jeduthun's sons (2 Chr. 20:19)—and two to Heman (Pss. 88–89). By their traditional ascriptions alone, a substantial majority of the canonical psalms, nearly two-thirds, can be traced back to David and the three Levites that Chronicles says were appointed to prophesy in the liturgy.

The Davidic liturgy is carefully arranged and orchestrated to offer fitting worship to God, to render to God what is God's due. This worship is not a ritual performance in which one mechanically discharges a debt to God. The liturgy is ordered in such a way as to bring worshipers into communion with the living God. The liturgy is an *imitatio Dei* (Levenson 1986: 36–37), a participation in the blessings of his eternal covenant—the covenant inaugurated in creation; renewed in the covenants with Noah, Abraham, and Israel at Sinai; and realized ultimately in the covenant with David. In the liturgy, the people share in God's Sabbath rest and commemorate both his primordial act of creation and his separation of Israel to be his people, a kingdom of priests. This was symbolized by the cloud that filled the temple and the fire that came down from heaven to accept Solomon's sacrifices. It is the promise of God himself—that if his people seek him with a humble heart, they will find him.

There is a tender mercy to the God of Chronicles that for some reason commentators tend to overlook. Until the temple, only his elect servants could see God or hear his voice and expect to live (Exod. 3:6; 20:19; 33:20; Judg. 6:22–23; 13:22; Deut. 5:23–26; Isa. 6:5). The gulf between creature and Creator is not erased by the temple: God remains utterly transcendent and holy, and his people remain utterly unworthy to receive him. Yet as he did in Eden in the beginning, God in his mercy now dwells with his people and personally invites them: "Seek my face" (2 Chr. 7:14; cf. 6:42; 30:9, 18–19). God's revelation to Solomon is filled with anthropomorphic language expressing the intimacy of the relationship he is offering to Israel. In the temple, God's eyes are open and his ears are attentive to their prayer, and he pledges, "My heart will be there for all time" (7:15–16).

How does the liturgy bring about this intimate communion with God? It is not possible to reconstruct any original order of the temple liturgy (but see Kleinig 1993: 101–3). From the Chronicler's account we can, however, identify its key elements as the offering of sacrifice accompanied by prayers and songs of remembrance (*zākar*), thanksgiving (*hôdâ/tôdâ*), and praise (*hillēl*; 1 Chr. 16:4). The essential content of the divine word proclaimed in the liturgy and the prayers by which Israel responded to that word are summarized in the short hymnlike refrain sounded throughout Chronicles:

> O give thanks [*hôdâ*] to the LORD, for he is good [*tôb*];
>    for his steadfast love [*hesed*] endures for ever [*ʿôlām*]! (1 Chr. 16:34)

This refrain again shows the interpenetration between the psalms and the Chronicler's vision of worship (1 Chr. 16:41; 2 Chr. 5:13; 7:3, 6; 20:21; cf. Pss. 106:1; 107:1, 8, 15, 21, 31; 118:29; 136; Jer. 33:11). It is heard throughout the Psalter and in some places seems like it might have served as an entrance antiphon in the temple liturgy, especially in prayers for the *tôdâ* (Ps. 100). This refrain roots Israel's liturgy of sacrifice and praise in its *Heilsgeschichte*, the sacred story of the people recounted in the biblical narrative, the story of the covenant (Levenson 1986: 34). The language is covenantal. God's goodness and steadfast love, his *tôb* and *hesed*, are expressions of the covenant bonds of kinship that he has established forever (*lĕʿôlām*) with his covenant people. The covenant is the foundation and reason for God's acts of salvation and the surety of his pledge to deliver his people in the future (Jer. 33:11; 1 Macc. 4:24).

The covenant is what gives the temple worship its transcendent realism. In the temple liturgy, through the cultic act of praise and thanksgiving offered as sacrifice, the Israelites enter into the presence of the God who created heaven and earth, the God who himself has entered into history and by his covenant has set them apart to be his people, the God who has shown them his steadfast love in delivering them from their enemies and giving them rest in the land he promised to their fathers, the God who on this very mountain swore by himself to make this people the source of blessing for all the nations of the world.

This is how God is invoked in the royal prayers found in Chronicles. And the Chronicler presents the verbal sacrifice of thanksgiving and praise as the only response worthy of the revelation of this great God, with whom none can compare in heaven or on earth. The first thanksgiving that David appoints to be sung sets the tone for worship in the kingdom:

> O give thanks to the LORD . . .
>     make known his deeds among the peoples! . . .
> Sing praises to him,
>     tell of all his wonderful works! . . .
>     Tell of his salvation from day to day.
> Declare his glory among the nations. . . .
> O give thanks to the LORD, for he is good;
>     for his steadfast love endures for ever! . . .
> O God, of our salvation, . . .
>     save us from among the nations,
> that we may give thanks to thy holy name. (1 Chr. 16:8–9, 23–24,
>     34–35)

In its worship, Israel understands itself as a people saved out of the nations and called to give thanks and to praise the name of the God who creates and redeems. Thanksgiving is more than an expression of gratitude: it is a calling, a vocation to proclaim God's salvation and glory to the nations, to make known his wondrous deeds. In the Psalter we frequently hear: "I will give thanks to thee, O LORD, among the peoples; I will sing praises to thee among the nations" (Pss. 9:1; 26:7; 57:9; 75:1; 105:1; 108:3; 122:1–4; cf. Isa. 63:7–9).

There is a similar missionary element in the worship of the Chronicler's temple. Solomon, in his dedication prayer, speaks of "foreigners" as hearing of God's great name and his mighty hand and outstretched arm—all his deeds of salvation. The temple, as Solomon envisions it, is to be a house of prayer for all peoples, a place where God displays his goodness and his reign over creation, "that all the peoples of the earth may know thy name and fear thee, as do thy people Israel" (2 Chr. 6:32–33).

This is a remarkable statement of universalism. Placed on the lips of Solomon, it anticipates Isaiah's prophecies that the nations, even the traditional enemies of Israel, would one day stream to Zion to worship before God (Isa. 2;

19:16–25; 60:14; 61:9; 62:1–2; 66:21–23; cf. Jer. 3:16–17). And as the Chronicler's account of Solomon's reign began with a foreign king's praising the Lord God of Israel (2 Chr. 2:12), it concludes by observing Solomon's benevolent rule over "all the kings of the earth," who bring him tributes of gold, myrrh, spices, and more (9:23, 26).

Solomon, son of David—heir to the oath that God swore to Abraham, Isaac, and Israel, his fathers—is now the king of kings. Abraham's sacrifice, offered in obedience to God's command, opened the world to God's blessings; his faithfulness triggered the first recorded oath sworn by God himself in the biblical canon: "By myself I have sworn, says the LORD, because you have done this, . . . I will indeed bless you. . . . And by your descendants shall all the nations of the earth bless themselves, because you have obeyed my voice" (Gen. 22:16–18; Wenham 1995: 102).

Now on the site where that oath was sworn, in the liturgical empire of Solomon, we see the beginnings of this oath's fulfillment. But Chronicles teaches poignantly that God's promise must ever be matched by the obedience of Abraham's children to his commandments, by their free and joyful offering of their whole hearts in worship in the temple, the house of sacrifice built upon the ashes of Moriah (1 Chr. 29:17–22).

In the Chronicler's vision of worship, we glimpse what Abraham's sacrifice was intended to point to in the economy of salvation. In Chronicles we see evidence of a transformation that we can also trace in the Psalter: prayer and song moving toward sacrifice, and sacrifice moving toward prayer and song. There is no religion without sacrifice, but the sacrifice that God requires ultimately is not about animals: it is the sacrifice of praise and thanksgiving, offered in joy and gladness "with a whole heart and with a willing mind" (28:9). As in the Psalms, in Chronicles we find that prayer, the praise and thanks of the lips, comes to be seen as the most acceptable and pleasing sacrifice to God (Pss. 50:14, 23; 51:16–17; 69:30–31; 141:2; Kugel 1986: 123; also Westermann 1981: 30).

This new understanding of worship and sacrifice reflects new ideas about life and the believer's relationship to God, new ideas rooted in Israel's own experience of exile and restoration. Worship becomes a thanksgiving for the gift of life, a gift experienced in the most dramatic terms as a ransoming from evil and a salvation from death. Gese observes that in the tôdâ "life itself can be seen as overcoming the basic issue of death by God's deliverance into life" (1981: 131).

In a profound way life itself becomes liturgical. To live is to be in God's presence in the temple, while to be apart from the temple is death (Ps. 30; Anderson 1991: 27–28). In the liturgy, the believer realizes redemption, which is actualized in the performance of the cultic acts of praise and thanksgiving offered as sacrifice (Kugel 1986: 127). In the liturgy, God hears their prayer, his marvelous deeds of protection and deliverance in the past are remembered, his protection and deliverance in the present are assured. According to Saul Zalewski's unpublished doctoral dissertation on cultic officials in Chronicles, the temple psalms recall God's mighty acts in order to "evoke the repetition of those acts in the present" (quoted from Kleinig 1993: 19).

The worship of the temple is, then, both performative and formative. It is pedagogy and mystagogy. It is performative and mystagogical in that through their offering of the sacrifices of praise and thanksgiving, believers are drawn into the reality and the mystery of their redemption. It is formative and pedagogical because through the repetition of their cultic duties, the people's hearts and minds and wills are being shaped: they are becoming what they pray, people of praise and thanksgiving, the kingdom of priests, the *qāhāl/ekklēsia*.

The prophets of the exile envisioned Israel's restoration as being characterized by the *tôdâ*. "Out of them shall come songs of thanksgiving [*tôdâ*]," said Jeremiah (30:19). Isaiah saw a new Eden filled with "thanksgiving [*tôdâ*] and the voice of song" (51:3). Perhaps these promises were in the back of the Chronicler's mind as he wrote to his audience in the early years after the exile. David led his people to pray, "And now we thank thee, our God, and praise thy glorious name" (1 Chr. 29:13). And in the first liturgy celebrated in the temple, the people gave thanks and were "joyful and glad of heart for the goodness that the LORD had shown to David and to Solomon and to Israel his people" (2 Chr. 7:10).

The Chronicler's vision of worship is that of Israel as leading the nations, and indeed all creation, in the offering of a great *tôdâ* to the Creator, *yhwh 'ĕlōhîm*. The seeds of *tôdâ* spirituality in Chronicles flowered in later Judaism. Philo, writing on the eve of the Christian era, believed that creation itself had a destiny of praise: "Surely it is the fitting lifework for the world that it should give thanks to its Creator continuously and without ceasing, . . . to show that it hoards nothing as treasure but dedicates its whole being as a pious offering to God who created it" (*Who Is the Heir of Divine Things?* 200). Several hundred years later *Pesiqta de Rab Kahana* promises: "In the coming [messianic] age all sacrifices will cease, but the thank offering will never cease; all [religious] songs will cease, but the songs of thanks will never cease" (quoted from Gese 1981: 133).

This glorious vision of a world in thanksgiving is anticipated in the first thanksgiving sung by David at Zion (1 Chr. 16:7–42). David's song envisions praise as flowing from Zion in ever-widening circles, beginning with the thanksgiving of Israel and moving to the nations, to the families of the earth, and finally to all the heavens and all the earth, the seas and fields and woodlands:

> O give thanks to the LORD, . . .
> O offspring of Abraham. . . .
> Sing to the LORD, all the earth! . . .
> O families of the peoples . . .

> Worship the LORD . . .
>     all the earth. . . .
> Let the heavens be glad, and let the earth rejoice. . . .
> O give thanks to the LORD, for he is good;
>     for his steadfast love endures for ever!

The world is made for praising the glory of the LORD's name. This is the goal of the covenant revealed in the temple age; it is the mission given to the liturgical empire of Israel, the kingdom of God on earth.

## Christian Interpretation

For the Christian interpreter, 2 Chr. 1–9 sheds light on Christ, his church, the Eucharist, and the meaning of worship.

Beginning in the New Testament, Christian tradition has understood Christ as both a new and greater Solomon and a new and greater temple. Compared to Solomon, Jesus is the true son of David (1 Chr. 29:22; 2 Chr. 1; Matthew 1:1; Luke 18:38) and the true Son of God (1 Chr. 17:13; Matthew 14:33; 16:16). As Solomon did, Jesus receives tribute from representatives of the nations (2 Chr. 9:23–24; Matthew 2:11). Solomon is the wise man (2 Chr. 1:10–12; 9:3, 5–7) who built the Lord's house (2:4) upon a great foundation stone (1 Kgs. 5:17; 7:10; Matthew 7:24–25; Acts 7:47). But Jesus is greater than Solomon (Matthew 12:42; Luke 11:31; cf. Matthew 6:29; Luke 12:27). He is the incarnation of the divine wisdom (Matthew 11:19; 12:42) and the messianic "man of peace" (1 Chr. 22:9; Ephesians 2:13–22; Kreitzer 2007). He builds a temple of living stones indwelt by the Spirit (Matthew 16:18; Ephesians 2:19–22), the church, the *qāhāl/ekklēsia*. The church, like Solomon's temple, is the spiritual house of sacrifice (1 Peter 2:5) and the temple of the living God (2 Corinthians 6:16); every believer is a temple made holy by the Spirit (1 Corinthians 6:19).

Ultimately, Christ is the new temple; the temple is his body (John 2:21). Indeed, he is "greater than the temple" (Matthew 12:6). Thus we find in Chronicles material for reflection on the meaning of the incarnation as well as for key topics in the relationship between Christ and the church. The Chronicler's vision of a temple people and the nation as a *qāhāl/ekklēsia* gives solid biblical grounding to the typologies of later traditions, such as those in the fifth-century writings of Augustine:

> The temple that Solomon built to the Lord was a type and figure of the future church as well as the body of the Lord. For this reason Christ says in the Gospel: "Destroy this temple and in three days I will raise it up again" [John 2:19]. For just as Solomon built the ancient temple, so the true Solomon, the true peacemaker, our Lord Jesus Christ, built a temple for himself. Now Solomon means peacemaker; Jesus, however, is the true peacemaker, of whom St. Paul says: "He

is our peace, uniting the two into one" [Ephesians 2:14]. The true peacemaker brought together in himself two walls coming from different angles and himself became the cornerstone. One wall was formed of the circumcised believers and the other of the uncircumcised gentiles who had faith. And of these two peoples he made one church, and with himself as the cornerstone and, therefore, the true peacemaker. (*On the Psalms* 127.2)

This typology is a staple of patristic and medieval interpretive tradition and is indispensable for a right understanding of what Christ intended for his church. What we find in Chronicles are the biblical foundations of this typology. Again we hear in Venerable Bede (circa 730):

The house of God which King Solomon built in Jerusalem was made as a figure of the holy and universal church which, from the first of the elect to the last to be born at the end of the world, is daily being built through the grace of the King of Peace, namely, its Redeemer. . . . He became the temple of God by assuming human nature and we become the temple of God through "his Spirit dwelling in us" [Romans 8:11]. It is quite clear that the material temple was a figure of us all, that is, both of the Lord himself and his members, which we are. But it was a figure of him as the uniquely chosen cornerstone laid in the foundation, and of us as the living stones built upon the foundation of the apostles and prophets, that is, on the Lord himself. (*On the Temple* 1.1)

The Chronicler's vision of the kingdom as a *qāhāl/ekklēsia* is the Old Testament substructure for Jesus's identification of the church (*ekklēsia*) with the temple and the kingdom in Matthew 16:18. Reading this text in light of the Chronicler, we notice a series of terms and concepts that are uniquely attributable to the Chronicler: kingdom and church, divine fatherhood and sonship, temple and foundation stone.

Finally, 2 Chr. 1–9 offers unique insights into the Old Testament roots of the Eucharist, Christian worship, and the liturgical consummation of history (Hahn 2005d). In Chronicles the testimony we find of a movement toward "verbal sacrifice" offers us insights into the early Christian notions of "spiritual worship" (*logikē latreia*, Rom. 12:1; and *eucharistia*), which in Philo and some versions of the Old Testament are used to translate *tôdâ* (Driscoll 2009). The importance of thanksgiving and praise in the temple liturgy provides fertile avenues for exploring not only the origins of the Eucharist but also the connection between *tôdâ* spirituality and Christology.

Leithart accurately describes the Chronicler's vision: "Worship is the goal of humanity, and worship is also the means by which Israel is to realize her mission among the nations" (2003: 29). The Chronicler's vision of the temple age as a new Sabbath opens important lines of inquiry for a liturgical theology. Chronicles, in drawing together the typologies of creation and the tabernacle, makes it possible to read canonically with a sacramental or liturgical hermeneutic and to see that, as Pope Benedict XVI writes, "creation is oriented to the Sabbath, which is the sign of the covenant between God and humankind. . . . Creation exists for the sake of worship" (Hahn 2009a: 118).

This in turn opens up new ways for understanding the telos and trajectory of biblical history and the biblical vision of humans as made for worship.

# 6

---

## In Rebellion since That Day

---

*After the House of David Is Divided (2 Chr. 10–28)*

**Major Divisions of the Text**

1. Kingdom of Israel is divided (10:1–13:22)
   Rehoboam's kingship is contested (10:1–15)
   Northern tribes secede (10:16–19)
   Rehoboam reigns in the southern kingdom (11:1–23)
   Rehoboam forsakes the Lord but humbles himself (12:1–16)
   King Abijah calls the north to return (13:1–12)
   Jeroboam's refusal and civil war (13:13–22)
2. Asa, a model of the good king (14:1–16:14)
   Asa seeks God and is blessed (14:1–15)
   Azariah's prophecy and Asa's obedience (15:1–9)
   Asa and the people swear a covenant oath and are blessed (15:10–19)
   Asa's foolish alliance with the king of Israel (16:1–14)
3. Jehoshaphat, a model of the good king (17:1–21:1)
   Jehoshaphat seeks God and is blessed (17:1–19)
   Jehoshaphat's foolish alliance with the king of Israel (18:1–19:3)
   Jehoshaphat's administrative reforms and religious renewal (19:4–11)
   Jehoshaphat's faith that God fights Israel's battles (20:1–21:1)
4. Judah and the house of King Ahab of Israel (21:2–22:12)
   Jehoram, a type of the unfaithful king (21:2–20)
   Ahaziah walks in the ways of Ahab (22:1–9)
   Athaliah seeks to destroy the royal family of Judah (22:10–12)

139

5. An era of decline (23:1–28:27)
      The priest Jehoiada saves Joash and the Davidic line (23:1–21)
      The reign of Joash, a good king who turns bad (24:1–27)
      The reign of Amaziah, a good king who turns bad (25:1–26:2)
      The reign of Uzziah, who was false to the Lord (26:3–23)
      The reign of Jotham, who did what was right (27:1–9)
      The reign of Ahaz, the most faithless of kings (28:1–27)

## Synopsis of the Text

The golden age of Solomon gives way to the reality of sin and division: "the kingdom of the LORD in the hand of the sons of David" (13:8) is divided into rival kingdoms in the north and in the south. From this point forward in his narrative, the Chronicler traces the fortunes of the southern kingdom, which preserves the house of David, through nineteen kings—until 586 BC, when invading Babylonian forces seize Jerusalem, destroy the temple, and take the southerners into exile. In the Chronicler's account of individual kings, we see his prophetic instructions for the people of his own day, explaining the meaning of the exile and how they should live in anticipation of the restoration.

## Theological Exegesis and Commentary

### Believe in His Prophets: History as Prophecy and Pedagogy

If Solomon's reign is represented as a new creation in 2 Chr. 1–9, the events that follow his death can be understood only as a new fall from grace. From the glorious vision of the royal son of David's ruling peacefully over all the nations of the earth, worshiping the God of creation at Zion in the house where he has chosen for his name to dwell, the Chronicler immediately plunges his readers into the chaos of tribal rivalry and civil war, the disunity of schism caused by human pride, ambition, and sin.

Within the narrative universe that the Chronicler has created, it is a strange, unsettling, and unexpected turn of events, to say the least. Up to this point the Chronicler has described world history as reaching its zenith in the covenant with David, the establishment of his kingdom at Jerusalem, and the building of the temple by his son and anointed successor, Solomon. More than the story of a nation, Chronicles has been the history of God's purposes for creation. All that has gone before—from the first man, Adam; through the father of their people, Abraham; and the great servants of God, Moses and David—has been about bringing God's purposes to a new level of fulfillment. This was why God had brought his people out of the house of bondage in Egypt by his mighty arm and led them into the land of the promise.

The kingdom of Israel was the kingdom of God on earth, under the heir to the throne of David, the beneficiary of God's eternal covenant. It was a liturgical empire ordered to wisdom and worship, to living according to the law given by God, offering continual sacrifices of praise and thanksgiving to the God of all creation. Through the wisdom of its law, the glory of its worship, and the sanctity of its people, Israel would be a light to the nations, bringing the blessings of God to all the families of the earth, in fulfillment of the oath that God had sworn to his faithful servant, Abraham (Gen. 22:16–18).

All this had been evoked in symbolic terms and imagery in the Chronicler's account of Solomon's reign, culminating with the kings of the earth as making pilgrimage to Jerusalem, to pay homage to Israel's king and Israel's God; in the temple liturgy, God's presence had filled the house, and he had accepted their sacrifices with fire sent down from heaven. Yet as the reader turns the page, within a matter of verses, in the span of less than one generation, all this glorious history appears to have been forgotten. In its place the Chronicler gives us an account of a crude interregnum power struggle.

The final third of Chronicles, which covers a period of about four hundred years from roughly 930 BC to 538 BC (2 Chr. 10–36), plays out in the long shadow of this power struggle and its tragic outcome: the fracture of Israel's monarchy and the shattering of the kingdom of God on earth. The Chronicler traces the basic outlines of the biblical historical narrative. He tells how the kingdom was divided after Solomon—ten tribes forming a northern kingdom, with its capital at Samaria; and the tribes of Judah and Benjamin remaining in the south, with their capital at Jerusalem. He traces the fortunes of the southern kingdom, which preserves the house of David, through nineteen kings, until 586 BC, when invading Babylonian forces seize Jerusalem, destroy the temple, and take the southerners into exile. He presumes that his audience knows that the northern kingdom, which the Chronicler considers illegitimate and apostate, meanwhile tottered along under its own succession of nineteen kings before eventually Samaria was captured by the Assyrians and the northerners were taken into exile in 722 BC.

The Chronicler's readers know the story all too well. Even after decades spent in physical and political exile, they still feel as if they are in bondage to the nations. Their faith is not so much shaken as it is confused. The anguish and confusion can be heard in their prayers and liturgical texts:

> LORD, where is thy steadfast love of old,
>     which by thy faithfulness thou didst swear to David? (Ps. 89:49)

> Save us, O LORD our God,
>     and gather us from among the nations,
> that we may give thanks to thy holy name
>     and glory in thy praise. (Ps. 106:47)

The Chronicler's task is not to offer a recitation of succeeding kings but to provide a theological explanation for what God has been up to in the long history of the divided monarchy and the resulting exile. Throughout his account, the Chronicler's audience had many questions in their minds: If Israel is God's chosen firstborn, why has it suffered so much, and why is it not the ruler of nations? If God's covenant with David is forever, why is the Davidic king not respected, and why is his kingdom divided? If the temple was God's house, why did he allow it to be destroyed? The prophets had promised a glorious restoration: why has that not materialized?

Through his use of inner-biblical allusions and typologies, the Chronicler has been answering these questions all along. But in this penultimate and longest section of his work, his pastoral agenda moves closer to the surface. Prophetic messengers emerge to deliver blunt assessments of the behavior of kings. The Chronicler himself narrates with an increasingly authoritative voice, telling his readers with certainty of the divine hand behind historical events. Persistent themes and features of his work become more pronounced in his writing of this period, such as his emphasis on the law (*tôrâ*) as the foundation of covenant faithfulness and the teacher and shaper of the kingdom spirituality of God's people. He continues to make extensive use of typology and inner-biblical references. Exodus imagery moves to the fore, perhaps as a nod to the prophets who had described the restoration from exile as a new exodus.

The Chronicler is not presenting a bare record of historical facts; instead he is making a prophetic interpretation of the historical record, giving special attention to the moral and spiritual levels of causality that helped to shape that history and explain its tragic outcome. In recounting the years after Solomon and the division of the kingdom, the Chronicler assigns a crucial role to the ministry of prophets, seers, and men of God. He virtually ignores the prophets who appear in other biblical accounts of this period, such as the miracle-workers Elijah and Elisha and the so-called literary prophets Isaiah and Jeremiah. Yet at the same time he tells of several prophets not mentioned anywhere else in the Bible. Of the eighteen prophetic speeches in Chronicles, fourteen are without parallel elsewhere in the canon (Beentjes 2001: 45–46). These speeches, often filled with intertextual allusions, reflect the Chronicler's own vocabulary and thematic concerns. They also fit into the wider pattern of prophetic discourse in Chronicles.

In this section of his work, it becomes even more apparent that the Chronicler considers himself to be delivering a prophetic word to his people in the period after the exile. The Chronicler's prophets function together with his narrative to help him comment not only upon Israel's past but also upon present conditions. Fishbane puts it well in describing the interweaving of prophecy and narrative in Chronicles:

> The Chronicler does not merely use his narrative voice—the authoritative voice of impersonal history—but employs the confrontative, exhortative, and instructive

voice of prophetic personae as well. In the course of the historical exposition, moreover, both voices—refracted through the stylistic forms of reported speech and reported events—reinforce each other. The prophetic oratories serve to set the course of the narrative reports and to exemplify them, while the narrative reports reciprocally comment upon these speeches and teach through them. . . . The continuous oscillation is, in its effect, part of the expository power of the Chronicler. Added to it is his aggadic ability to teach *through the traditions.* . . . This content confronted [the Chronicler's readers] as a *traditum*, as *the* authoritative version of the ancient *traditio* made present as witness and as challenge. No less than his prophetic personae, then, the Chronicler's narrative addressed his generation, in the twilight of classical prophecy, with a "prophetic" voice. (Fishbane 1985: 391–93, emphasis original)

Chronicles offers an authoritative haggadic or homiletic commentary on the historical record. But often in his history of the divided monarchy, his haggadic commentary has another layer of meaning intended for his contemporaries (Schniedewind 1997: 222). When he has the good King Jehoshaphat cry out, "Hear me, Judah and inhabitants of Jerusalem! Believe in the LORD your God, and you will be established; believe his prophets, and you will succeed" (2 Chr. 20:20), it represents also his cry to his contemporaries. When he remarks with great sadness at the end of his work, "They kept . . . scoffing at his prophets . . . till there was no remedy" (36:16), this sad legacy of history is made a lesson for his contemporaries.

Again this is more than a commentary on the past. In writing on this period, the Chronicler fashions his history to be an increasingly obvious and ominous warning to the generation that has returned to rebuild the temple and the kingdom. The Chronicler's answers to his contemporaries become even more straightforward in these final pages of his work. Why did the chosen people suffer? Because they failed to live by *tôrâ* and failed to heed the warnings of God's messengers; exile and the demise of the temple followed as inevitable outcomes. So long as people continue to sin and practice idolatry, the kingdom will remain divided, the exile will continue, and Israel will live under foreign domination. Yet what also comes to the fore in this period is the Chronicler's testimony to the unfathomable depths of God's mercy. As surely as sin will be punished, God's mercy is available to those who turn to him in humility and repentance.

With these broad thematic markers in place, these themes are now developed in the Chronicler's narrative. Second Chronicles 10–36 is long, occupying more than one-third of the work; it contains 621 of the work's 1,765 verses (Johnstone 1997: 2.12). And the Chronicler's version of events during this period differs markedly from the version found elsewhere in the biblical history (i.e., 1–2 Kings). This is especially true of the period just after the death of Solomon. As Knoppers observes, "Perhaps nowhere else does Chronicles diverge more radically from Kings than in depicting the period of the secession and early divided kingdom" (1990: 430).

## So the King Did Not Listen: The Kingdom Is Divided

In terms of the Chronicler's narrative, the scene in 2 Chr. 10 marks a strange and abrupt change in mood that seems almost to deliberately frustrate readers' expectations. After his glorious forty-year reign, Solomon is buried, and his son Rehoboam assumes charge of the kingdom. From that point forward, none of the events that follow make sense within the strict narrative logic of the Chronicler's story line; the drama that results is puzzling and troubling. Rehoboam travels to Shechem, where "all Israel" has gathered "to make him king" (10:1). This apparently straightforward reportage conceals a host of historical questions. Why Shechem? Should the scene not be in Jerusalem, the city of David? Should not Rehoboam be king simply by virtue of being Solomon's son, heir to the promises of God's eternal covenant with David? What business does Israel have in "making" him king?

Shechem, located about thirty miles north of Jerusalem, was undoubtedly a venerable site in Israel's sacred tradition. Abraham built his first altar there at the oak of Moreh (Gen. 12:6–7). It was also the site of Joshua's famed covenant renewal after the conquest of the promised land (Josh. 24:1–28) and the place where the patriarch Joseph's bones were interred after being brought up from Egypt (24:32). Nonetheless, there is no precedent and no immediate justification for holding the coronation of a Davidic king there.

As the preceding chapters in Chronicles emphasize, the capital of the kingdom, indeed the center of creation, is Jerusalem. "I chose no city in all the tribes of Israel in which to build a house, that my name might be there," Solomon had said in quoting God's covenant with David (2 Chr. 6:5; cf. 6:38). That is what makes the events that transpire after Solomon seem so strange and disconcerting.

The reader has been led to expect that Jerusalem would be the only legitimate site for the crowning and anointing of God's covenant king; such a coronation would be celebrated by the *qāhāl/ekklēsia* with a grand temple liturgy of covenant renewal, in the style of David and Solomon. In the days before the temple, the people had anointed David king at Hebron and had ratified Solomon's accession to the throne at Jerusalem (1 Chr. 11:3; 29:22). These were occasions of joy and sacrifice to the God of their fathers. Nothing like that is mentioned in 2 Chr. 10. In the other account of this episode found in the Bible, Rehoboam comes before "all the assembly of Israel" (*kōl-qĕhal yiśrā'ēl*; 1 Kgs. 12:3). The Chronicler conspicuously does not carry this language over in his account of the affair; "all Israel" has gathered, but not the *qāhāl*. This is one of several subtle but important changes he introduces into his source material to underscore his interpretation of the historical record (Raney 2003: 95–97; Zvi 2006: 118). For him the term *qāhāl* is reserved for the solemn liturgical assembly of the people, under their Davidic king and in the presence of God. God is not on the agenda at Shechem.

The gathering at Shechem seems less like a coronation than a confrontation. Rehoboam is greeted not with joy and celebration but with a representative delegation of the northern ten tribes, come to demand concessions and dictate the terms for their continued allegiance to the king (Johnstone 1997: 2.24; Selman 1994b: 360). They are led by a new character, Jeroboam, who is said to have returned from Egypt, where he had fled from King Solomon. This confronts the reader with still another set of questions. Who is this Jeroboam? Why did he flee Solomon? Why is he so powerful among the people? What are we to make of their complaints of a "heavy yoke" imposed by Solomon (2 Chr. 10:4)?

The reasons for the conflict at Shechem are almost impossible for readers to comprehend solely on the basis of the Chronicler's narrative. Here, perhaps more than anywhere else, we see evidence of his presumption that his audience already knows Israel's history. In this case he presumes that his readers already know the tradition that Solomon imposed forced labor on the population of Israel (1 Kgs. 5:13–18; 11:28). However, perhaps adding to the reader's perplexity, the Chronicler has earlier asserted a contradictory tradition—that Solomon did *not* impose forced labor on the Israelites, only upon foreigners (1 Kgs. 9:20–22; 2 Chr. 8:7–9; Zvi 2006: 135–36nn22–23; Williamson 1982: 201–2).

The Chronicler did refer in passing to a prophecy concerning Jeroboam—just four verses before bringing him onto the stage of his drama (9:29)—but the contents of this prophecy are not recounted and again would not make sense within the Chronicler's narrative orbit (Frisch 2000). In the biblical history, the prophet Ahijah tells Jeroboam that God will tear the kingdom from Solomon's hands because of his idolatry and give Jeroboam rule over ten of the tribes (1 Kgs. 11:26–40; cf. 11:4, 6, 9). The literary problem is that within his narrative the Chronicler has told his reader nothing but good things about Solomon's reign and certainly nothing about idolatry or political oppression. Thus the tribes' complaint seems to come out of the blue in Chronicles, and Rehoboam's resulting deliberations with his counselors only further the confusion.

There is no easy resolution to the literary and narrative issues raised. Again we need to keep in mind the Chronicler's pastoral aims. In describing the confrontation at Shechem, he aims to provide his readers with more than an etiology of the schism that split the monarchy into rival kingdoms in the north and south. He does offer them an authoritative interpretation of the biblical record from the perspective of salvation history and the plan of God. With vivid portraits of historical personages mixed with carefully chosen prophetic speeches and narratives, he at the same time is teaching his contemporaries how to serve God rightly in the present and how to avoid repeating the mistakes of the past.

Retelling the story of the kingdom's breakup, the Chronicler's account is painted in irony. At this crucial juncture when the sons of Israel are about to be divided, the Chronicler makes a subtle allusion to their origins, to the historical moment when they were established as God's people in their deliverance from bondage in Egypt. The drama here, as in the exodus, turns on a wordplay involving the word 'bd (serve/service), which has a range of meanings—from slave labor to royal service or liturgical worship.

In Exodus, Israel is locked in "hard service" ('ǎbōdâ qāšâ) under Pharaoh (1:14; 6:9) but demands freedom to "serve" ('ābad) the Lord (4:23; 7:16; 8:1; 9:1). In a similar way the northern tribes seek release from their "hard service" ('ǎbōdâ qāšâ) as a condition of their "serving" ('ābad) Rehoboam (2 Chr. 10:4–5). There are incidental parallels in both accounts: a three-day time period (Exod. 3:18; 5:3; 8:27; 2 Chr. 10:5, 12), the important participation of "the elders" (zěqēnîm; Exod. 3:16, 18; 4:29; 2 Chr. 10:6, 8, 13), and the use of the relatively rare term "yoke" ('ōl) to describe the tribes' and Israel's slavery in Egypt (Lev. 26:13; 2 Chr. 10:4, 9, 10, 11, 14).

The dark irony at Shechem is that the Davidic King Rehoboam assumes the role that the Egyptian king plays in the exodus account. His intransigence parallels Pharaoh's stubborn refusal of the Israelites' requests. In Exodus, "Pharaoh's heart was/remained hardened, and he would not listen to them" (7:23; 8:19). In 2 Chronicles, all Israel sees that "the king did not hearken to them" (10:16; cf. 10:15). Pharaoh responds by not only rejecting the people's request but by also making their workload even heavier (kābēd 'ǎbōdâ; Exod. 5:7–9); Rehoboam vows to add to the people's already-heavy yoke (2 Chr. 10:11, 14). The "chastisement" (yāsar) he threatens, "scorpions," is mentioned elsewhere only as one of the tribulations imposed on Israel in the wilderness (Deut. 8:15). The adjective used to describe Rehoboam's response to the people, qāšeh (2 Chr. 10:13), is the same one used to describe the harsh treatment of the Israelites under Pharaoh (Exod. 1:14; Deut. 26:6; cf. Exod. 6:9).

The implication of the Chronicler's analogy is that as Pharaoh's heart was hardened by divine design (Exod. 7:3, 14, 22; 9:35) so too was Rehoboam's. As Pharaoh refused to humble himself before God (9:17; 10:3), neither would Rehoboam humble himself to accept the responsibilities of covenant kingship. What was expected of the king as the servant of God and the keeper of his covenant is symbolized in the Chronicler's account by the wise advice of the elders who had served in Solomon's administration. Tellingly, the Chronicler uses the word 'zb (to forsake) to describe Rehoboam's rejection of their counsel (2 Chr. 10:8; 12:1). This is the same word he uses elsewhere throughout his work to describe the rejection of God's covenant law.

"So the king did not hearken to the people; for it was a turn of affairs brought about by God that the LORD might fulfil his word," the Chronicler says, referring to Abijah's prophecy to Jeroboam (10:15; also 11:4; cf. 1 Chr. 10:14). This prophetic word, known to his readers from 1 Kings, remains unquoted in the Chronicler's work; nonetheless he accepts this as the motive for the division of the kingdom. Behind the incidentals of historical causality, the

Chronicler sees the agency of divine providence. Again, the Chronicler wants his readers to remember that God is in charge of history, even if his designs might not always be so readily detectible or explicable.

The Chronicler's God, however, is not some puppeteer pulling the strings on his creations. Although the monarchy's division is ultimately of God (2 Chr. 11:4), the drama is sketched in terms of the free choices and ambitions of Rehoboam and Jeroboam and their respective constituencies. According to the Chronicler's assessment, there is no shortage of blame to go around. In addition to portraying Rehoboam as behaving in a pharaoh-like manner, the Chronicler adds the judgment of his son and successor, King Abijah, who delivers an important speech to Jeroboam in the presence of the people of the north (13:4–12). Abijah faults his father for being too "irresolute" or "faint-hearted" regarding "certain worthless scoundrels" (13:7).

### The Covenant of Salt and the Rebellion of the North

The Chronicler casts an even dimmer eye on Jeroboam and the secessionists of the north. They are in "rebellion [*pāšaʿ*] against the house of David," he remarks, using a term that in the prophetic writings denotes a personal rejection or transgression against God and his covenant (2 Chr. 10:19; cf. Isa. 1:2; 43:27; 46:8; 53:12; 59:13; 66:24; Jer. 2:8, 29; 3:13; 33:8; Ezek. 2:3; 18:31; 20:38; Dan. 8:23; Hos. 7:13; 8:1; Zeph. 3:11). To reject the "house of David" is to reject the Davidic covenant by which God swore to establish David's house forever (1 Chr. 17:10, 17, 23–24, 27; cf. 2 Chr. 21:7). For the Chronicler, the covenant is the key to the kingdom. In his speech, Abijah chastises Jeroboam and the north: "Ought you not to know that the Lord God of Israel gave the king-ship over Israel for ever to David and his sons by a covenant of salt?" (2 Chr. 13:5). A covenant of salt is meant to last forever (Num. 18:19; Lev. 2:13; Japhet 1997: 453–55). And, as Abijah continues, the covenant with David established "the kingdom of the Lord in the hand of the sons of David" (2 Chr. 13:8).

What God has established, the Chronicler says, no one should presume to destroy. Yet this is what the people of the north, led by Jeroboam, have done. Their emancipation declaration—"What portion have we in David? We have no inheritance in the son of Jesse"—is a deliberate and defiant reversal of the people's original pledge of allegiance to David (10:16; cf. 1 Chr. 12:18; 2 Sam. 20:2). Pointedly, the Chronicler does not recount Jeroboam's election as king of the north (1 Kgs. 12:20) and recognizes him only as a rebellious "servant of Solomon" (2 Chr. 13:6–7).

In contrast to the fairly neutral account of his reign found in 1 Kings, the Chronicler sketches Jeroboam in dark paradigmatic strokes. From his initial rebellion, Jeroboam quickly leads the northern tribes into apostasy. He rejects the temple and the priesthood of Aaron and the Levites, driving out the "priests of the Lord" and replacing them with priests of his own to offer sacrifices to the goat-gods in the high places. He creates his own gods for the people and, in another echo of the exodus years, fashions golden calves for them to worship and carry into battle (13:8). As final proof of his revolt against God, he resists Abijah's entreaties and instigates a horrible internecine war that leaves a half million dead (13:17).

For the Chronicler, the northern kingdom is illegitimate and stands in defiance of God's covenant will. Within the terms of the Chronicler's teaching, the north is guilty of more than breaking up an earthly political union. Its rebellion is against "the kingdom of the LORD in the hand . . . of David" and results in the frustration of God's will, for without the united kingdom of all Israel, God's covenant blessings cannot flow to the nations. The north has made itself "like the peoples of other lands," who serve "what are no gods" (2 Chr. 13:8–9; cf. Deut. 32:17; Isa. 37:19; Jer. 2:11; 5:7; 16:11). The epithet "walked in . . . the way of Israel" becomes the Chronicler's abbreviation for idolatry, sin, and apostasy (2 Chr. 17:4; 21:6, 13).

The remnant in Jerusalem, the tribes of Benjamin and Judah, constitutes the heart of the true kingdom. Abijah's speech gives us the markers of their faithful covenant identity: their loyalty to the Davidic line; the capital at Jerusalem, "the city which the LORD had chosen out of all the tribes of Israel" (12:13); and temple worship under the ministry of the priestly sons of Aaron and the Levites. Thus Abijah can say, "As for us, the LORD is our God, and we have not forsaken him" (13:10).

The Chronicler does not write off the northern tribes; nor is there anything like a sustained antinorthern or anti-Samaritan polemic (Japhet 1997: 313–28). From this point onward, Chronicles is a history of the southern kingdom, and the north is mentioned only when it comes in contact with the south. But it is also true that every contact between north and south is registered carefully, including some not mentioned elsewhere in the Bible (Williamson 1977: 114). This is an important indicator of the Chronicler's real attitude toward the north. The north remains crucial to his narrative even in absentia. He is quite conscious that the division of the kingdom is an open wound that continues to shape the reality of his audience. Thus comes his summary statement: "So Israel has been in rebellion against the house of David *to this day*" (10:19).

The revolt of the north does not cause it to forfeit its hereditary rights as children of Israel or its opportunity for repentance. The northerners still retain their fraternal relationship with the south, and they can still lay claim equally and legitimately to the title "Israel." Earlier in his work, the Chronicler has no less an authority than David himself, who said, "Send abroad to our brethren who remain in all the land of Israel" (1 Chr. 13:2). This seemingly deliberate anachronism shows Israel's true king calling for reconciliation and restoration, for the uniting of the kingdom through the reunion of the brethren of north and south (but see Williamson 1982: 114). When the prophet Shemaiah arrives to dissuade Rehoboam from waging war to restore the kingdom, he too describes the secessionists as "brethren" (2 Chr. 11:4; cf. 28:8, 11; 1 Chr. 12:40). And in his speech, Abijah calls them "sons of Israel" and urges them not to fight against "the God of your fathers" (2 Chr. 13:12).

Japhet believes the Chronicler's attitude was already anticipated in his unique genealogical interpretation of the birthright transfer from Israel's firstborn, Reuben, to the sons of Joseph. The tribes of Joseph's sons, Ephraim and Manasseh, are associated with the northern kingdom (1 Chr. 5:1–2). Hence the northern tribes are seen as the rightful "firstborn" (bĕkôr) of Israel (Jer. 31:9); the Chronicler even identifies the northern kingdom of Israel as "Ephraimites" (2 Chr. 25:7). But while these northern tribes bear the birthright, as the Chronicler stated in his genealogy, Judah was "strong" and a "prince" among his brothers, an affirmation that the Davidic kingship belongs to Judah.

The point is that the sins of the north do not strip the people of their identity as true Israelites, any more than do the sins of the south. The rabbinic proverb still holds: "Though he sinned, he is Israel" (Babylonian Talmud, *Sanhedrin* 44a; quoted from Japhet 1997: 324n216). Although his preferred shorthand is to refer to the northern kingdom as "Israel" and the southern kingdom as "Judah," the Chronicler at various points refers to both north and south with variations on the term "Israel" (Williamson 1977: 110; cf. 97–118):

|  | north | south |
| --- | --- | --- |
| "Israel" | 2 Chr. 10:16, 19; 11:1 | 2 Chr. 12:6 |
| "people of Israel" | 2 Chr. 10:18 | 2 Chr. 10:17 |
| "all Israel" | 2 Chr. 10:1, 3, 16; 11:13; 13:4, 15 | 2 Chr. 11:3; 12:1; 24:5; 28:23 |

The Chronicler's use of "all Israel" (kōl yiśrā'ēl) in the period of the divided monarchy is sadly ironic. The term evokes the unity of the twelve tribes under the Sinai covenant (Exod. 18:25; Deut. 1:1; 5:1; 13:11; 27:9; 31:1; Josh. 3:7; 4:14; 23:2). It is telling that the north under Jeroboam is described as kōl yiśrā'ēl precisely at the moment when it is bringing about the destruction of the kingdom (2 Chr. 10:16). Throughout the divided monarchy, the Chronicler occasionally refers to both north and south by kōl yiśrā'ēl, as if to emphasize each one's need for the other in order to realize its completion and fullness.

The Chronicler hopes for the reunion of "all Israel" under the Davidic king. This hope is never far from the surface of his narrative and shapes his handling of the historical material. He writes a frankly pedagogical history, offering his readers both exhortation and examples of how full restoration can take place. This begins almost immediately in his account of the divided monarchy and sets a pattern. Early in Jeroboam's reign, priests and Levites defect from the north to return to Judah and Jerusalem; many others "came after them from all the tribes of Israel to Jerusalem to sacrifice to the LORD, the God of their fathers" (11:16). This is a model that the Chronicler wants to inspire his contemporaries in Samaria and the north to follow.

### To Serve God or Be a Slave to the Kingdoms of the Earth

The Chronicler's account of Rehoboam's reign is much longer than the account found in 1 Kgs. 14:21–28 and is essentially a theological exegesis of the history found there (2 Chr. 11–12). The brief report in 1 Kings says that the people fell away from the faith during Rehoboam's tenure and that during that period Pharaoh Shishak of Egypt invaded Israel. The Chronicler's report acknowledges these same facts but makes two significant changes: he shifts the focus and the blame from the people to Rehoboam; through an exegesis that relies on typology and analogy, he establishes a cause-and-effect relationship between Israel's sin and its punishment by Egypt.

Strength is a leading motif in the Chronicler's treatment of Rehoboam (Japhet 1993: 676). Rehoboam's top priority is to build his defenses against an attack, especially from the northern kingdom. He builds "cities for defense," outfitting them with spears and swords (2 Chr. 11:5–12), and his reign is characterized by the repetition of words such as "fortified," "fortress," and "strength" (11:5, 11, 12, 17, 23). But human strength in Chronicles is usually a precursor to a fall from faith, for the only true strength comes from relying upon God; human strength and success are an illusion and a snare, a temptation to live as if one has no need for God.

Thus, when Rehoboam is "established" (*kûn*) and "strong" (*ḥzq*), he "forsakes" (*'zb*) the law of the Lord and leads "all Israel" into sin with him (12:1). This is paradigmatic language for the Chronicler. To "forsake" for him carries a range of meanings, from failing to offer fitting worship to God (13:10–11; 21:10–11; 28:6; cf. 28:1–4) to outright idolatry (7:19, 22; 24:18; 34:25; Williamson 1982: 246). Israel is intended to be a liturgical empire. The king's chief priority is not national defense or economic administration. The king is anointed for one essential task—to ensure the right worship of God and by this worship to bring about the sanctification of Israel and the blessing of the nations. This is the standard against which kings are judged throughout the remainder of the work.

In saying that Rehoboam and the people forsook the law of the Lord, the Chronicler is making a theological commentary on the false worship reported in 1 Kgs. 14:22–24. But he goes much further. He posits this forsaking of God as the *cause* for Shishak's invasion, using the conjunctive *kî* and his term for covenant infidelity: "Because [*kî*] they had been unfaithful [*mā'al*] to the LORD, Shishak king of Egypt came up against Jerusalem" (2 Chr. 12:2). Chronicles is perhaps making explicit what the earlier historical record only implied. This, however, marks a significant theological rereading.

Fishbane compares what the Chronicler does to the later rabbinic exegetical technique known as *sĕmûkîn* (conjunctions), in which nearby texts are used to interpret each other. In interpreting Shishak's invasion in light of Israel's apostasy, the exegesis of Chronicles yields "insights into the workings of divine providence and historical causality," Fishbane writes. He adds: "By means of this aggadic [homiletic] exegesis, in fact, he was able to project his own values into his sources and so instruct his generation concerning its past *for the sake of its present*" (1985: 399–401, emphasis original).

In the encounter between the prophet Shemaiah and Rehoboam, the Chronicler drives home his point to his generation. The prophet announces that because they have "abandoned" (ʿzb) God, God has "abandoned" (ʿzb) them. But that is not the end of the story. Upon receiving this prophetic word, the king and his men "humble" (knʿ) themselves and submit to God's righteousness. Knʿ is a key theological term in 2 Chronicles and is used four times in this episode alone (12:6, 7 [twice], 12). Indeed, this episode marks the first historical test of God's promise to Solomon that he would forgive and heal those who "humble" (knʿ) themselves and "turn" (šûb) from their evil ways (2 Chr. 7:14; also 30:11; 32:26; 33:12, 19, 23; 34:27; 36:12; cf. Lev. 26:41). True to his word, in response to Rehoboam's humble submission, God relents.

Sin must be punished, but God's mercy and steadfast love for his servant David save Israel from utter destruction. God gives this word to Shemaiah: "They have humbled themselves; I will not destroy them, but I will grant them some deliverance. . . . Nevertheless they shall be servants to him [Shishak], that they may know my service and the service of the kingdoms of the earth" (2 Chr. 12:7–8).

The Chronicler continues to interpret the breakup of the monarchy in terms of the exodus tradition. Is it coincidental that the confession Rehoboam makes in humbling himself before God—"The LORD is righteous" (12:6)—is the exact confession that Pharaoh made during his confrontation with Moses and Aaron (Exod. 9:27)? Rehoboam's sin is to turn away from the *tôrâ* given to Moses and Israel at Sinai. And because of his sin, in which he was joined by "all Israel," the children of God lose the freedom won for them through the exodus; once more they fall into servitude to an Egyptian pharaoh. Once more, the divine message is delivered with a wordplay on "serve" (ʿbd). Japhet interprets the Chronicler's meaning well: "Here, again, we find an implied causality: to avoid the Lord's service leads to slavery, while to serve God—the source of human well-being—is liberation" (1993: 680).

Shemaiah's oracle no doubt was intended to have a poignant double meaning for the first hearers of Chronicles, for the lesson that the prophet speaks is the lesson the Chronicler hopes his audience will learn from their own exile. Exiled because of their unfaithfulness (1 Chr. 9:1; 2 Chr. 36:15–16), they too must learn the difference between service of the living God and slavery among the nations. They too face the choice of living out their vocation as God's servants or being given over to servitude to foreign tyrants.

### To Seek the Lord and Keep His Tôrâ

In his account of Rehoboam, the Chronicler establishes the pattern that will continue with slight variations throughout the rest of his work. His story of

Rehoboam is painted in gray, not in black and white. The Davidic king is not often all bad. Often he starts out good and ends up bad. In Rehoboam's case he rebounded from his pharaohesque handling of Jeroboam's rebellion. For three years he kept the way of David and Solomon and maintained Judah as a refuge for those who set their hearts to seek the Lord. But he strayed from the *tôrâ* and led the people into sin too. Although he humbled himself and averted destruction, he cannot escape the Chronicler's summary verdict: "And he did evil, for he did not set his heart to seek the LORD" (12:14).

Here is the criterion by which kings are judged in Chronicles: Did they "seek" (*dāraš*) God? This seeking terminology is a distinctive mark of the Chronicler and has few parallels in the biblical materials he drew from (Begg 1982: 129–31). *Dāraš* in Chronicles describes far more than a vague religiosity or religious feeling. It is a concrete and all-embracing attitude toward life. To seek God is the filial spirituality proper to the children of the covenant; it is an act of the will by which believers dedicate themselves to serving God's covenant purposes; *dāraš* includes worshiping God in the sacrificial temple liturgy, observing his law, and refusing to tolerate the corrosive influence of idolatry and injustice in the midst of God's kingdom. There is also something distinctively Davidic about the concept. It was the dominant note of David's first great psalm of thanksgiving: "Let the hearts of those who seek the LORD rejoice! Seek the LORD and his strength, seek his presence continually!" (1 Chr. 16:10–11). David's final instructions to both Solomon and to the *qāhāl/ekklēsia* include the command to "seek" God (22:19; 28:8, 9). And in God's response to Solomon's dedication of the temple, he too establishes this as the characteristic note of the people's relationship with him (2 Chr. 7:14).

Seeking the Lord becomes the leading motif with the "renewal kings" who arise in the period of the divided monarchy, beginning early with Rehoboam's grandson: King Asa, son of King Abijah. As with the accounts of Rehoboam and Abijah, the Chronicler's account of Asa's reign is again longer than that found in his biblical source and has a different accent (1 Kgs. 15:9–24). He inaugurates his tenure by "command[ing] Judah to seek [*dāraš*] the LORD, the God of their fathers, and to keep the law [*tôrâ*] and the commandment" (2 Chr. 14:6); as in his treatment of Rehoboam (12:1), again the Chronicler places importance on the Mosaic *tôrâ* as the foundation of life in the kingdom. Asa proceeds to uproot all the foreign altars and idolatrous sites in Judah and through his total reliance upon the Lord is able to defend the kingdom against the imminent attack of a million-man Ethiopian army.

The people build and prosper, and the kingdom is said to be at "rest" (*šāqaṭ*) and at "peace" (*nûaḥ*), a point made five times in 14:1–7 (*šāqaṭ* in 14:4, 5; *nûaḥ* in 14:6, 7; cf. *šālôm* in 15:5 and *nûaḥ* in 15:15). This rest and peace are presented as the fruits of the people's faithful seeking of the Lord. Asa declares: "The land is still ours, because [*kî*] we have sought [*dāraš*] the LORD our God; we have sought [*dāraš*] him, and he has given us peace [nûaḥ] on every side [missābîb]" (14:7). This language hearkens back to God's covenant promises concerning Solomon: "I will give him peace [nûaḥ] from all his enemies round about [missābîb], . . . and I will give peace [šālôm] and quiet [šeqeṭ] to Israel in his days" (1 Chr. 22:9). These promises in turn point back to Deuteronomy, where Moses pledged that rest would be the inheritance of God's covenant people (Deut. 12:8–11; Josh. 11:23; 14:15; 21:44; 23:1).

Asa is the first of several new-Solomon figures in the Chronicler's royal history. In restoring and recapitulating the ideals of the Davidic kingdom, his reign anticipates the definitive restoration of the kingdom in fidelity to the covenant and Israel's entering fully into the peace and rest that God promised to his people.

Following a description of Asa's victories in battle, the Chronicler introduces a prophetic figure, Azariah, who exhorts the king and people to still deeper renewal. Azariah does not appear elsewhere in the biblical histories and is not identified here technically as a prophet; he comes as an authoritative messenger who speaks and acts under the power of "the Spirit of God." His discourse, addressed to Asa and "all Judah and Benjamin," reflects a deep spiritual appropriation of Israel's scripture. The substance of his message is a restatement of David's instructions to Solomon upon his accession to the throne: "The LORD is with you, while you are with him. If you seek [dāraš] him, he will be found [māṣā'] by you, but if you forsake ['zb] him, he will forsake ['zb] you" (2 Chr. 15:2; cf. 1 Chr. 28:9).

This broad covenantal principle articulated, the messenger proceeds to apply it by offering a sweeping if enigmatic overview of Israel's history (2 Chr. 15:3–6). His reference points remain obscure. He could be speaking of the chaotic period of the judges or foretelling a future time; both the Greek Septuagint and the Latin Vulgate understand this passage as a prophecy of future events (Beentjes 2001: 51), which opens interesting interpretive possibilities. However, in the context of the Chronicler's narrative, it seems more likely that Azariah's words should be taken as an oblique commentary on the first quarter-century of the divided kingdom (Johnstone 1997: 2.66). This is the stance taken by the Targum on 2 Chr. 15:3–7.

Following this interpretive line, the north has indeed for a long time alienated itself from the true God since it has embarked upon the worship of false and strange gods. The north has been without a teaching priest, having expelled the Levites and the sons of Aaron; and it has placed itself in opposition to the law of Moses. These points have all been documented thus far in the Chronicler's narrative of the years since Rehoboam. In addition, the narrative has supplied ample testimony to Azariah's further remarks. Since the breakup of the kingdom and the brief Pax Solomona, both north and south, as well as the surrounding region, have been without "peace" (šālôm), as the people have been broken apart, nation against nation and city against city.

From start to finish, the language of Azariah's discourse is drawn from the prophets. Azariah's description of Israel as being a long time without God, priest, or law (15:3) is an "exegetical revision" (Fishbane 1989: 15) unmistakably patterned after Hosea's description of the northern exiles (3:4; Beentjes 2001: 51). As Hosea saw the children of the exile "dwell[ing for] many days without king or prince, without sacrifice or pillar, without ephod or teraphim," so Azariah too speaks of "a long time" (lit., "many days") and adopts the prophet's triple use of "without."

Azariah describes a period when "there was no peace to him who went out or to him who came in" (2 Chr. 15:5)—an allusion to Zechariah's vision of the exile, when there was "no safety . . . for him who went out or came in" (Zech. 8:10; Beentjes 2001: 52). The dramatic, rare expression that Azariah uses to describe the "great disturbances" in the land, mĕhûmōt rabbôt (2 Chr. 15:5), stems from Amos's prophecy concerning the chastisement of Samaria and the northern kingdom (3:9). Finally, his exhortation to Asa and the people, "Do not let your hands be weak, for your work shall be rewarded" (2 Chr. 15:7), combines language from two prophecies addressed to the exiles of the north: Zephaniah's encouragement "Let not your hands grow weak" (3:16) and Jeremiah's assurance "Your work shall be rewarded" (31:16).

Fishbane characterizes Azariah's speech as an "exegetical anthology" (1989: 15): old prophecies and material from the Pentateuch are fashioned into an "aggadic blend" designed to draw contemporary lessons from the exile (1985: 389–90). Schniedewind concludes that Azariah functions as an "inspired messenger," who provides "inspired interpretation of authoritative texts which revitalized the Word of God anew for the post-exilic community" (1995: 127). The questions for us are, What message is the Chronicler trying to communicate to his postexilic audience? How does his theological exegesis contribute to this message?

The clue is that Azariah's inspired discourse is composed entirely from exilic prophecies. Upon closer reading, we find that the immediate context for each of the prophecies he quotes is a divine promise of salvation and restoration for a faithful remnant who are assured that they will once more live in the presence of God. Azariah quotes Hosea's reference to a vacant throne and the absence of temple sacrifices and venerable cultic traditions. In the very next verse of his prophecy, Hosea (3:5) promises that "afterward the children of Israel shall return [šûb] and seek [biqqēš] the LORD their God, and David their king." Azariah's quotation from Amos's prophecy (3:12) includes the prediction that a remnant of exiles will be saved as a "shepherd rescues from the mouth of the lion two legs, or a piece of an ear."

He also quotes from a passage in which Zechariah promises God's "return" (šûb) to Zion, the building of a new temple, and the saving of a remnant of God's people from the east and the west (8:3–8). In this prophecy Zechariah also promises "peace" (šālôm) in the land following restoration (8:12; cf.

2 Chr. 15:5) and frames his prophecy with a call to courage: "Let your hands be strong" (Zech. 8:9, 13). Azariah's use of a similar expression to encourage Asa is drawn from another passage where Zephaniah promises to "bring home" and "gather together" all Israel under "the King of Israel, the LORD" (3:15, 20). Finally, Azariah draws from a long, poetic expression of filial love for scattered Ephraim found in the prophet Jeremiah (31:9, 20). In this prophecy too we find a divine pledge to save a remnant (31:7) and to once more be "the God of all the families of Israel" (31:1).

In the intensity of this intertextual imagery we see the Chronicler's pastoral agenda. He wants to encourage his postexilic remnant readership to persevere in their task of completing the work of restoration in accord with the vision of the prophets, seeking to reunite their divided northern brethren, and purifying the land of idolatry. Indeed, these are the three pillars of the renewal program that Asa launches in immediate response to Azariah's speech (2 Chr. 15:8–9). There can be little doubt that in hearing Azariah's words, the Chronicler's audience registered his intentional echoes of Deuteronomy:

> Take heed to yourselves, lest you forget the covenant of the LORD your God. . . . And the LORD will scatter you among the peoples. . . . But from there you will seek [*biqqēš*] the LORD your God, and you will find [*māṣā'*] him, if you search after [*dāraš*] him with all your heart and with all your soul. When you are in tribulation [*baṣṣar*], . . . you will return [*šûb*] to the LORD your God and obey his voice, for the LORD your God is a merciful God; he will not fail you or destroy you or forget the covenant with your fathers which he swore to them. (Deut. 4:23, 27, 29–31)

This promise gave hope to the prophets Jeremiah and Hosea, who quoted it in their preaching to the scattered exiles (Jer. 29:13–14; Hos. 5:15; cf. Isa. 55:6; 65:1; Japhet 1993: 720). And this promise holds a particular power for the Chronicler also. With unmistakable echoes, Azariah assures the people that if they "turn" (*šûb*) to God in their "distress" (*baṣṣar*) and "seek" (*biqqēš*) him, they will "find" (*māṣā'*) him.

### King Asa and the People Swear a Covenant Oath

This Deuteronomic promise, mediated by Azariah, is shown to be powerfully if partially fulfilled in the dramatic covenant renewal ceremony that Asa organizes at Jerusalem (15:8–15). The people scattered by the monarchy's breakup find God in seeking after him with all their heart and soul. In swearing their covenant oath, they realize God's own fidelity to the oath he swore to David. The groundwork for Asa's covenant is laid by the three-pronged renewal inspired by Azariah's preaching. First, Asa eradicates the vestiges of idol worship in Judah, Benjamin, and parts of Ephraim, indicating that his influence has already begun to extend into the northern kingdom. Second, he restores the altar in the temple (cf. 29:18; 33:16). Third, he gathers "all Judah and Benjamin," along with "great numbers" of faithful Israelites from Ephraim, Manasseh, and Simeon—tribes affiliated with the north.

They gather "at Jerusalem in the third month of the fifteenth year of the reign of Asa." Following the Targum on 2 Chr. 15:11, commentators generally take this to mean that Asa's covenant was made on Pentecost or the Feast of Weeks, which was observed annually on this day (Exod. 23:16; 34:22; Lev. 23:9–21; Num. 28:26–31; Deut. 16:9–10, 16; De Vries 1997: 108–10; Fitzmyer 1998: 233–34; N. Wright 1992: 234n73). The Feast of *Šābuʿôt* originated in the Mosaic legislation as a celebration of the wheat harvest and a joyful thanksgiving for the blessings of the earth. By postbiblical Judaism, the feast had come to commemorate the giving of the law of the covenant on Mount Sinai, an event that occurred in the third month after Israel's liberation from Egypt (Exod. 19:1). Essentially, the feast evolved into an annual thanksgiving for God's gift of the *tôrâ*; in the context of this feast, the people renewed their commitment to the Sinai covenant. The book of *Jubilees*, written some four centuries after Chronicles, describes *Šābuʿôt* as being first "celebrated in heaven" and later on earth by Noah, Abraham, and Isaac. Israel, according to *Jubilees* 6.17–20, is commanded to observe the feast forever "in order to renew the covenant in all (respects), year by year." In the Chronicler's depiction of Asa's covenant, we likely see the origins of later Judaism's conception of *Šābuʿôt* as a celebration of Sinai and the *tôrâ* (Berlin and Brettler 2004: 1789; Fitzmyer 1998: 233).

There is definitely a covenant-renewal feel to Asa's ceremony:

> They sacrificed to the LORD on that day . . . seven hundred oxen and seven thousand sheep. And they entered into a covenant to seek the LORD, the God of their fathers, with all their heart and with all their soul. . . . They took oath to the LORD with a loud voice, and with shouting, and with trumpets, and with horns. And all Judah rejoiced over the oath; for they had sworn with all their heart, and had sought him with their whole desire, and he was found by them, and the LORD gave them rest round about. (2 Chr. 15:11–12, 14–15)

The language here is the same as that used by David in describing the covenant obligations of the people and their king. As Solomon and the people were enjoined to serve God with their whole heart and soul (1 Chr. 22:19; 28:9), so Asa and the people enter into a covenant to seek God with all their heart and soul. David told Solomon that if he sought God, he would find him (28:9); in making their covenant, Asa and the people rejoice because they sought God and found him. And as God gave Israel "peace on every side round about" in the time of Solomon (22:18), so God grants the people "rest round about" as a response to Asa and the people's covenant oaths.

In this covenant scene, the Chronicler continues his portrayal of Asa as a new Solomon. In the covenant they enter into and the oath they swear, Asa and the people are renewing their commitment to the Davidic covenant. As the people did in Solomon's day (1 Chr. 29:23–24), the people here are pledging allegiance to the king. Yet at the same time, they are renewing the Sinai covenant that made Israel a "kingdom of priests" and rededicating themselves to live according to the law of Moses (but see Williamson 1982: 270–71).

Throughout his work the Chronicler has insisted that the *tôrâ* of Sinai is the sole law of the kingdom. His emphasis on the *tôrâ* is one of the distinctive marks of his interpretation of the historical record. This emphasis becomes more pronounced as his treatment of the divided monarchy progresses. The *tôrâ* was the foundation for David's original vision of the kingdom (1 Chr. 16:40). In the era of the divided kingdom, the Chronicler appeals to this *tôrâ* under various labels: "the book of Moses" (2 Chr. 25:4), "the law of Moses" (23:18; 30:16), "the law of the Lord" (1 Chr. 16:40; 2 Chr. 31:3; 35:26), "the book of the law of the Lord" (17:9; 34:14), "the book of the law" (34:15), and simply "the book" (34:15, 16, 21, 24; Shaver 1989: 75n5). The law is the touchstone for every renewal found in the Chronicler's narrative, and in almost every case the Chronicler's emphasis on the *tôrâ* has no precedent in the parallel accounts found in his historical sources (cf. 2 Kgs. 11:17–20 and 2 Chr. 23:16–17, 20–21; cf. 2 Kgs. 23:28 and 2 Chr. 35:26). Thus it seems highly likely that Asa's covenant is a renewal of Israel's dedication to the *tôrâ* under the Sinai covenant.

In his temple-dedication prayer, Solomon interpreted God's covenant promises to David in terms of Sinai: "There shall never fail you a man before me to sit upon the throne of Israel, if only your sons take heed to their way, to walk in my law [*tôrâ*] as you have walked before me" (2 Chr. 6:16; cf. 1 Chr. 22:12–14). This language, which has no parallel in 1 Kgs. 8:25, conditions the health and continuity of the kingdom on the king's adherence to the *tôrâ*. Thus, when Rehoboam failed to keep the law, the kingdom was divided, and the land fell into "lawlessness" (2 Chr. 12:1; 15:3). Asa's first task is to call people not only to seek God, but also to keep the law (14:4). All this suggests that we should understand Asa's covenant in a similar way. The oath that Asa and the people swear is an oath to both seek God and keep his *tôrâ*. Like the people whom Moses gathered at Sinai (Exod. 24:3–8), the people gathered by Asa at Jerusalem have come to swear an oath to live by God's covenant law, and they seal their covenant oath with sacrifice.

The oath-ritual suggests that there is a certain self-maledictory character to the oath sworn by Asa and the people. Not only are they swearing to live by the *tôrâ*; they are also agreeing to suffer the consequences if they fall away from God and his covenant. Those who fail to seek God (2 Chr. 15:13; cf. Deut. 13:6–11) face capital punishment. The animals they sacrifice are symbolic of the fate that awaits them if they violate the oath (Hahn 2009b: 50–56). This is consistent with the Mosaic precedent. The covenant promised blessings for faithfulness and warned of curses for failure (Deut. 28). Later in the Chronicler's history of the monarchy, he will show the people under King Josiah as entering into a similar covenant after having come to realize the gravity of the curses written in the book of the law (2 Chr. 34:14, 19–21, 24–25).

Asa and the people, then, are yoking themselves to the terms of the Sinai covenant, which provides the juridical and liturgical foundation of the Davidic covenant. The pattern of covenant conditionality, of blessing and curse, has been articulated again and again in Chronicles. David had told Solomon that he would prosper if he cleaved to the law, but that if he forsook God, he would be cast off forever (1 Chr. 22:11–13; 28:9–10). God warned Solomon too that if he and the people turned aside from the commandments, they would be plucked up from the land and the temple would be destroyed (2 Chr. 7:19–20). The account of Asa's covenant oath is meant to summon those earlier warnings, not only as a commentary on the divided kingdom, but also as warning for the Chronicler's audience. They are heirs to the oath sworn long ago by their ancestors in the time of Asa. The Chronicler's subtext here is divine justice. The exile that the people have lived through was not the capricious act of a vindictive God. The exile was the just punishment for the people's violating the oath that their ancestors swore to God in entering into his covenant.

### The Cycle of Fidelity and Infidelity

Asa's covenant renewal also suggests a recapitulation of the true kingdom glimpsed under Solomon, as seen in the abundance of Sabbath and "seven" imagery. The people's extravagant sacrifices, which recall the great covenant liturgies of David and Solomon, are described symbolically in terms of multiples of seven: "seven hundred oxen and seven thousand sheep" (2 Chr. 15:11; cf. 1 Chr. 29:20–22; 2 Chr. 7:4). Throughout this episode is a wordplay on *šbʿ* (seven), especially in the notion of oath-swearing or *šābaʿ* (lit., "to seven oneself"). Finally, the people are given "rest round about," another echo of the Sabbath of creation.

The Chronicler is keenly aware of the relationship between oath-swearing and covenant-making. The divine covenant oaths sworn to Abraham at Moriah and to David at Zion are pivotal for the Chronicler's vision of Israel's history and destiny. This is the background for what the Chronicler is showing with Asa. The Chronicler's treatment of covenant oath-swearing is one of his most underappreciated contributions to our understanding of the biblical worldview.

In the account of Asa's oath, as elsewhere in Chronicles, covenant and oath are used as parallel terms: "And they entered into a covenant to seek the LORD. . . . They took oath to the LORD. . . . And all Judah rejoiced over the oath" (2 Chr. 15:12, 14, 15; cf. 1 Chr. 16:16). The Chronicler's treatment is in line with the pattern found elsewhere in the Bible. As Tucker observes: "The parallel between covenant and oath is widespread throughout the Old Testament. . . . Covenants—both those among human partners and those between

God and man—are also called oaths. . . . The oath was essential to the covenant and the oath form was the heart of the covenant form" (Deut. 29:12;
Pss. 89:3, 4; 105:9; Ezek. 17:19; Tucker 1965: 500–501; Hahn 2009b: 50–59).

The self-maledictory character of biblical oath-swearing is seen in an oath
being a self-pledge made in the presence of God, a promise joined to the invocation of the name of God for help, whereby the oath-swearer comes under the
divine judgment signified by the conditional self-curse. Asa's oath binds the
people to the law of the covenant and its attendant blessings and curses. Thus
there is here a subtle anticipation of the exile, with exile being the covenant
curse par excellence. Having sworn an oath to live by the covenant, the people
are setting themselves up to be judged according to the terms of that covenant.

Yet there is another dimension of the covenant oath necessary to understand
the Asa episode. Why are the people described as being jubilant over the oath
they have sworn? Why is their oath accompanied by a great sacrificial celebration, with loud singing and the playing of trumpets and horns? There is a real
sense of oddity here. As McCarthy notes, the Chronicler here and elsewhere
adapted his source material "to make liturgy central to the covenant-renewals,"
not only the renewal of Asa, but also later of Hezekiah and Josiah. McCarthy
suggests that a deliberate pattern of covenant renewal may be presented in
the Chronicler's treatment of the divided monarchy period. He notices that
every fourth or fifth king renews the covenant, suggesting perhaps some sense
of "ritual periodicity" to these celebrations (1982: 28–29).

This legally binding nature of liturgy and the liturgical element of the law
shows that for the Chronicler the covenant is a liturgical relationship, a communion with the God of Abraham, Isaac, and Israel. As McCarthy states, the
Chronicler's approach to the covenant is "almost entirely cultic, dealing with
a total liturgical relationship. When the community worshiped as it should,
it and its members were one with God. Hence the covenant-renewals: their
thrust is to revalidate the cult, make it pure so that God *can* be there with his
people. Hence the rejoicing: the community feels itself again what it should
be" (1982: 32).

Asa's covenant renewal is a celebration of the divine presence or, better, the
restoration of the *qāhāl* to communion with the divine presence. The clue to
understanding Asa's liturgical celebration is to compare it to the celebration
of David and the people at the restoration of the ark (1 Chr. 16). David's
celebration too was characterized by rejoicing, ritual song, and sacrifice. In
the song of thanksgiving appointed for that occasion, the people celebrate the
"covenant" made with Abraham and the "oath" sworn to Isaac. The people
there rejoiced before the ark of the Lord, as they gave thanksgiving and praise
in the very presence of God. What David established that day amounted to a
perpetual adoration of the presence of God in the ark (16:6, 37).

What Asa and the people are celebrating is the renewal of that relationship
with the divine presence. God's presence is the cause of their joy. Again, this

communion with the divine presence is a constitutive element of the covenant oath. Neusner surveys the biblical evidence and explains that the swearing of a covenant oath is done in the presence of God: "In every practical context imaginable, God is present at the taking of the oath. . . . When an oath is taken, God is in attendance. So the oath may be compared to an act of prayer, which God likewise attends" (2004: 231–32).

Renewing the covenant of David, the people bind themselves to the original divine oath sworn to Abraham. Here at Jerusalem, at the temple built on Moriah, the very place where God had sworn an oath to bless all the nations in Abraham's seed, the people rejoice to be counted children of that promise.

The good king Asa has renewed the covenant and the temple liturgy. He has rightly assumed the most important rule of kingship, the ordering of the people to worship and faithfulness to the covenant. In his renewal, which includes believers who have returned from the north, we sense the Chronicler's anticipating the healing of the broken kingdom. Yet in the Chronicler's telling, even the good king falls. He foolishly makes a covenant with the king of Syria to defend Judah from the belligerence of the northern kingdom. In the Chronicler's worldview, Asa should have "relied" (šā'an) upon God, not human strength (2 Chr. 16:8). Confronted with the prophetic word from Hanani, however, Asa does not humble himself but instead reacts with indignation. He is afflicted with a disease of the feet and dies unrepentant.

This cyclical pattern of fidelity followed by immediate infidelity continues throughout the Chronicler's reckoning of the monarchy (Raney 2003: 114). Asa's son, Jehoshaphat, a minor figure in the history found in 1 Kings, becomes a prominent and model king in the Chronicler's version of events. He is introduced with an array of Solomonic imagery. As Solomon did, so also Jehoshaphat establishes himself in his kingdom; the Lord is with him, and he is rewarded with wealth and honor. His concern is for right worship, the rooting out of idolatry, and the teaching of the law. He earns the respect of all the kingdoms of the land and is blessed with peace round about (2 Chr. 17:1–10; cf. 1:1).

As with Asa, so also with Jehoshaphat the Chronicler continues his portrayal of the kingdom as a liturgical empire. The power of the kingdom is the power that comes from reliance upon the living God. The kingdom expresses itself more truly just as it releases the divine power that defines it—in and through worship. Thus Jehoshaphat, like Asa before him, achieves an absolutely unexpected victory over his enemies through liturgical prayer and sacrifice. Facing an Ethiopian army a million men strong, King Asa went to the front lines, armed not with weapons but with a prayer: "Help us, O LORD our God, for we rely [šā'an] on thee!" And "the LORD," the Chronicler reports, "defeated the Ethiopians" (2 Chr. 14:11–12).

Faced with attack from the combined armies of the dreaded Moabites and Ammonites, Jehoshaphat turns to prayer and fasting and seeking the Lord.

He assembles the *qāhāl/ekklēsia* in the temple and leads the people in prayer. His prayer is a fine example of the spirit of humility that the Chronicler believes should characterize the king and the people (20:6–12). In this episode the Chronicler once more evokes the exodus tradition to make his point. The prophecy that Jahaziel delivers in the *qāhāl* (20:17) is a virtual paraphrase of Moses's exhortation when the people were about to cross the Red Sea (Exod. 14:13–14; Japhet 1993: 795). Selman points out that only in Moses's speech do we find the same combination of expressions as in Jahaziel's prophecy: "Do not be afraid," "take your stand," and "see the LORD's deliverance." Jahaziel's assertion that Israel will not have to fight but only to stand firm and watch is a deliberate variant of the promise of the exodus: "The LORD will fight for you" (1994b: 426–27).

Yet even the great Jehoshaphat, to whom the Chronicler devotes four almost entirely laudatory chapters, stumbles. Like his father, it is not that he descends into idolatry or apostasy. Like Asa, he is faithful in cultic matters and in keeping the law. He sins by presumption, by relying on a human alliance rather than on God. His tragic error will not reveal itself for another generation. The Chronicler reports only that Jehoshaphat "made a marriage alliance with Ahab," the ruler of the northern kingdom (2 Chr. 18:1). But he hints at the trouble to come when he reports that Ahab subsequently "induced" Jehoshaphat into joining him in an ill-advised military campaign. The verb here, *swt*, is the same used to describe Satan's seduction of David in his ill-fated census (18:2; cf. 1 Chr. 21:1).

Jehoshaphat's misstep indeed proves portentous since the marriage alliance almost leads to the extinguishing of the Davidic line. The reign of Jehoshaphat's son, Jehoram, and his wicked wife, Athaliah, the daughter of Ahab, marks a dark period in the monarchy, full of palace intrigue, fratricide, and growing corruption of morals and worship. The reigns of Joash, Amaziah, Uzziah, and Ahaz are characterized to varying degrees by patterns of ever-worsening faithlessness; only Jotham, who reigns between Uzziah and Ahaz, is commended by the Chronicler.

With Ahaz the kingdom descends to its lowest point: child sacrifice and all the "abominable practices of the nations whom the LORD drove out before the people" (2 Chr. 28:1–4). For this, God delivered Ahaz and a great number of his people into exile in Syria. It is the first great foreshadowing of the exile that is to come.

## Christian Interpretation

The division of the Davidic kingdom was a still-open wound for the Chronicler's first readers. Even after exile and the beginnings of the restoration, they lived every day with the political and theological implications of the split. They knew that the breakup of the kingdom and the subsequent exile called into question not only God's covenant promises to David, but also the purposes of God's election of Israel to be his chosen people and the source of blessings to all the nations of the world.

Anxiety for the restoration of the kingdom, so palpable in these pages of 2 Chronicles, animates much of the drama of the Gospels—which turns on the question of whether Jesus is the long-awaited son of David come to restore the everlasting monarchy that God promised to David. The anticipation can be heard in the voice of the apostles, who implored him after he had risen from the dead: "Lord, will you at this time restore the kingdom to Israel?" (Acts 1:6).

The division of the kingdom forms the subtext of much of the New Testament, from the Gospels' description of Jesus's ministry beginning in the region of the northern tribes (Zebulun and Naphtali) and concluding among the southern tribes in Jerusalem, to Paul's declaration: "All Israel will be saved" (Romans 11:26). During his roughly north-to-south itinerary in Luke, Jesus gathers disciples from all of these territories until, by the triumphal entry into Jerusalem, they have become a "multitude," forming the reunited kingdom of David (19:37).

The pattern of Davidic kingdom restoration runs like a scarlet cord through the Gospels. For instance, in the Gospel of Matthew, a sequence of events seems deliberately drawn to evoke this division. Christ appeals to all who are burdened and heavy laden and tells them that his yoke is easy (11:28–30). He follows this with a symbolic reenactment of an episode from the premonarchical life of David (12:1–8) and then the healing of a man with a withered hand (12:9–14).

All the vocabulary in these scenes is drawn from the biblical history of the division of the monarchy. Jeroboam and the northern tribes complain of the heavy "yoke" imposed by Solomon. Later, when a prophet complains against Jeroboam's division of the kingdom, Jeroboam "stretches out his hand" and orders that the prophet be seized. Immediately Jeroboam's hand is withered; he asks that it be "restored," and it is (1 Kgs. 13:1–6). All this language recurs in Jesus's healing of the man with a withered hand. He commands that the man "stretch out" his hand, and the man's hand is "restored." Luke's Gospel presses the point by noting that it was the man's "right hand" (6:6), thus making a clear allusion to Ps. 137:5: "If I forget you, O Jerusalem, let my right hand wither!" Jeroboam had "forgotten" Jerusalem (1 Kgs. 12:25–33). The language of restoration evokes hopes of the restoration and ingathering of the twelve tribes from exile (Hahn 2005b: 305n70).

Although this particular episode is not included in the Chronicler's account, his poignant treatment of the monarchy's division undoubtedly influenced the New Testament's understanding. We see this in Jesus's parables of the good Samaritan (Luke 10:25–37) and the last judgment (Matthew 25:31–46), which seem to allude to an episode late in the reign of the wicked King Ahaz (2 Chr.

28:5–15; Selman 1994b: 478; Spencer 1984). Good Samaritans, appalled by the violence that the northern kingdom visited upon their brethren in the south, bind up their wounds and provide food and clothing to the hungry and the naked. Also, the Chronicler's extensive use of exodus typology in these passages and his theology of retribution and mercy can be seen behind Paul's treatment of kingdom restoration in Romans 9–11. Like the Chronicler, Paul sees Pharaoh as being used by God for his purposes. And like the Chronicler, Paul envisions the sufferings of Israel as the occasion for repentance and the demonstration of God's mercy.

Finally, in the covenant with Asa, we have a window into the New Testament's understanding of the sacraments, the covenant oaths of the new covenant. By their oath, Asa and the people bound themselves to God and his covenant. This same act of "sevening oneself" is the foundation of the sacramental liturgy of the New Testament church (Hahn 2004), seen especially in Paul's treatment of the Eucharist. In the Eucharist, the believer binds oneself to God through the celebration of the sacrifice of the new covenant. The sacrament must be celebrated in a worthy manner. Those who do not celebrate worthily bring the judgments of the covenant upon themselves (1 Corinthians 11:27–32; cf. 10:16–22).

Chronicles influenced later Christian sacramental theology. In a tradition that dates back to the late first and early second century, the Latin word *sacramentum* was used to describe the binding "oaths" sworn by Christians in the eucharistic liturgy and the other sacramental liturgies. Among other ancient authorities, this usage can be found in Tertullian, Augustine, Jerome, Leo the Great, and Pliny the Younger. *Sacramentum* was also used to translate the early Christian term for the sacraments or "mysteries" (Greek *mystērion*). In a way similar to Asa's covenant renewal, the early church viewed the eucharistic liturgy as a covenant renewal; the notion of *sacramentum* was an indispensable part of covenant-making and covenant-renewing.

Perhaps too Asa's celebration of the feast of weeks is another dimension of the early Christians' approach to the sacraments. The great procession that accompanies the swearing of the oath under Asa anticipates later Christian liturgical processions of the eucharistic sacramentum. Asa's procession is premised on the idea that the covenant oath brings Israel into the living presence of God, binding the people to their God. This same principle is at work in Christian eucharistic devotion, as exemplified in such rituals as *Corpus Christi* devotions. Again, the depiction of Asa's covenant renewal shows evidence of biblical beginnings for sacramental understandings found in the New Testament and in the later Christian tradition (Hahn 2004).

# 7

## Exile and Return

*The Fall and Rise of the Kingdom (2 Chr. 29–36)*

**Major Divisions of the Text**

## Synopsis of the Text

Chronicles moves swiftly to its conclusion, in eight chapters taking readers from the Assyrian invasion and exile of the northern tribes in 722 BC to the end of the Babylonian exile of the southern tribes in 538 BC. In this section, the paradigmatic kingships of Hezekiah and Josiah stand out: each seeks to reunite the kingdom through liturgical renewals centered on the Passover.

## Theological Exegesis and Commentary

### Exile, Restoration, and the Hermeneutic of History

In the final chapters of Chronicles, the drama of history moves swiftly. In the matter of eight chapters nearly two centuries pass: from the Assyrian invasion and exile of the northern tribes in 722 BC, to the end of the Babylonian exile of the southern tribes in 538 BC. Still, the Chronicler's priorities are to the fore. A king who reigned for decades can be dispatched within a matter of a few verses, while the Chronicler will spend entire chapters on preparations for the Passover. As the Chronicler's grand narrative of world history seen through the eyes of the children of Abraham moves rapidly toward its conclusion, the Chronicler's prophetic historiography is aimed at more than documenting past events. He wants to address the crisis of faith in the postexilic generation caused by the destruction of the kingdom and the deportations of the people.

The Chronicler is writing in part to explain theologically how God could allow his kingdom and his chosen people to fall into such straits. And his efforts intensify, the closer his narrative draws toward the events leading to the exile. His burden is to demonstrate to his contemporaries that not only is the restoration of all Israel possible, as promised by the prophets: it also is God's deepest desire and the fulfillment of his plan for history. This explanatory purpose shapes the Chronicler's telling of this period of Israel's history, giving a deliberate patterning to his interpretation and recounting of events. Beneath what seems like a standardized recitation of successive kings, he is always articulating a profound interpretation of God's manner of acting in history. What God has done in the past is the prelude and prototype for understanding his presence and action in the present and how he will act in the future.

Readers of Chronicles are invited to see how the trauma of the exile came about as an inevitable consequence of the covenant infidelity, the *mā'al* of their forebears. The Chronicler's worldview allows no option of neutrality. A child of Israel is either for or against the God of his fathers. This perspective is articulated again and again in his history of this period. If Israel seeks God, they will find him. If they rely upon him, they will be sustained and prosper. But if they forsake God, they will be forsaken by him.

Sin has immediate consequences in the Chronicler's narrative. But the people's sin and God's retribution never has the last word for the Chronicler. Undeniably, there is punishment for every unfaithfulness. Yet for the sake of his covenant with David, God will not allow his people to perish. God's mercy is always available and is freely given. This is the most important lesson of the Chronicler's history, perhaps the single most important message that he wants to get across to his contemporaries. To serve the true God, people must repent and return; they must abandon their foreign gods and set their hearts to seek the Lord God of Israel in his house at Jerusalem. If they do not, their fate will be disaster.

Exile and return form the basic pattern of his understanding of history (Williamson 1982: 368). Sin leads to exile from God, corresponding to harsh service to foreign powers; reconciliation means humble return and restoration to the service and worship of God. As the Chronicler explained the origins of Israel's divided house with analogies and allusions to the exodus, he continues to use the patterns of God's past actions to interpret later events and shed light on the meaning of events in his own day (Fishbane 1989: 16–17). The prophets had described the restoration from exile as a new exodus and an ingathering of the scattered tribes; perhaps this theme has influenced the Chronicler's own vision of history and his intentions with this imagery.

The Chronicler, however, introduces a wrinkle into this new-exodus typology. In these final chapters of his work, an episode from immediately after the exodus becomes important: the golden-calf incident. This points to a deeper pattern at work throughout the Chronicler's history of the monarchy. The presence of a cyclical pattern of fidelity followed by immediate infidelity (Raney 2003: 114) represents the Chronicler's interiorization of a fundamental archetype in the biblical worldview. God's words on the occasion of the golden-calf incident are a good summary of this archetype: "They have turned aside quickly out of the way which I commanded them" (Exod. 32:8).

This is why later rabbis described this incident as Israel's "original sin" (Smolar and Aberbach 1968). Having received God's covenant, the people quickly or immediately descend into sin. Kearney (1977) notices that in the exodus narrative the golden-calf incident (Exod. 32–34) intervenes between God's giving of the instructions for creating the tabernacle (Exod. 25–31) and the people's building of the tabernacle (Exod. 35–40). The result is a pattern of creation (giving of the tabernacle instructions), fall (golden calf), and restoration (covenant renewal and building of the tabernacle). This same pattern can be noticed throughout the Old Testament, beginning in the garden of Eden. "Israel's story is seen as a direct parallel to Adam's," according to Morris's study of rabbinic interpretation (1992: 124; also Kaminsky 2000; Damrosch 1987; cf. Hahn 2005d: 120–21). As Adam sinned immediately after receiving God's blessing, so too did Israel. In his canonical reading, Anderson also observes: "The story of Adam and Eve . . . shows a striking number of parallels to Israel's larger national story. We might say that the entire narrative of the Torah is in a tersely summarized form. . . . Adam and Eve fall at the first and only command given to them. And like the nation Israel, the consequence of their disobedience is exile from a land of blessing" (2001: 207–8).

Throughout the canonical text, the bestowal of God's covenant blessing is followed almost immediately by sin and apostasy, most often in the form of idolatry. In addition to the golden-calf affair, one could point to the great sin of the second generation after the exodus, the sin at Baal-peor (Num. 25). The inauguration of the tabernacle sacrifices follows the same pattern. No sooner had the divine fire come down to signal God's acceptance of Israel's sacrifices, than two sons of Aaron came forward to offer a "strange fire," a profane offering. They were punished with instantaneous death (Lev. 9–10). As at Baal-peor and the golden calf, there was need for cultic and covenant renewal.

This pattern of "Israel sinning immediately upon receiving benediction" (Anderson 2001: 206) has been internalized by the Chronicler, and it shapes how he tells the history of the divided monarchy. The new Eden of Solomon and the temple is followed immediately by the rebellion of Jeroboam, who incidentally creates "golden calves" for his northern kingdom to worship. The pattern persists: blessing is followed by sin almost immediately, and sin results in exile or alienation from God. Good kings are followed by bad in Chronicles, but even good kings like Jehoshaphat and Asa fall into pride and sin and are in need of restoration.

The Chronicler's reflection upon history is influenced by the interpretation of the exodus found in Deut. 8. He seems to see a constant pattern of covenant testing at work in Israel's history. God is trying his people, testing their faithfulness, their wholehearted willingness to serve him, as seen in David's temptation in the census (1 Chr. 21). And in his farewell discourse David describes how God "tries" (*bḥn*) the heart of his servants (29:17). *Bḥn* (to put to the test) is used almost exclusively in the Prophets and Psalms to describe how God refines and "tests" the faithfulness of even his righteous servants (Pss. 7:9; 11:5; 17:3; 26:2; 66:10; 139:23; Job 23:10; 34:36; Jer. 9:7; 11:20; 12:3; 17:10; 20:12; Ezek. 21:13; Zech. 13:9).

This seems to be behind the Chronicler's highly patterned depictions of the kings. Success and faithfulness is followed by a temptation to pride and self-reliance. More often than not, this temptation comes in the form of riches and power or a military alliance with a foreign power. This pattern, along with the language of testing, is unique to the Chronicler's interpretation of the historical record. It represents his distinctive hermeneutic of history.

This interpretive principle, seen at work in many of his individual royal portraits, is made explicit only in the case of Hezekiah, the greatest of the post-Solomonic monarchs. At the end of his account of Hezekiah, the Chronicler interprets an episode in which envoys from Babylon come to seek his guidance (cf. 2 Kgs. 20:12–19): "God left him to himself [*ʿāzab*], in order to try [*nāsâ*] him and to know all that was in his heart" (2 Chr. 32:31). *Nāsâ* is the same term used to describe Abraham's "testing" in the Akedah (Gen. 22:1) and Israel's testing in the wilderness (Exod. 16:4; 20:20; Deut. 8:2, 16). Here the language is similar to Deuteronomy's explanation of Israel's testing: "God has led you these forty years in the wilderness, that he might humble you, testing [*nāsâ*] you to know what was in your heart, whether you would keep his commandments, or not" (Deut. 8:2).

The maxim that Deuteronomy expressed in interpreting the exodus ("As a man disciplines his son, the LORD your God disciplines you"; Deut. 8:5) guides the Chronicler's understanding and writing of Israel's history. Strong continuities of vocabulary and thematic concern run between Moses's speech in Deuteronomy and the Chronicler's reading of Israel's preexilic history. Humility before God—expressed in keeping his law, commandments, ordinances, and statutes—is a key theme. This is a large part of what the Chronicler means by "seeking" (*dāraš*) God. The cautionary streak of moral realism that runs through Deuteronomy is also strongly felt. Material well-being and prosperity—to be established and strong in the Chronicler's idiom—lead to presumption and the illusion of self-sufficiency. For Israel, this amounts to forsaking "the LORD the God of their fathers who brought them out of the land of Egypt" (2 Chr. 7:22; cf. Deut. 8:11–17). This is a paradigmatic definition of the roots of covenant unfaithfulness. For Israel, unfaithfulness to the covenant means mistaking its own power and strength as coming from its own hand. It is forgetting God's saving actions in Israel's history.

This is the template for the royal history from Rehoboam to Zedekiah in 2 Chr. 10–36. But this metahistory is intended as a lesson for the Chronicler's first readers. His history of this period plays out in the personal actions and decisions of kings who at every turn have a fundamental option: to seek God and his covenant will—or to forsake him. These are the same basic choices that the Chronicler's audience faces: to serve God and live—or to abandon his covenant and be cast out and scattered in servitude to foreign kings. Again the Chronicler has used the stark "life and good" or "death and evil" motif of Deut. 30:15–20.

The covenant that Israel's fathers entered into under Moses contained blessings as well as curses, as the people will rediscover in these final pages of Chronicles (2 Chr. 34:23–25). Punishment for sin can be postponed but cannot be evaded. Still, Chronicles is theodicy. It is about the plan of the Creator for his creation and the role of Israel in that plan. For the sake of his covenant with David, made to fulfill his promise to Abraham, God will redeem Israel. Kelly says it well: "The Chronicler is concerned primarily to highlight the offer of God's prevenient and undeserved mercy to a sinful yet penitent people—an offer, moreover, that is tied to the concrete form of the Jerusalem temple and its cultus of prayer and sacrifice" (2003: 226).

In these final pages, the Chronicler places importance on the restorative process envisioned at the dedication of the temple. In his private revelation to Solomon following the dedication, God himself had promised: "If my people who are called by my name humble themselves, and pray and seek my face, and turn from their wicked ways, then I will hear from heaven, and will forgive their sin and heal their land" (2 Chr. 7:14). This divine promise will become one of the organizing principles of the Chronicler's narrative of the final years of the kingdom.

### The Shape of the Kingdom

The shape of the kingdom—the visible institutional form of the kingdom that we can detect from Chronicles—is important for understanding the Chronicler's message to his audience. He is writing in a time of rebuilding, an era of reconstruction, not only of the temple but also of the structures of religious and political life. Some of the assumptions of the Davidic monarchy—for instance, its international dominance—no longer apply because the region is under Persian rule. Nonetheless, this and other aspects of the kingdom serve to animate and arrange the Chronicler's hopes for a Davidic restoration as the earthly expression of the kingdom of God (Kelly 1996: 156–215).

The Chronicler does not give a sustained or organized picture of the political administration or economic organization of the kingdom. But it is possible to identify key characteristics of the kingdom as the Chronicler understands it. First and foremost, the kingdom is established on the basis of God's covenant oath sworn to David (1 Chr. 17:10–14). It is not, then, a human creation; it is rather a gift of God's grace and is sustained by God's faithfulness to his covenant (2 Chr. 21:7). This covenant is eternal: it is a "covenant of salt," which is another way of saying that it is "for ever" (13:5).

Under the terms of this covenant, the king is "son of David," "son of God," and an "anointed one" (1 Chr. 17:13; Saebo 1980). He is both "king" and "priest," with two basic responsibilities: ensuring that the law of God is lived and proclaimed among the people, and ensuring that God is worshiped in the manner in which God has prescribed (1 Chr. 16:1–3; 2 Chr. 7:1–4). The temple and Jerusalem, the city of God and the city of David, are also central features of the kingdom as understood in Chronicles (6:6, 10–11). Thus the kingdom is most fully represented at worship, in its liturgical expression in the temple at Jerusalem, as the qāhāl/ekklēsia (30:25–27).

The kingdom is a liturgical empire, and its most important functionaries are the ministers of sacrifice: the "priests," under the leadership of the chief priest; and the "Levites," who increasingly in Chronicles are associated with the ministry of teaching the law (35:3). In addition to the chief priest who oversees the matters of the temple and religious practice, a "governor" (nāgîd) oversees the "house" of Judah and all matters of the kingdom (19:11). There is also a prominent role for the "queen mother," the mother of the king, who is mentioned in every account of the monarchy in Chronicles except for the last four kings (Andreasen 1983; Smith 1998; Sri 2005; Zlotnick 2001).

Finally, the kingdom is international in scope, and its law and its temple worship are meant to be the desire of the nations (9:23, 26). Through all its institutions, Israel is to show itself to be God's "firstborn" among all the nations, a holy nation, a "kingdom of priests" mediating the blessings of the Creator to all the families of the nations (6:32–33; cf. Isa. 56:7; Ps. 47:7–9).

These are the main features of the kingdom as the Chronicler depicts it. Such features do not constitute a utopian vision or an ideal type of the kingdom. As the Chronicler tells it, they were the basic characteristics of the Davidic kingdom in its historical prime and in its decline. These elements set the stage for his narrative of the final days of the kingdom and the temple.

### To Make Atonement for All Israel: Hezekiah Renews the Kingdom

The Chronicler presents Hezekiah as a new Solomon. In 1–2 Kings, an occasional king of Judah is compared, favorably or not, with "David his father" (Abijam in 1 Kgs. 15:3; Asa in 15:11, 24; Jehoshaphat in 22:50; Amaziah in 2 Kgs. 14:3; Jotham in 15:38; Hezekiah in 18:3; Josiah in 22:2). In Chronicles, use of this expression is sharply curtailed, reserved only for Solomon (2 Chr. 2:17; 3:1; 5:1; 8:14; 9:31) and two later kings—Hezekiah (29:2; cf. Sir. 48:22) and Josiah (2 Chr. 34:2, 3). It is as if the Chronicler wants to say that these three and these alone truly ruled as God's sons and kings over God's people in the tradition of the Davidic covenant. The importance the Chronicler assigns to Hezekiah is suggested by the amount of space he devotes to his reign: 117 verses, more than any other king in the work (Johnstone 1997: 2.188).

In the first day of his first month on the throne (2 Chr. 29:17), Hezekiah moves to restore the worship of the temple under the priests and the Levites. The sanctuary that Solomon built is to be rebuilt and reestablished by Hezekiah as the spiritual center of the kingdom. With deft symbolism, the Chronicler writes that Hezekiah "opened the doors of the house of the LORD" (29:3). His reign is characterized by his literal and metaphorical throwing open the doors of the sanctuary: he invites the people of Judah, the fallen-away children of the north, and even non-Israelites sojourning in the land to join him in worshiping the Lord, the God of Abraham, Isaac, and Israel.

Under Hezekiah's father, King Ahaz, the temple doors were shuttered and the temple lamps extinguished—again, both literally and metaphorically (28:24; 29:7). The people that were called to seek God's face had "turned away their faces . . . and turned their backs" (29:6; cf. 7:14). They had been "unfaithful" (*mā'al*) and had "forsaken" ('*zb*) God (29:6); the result has been political catastrophe, as Hezekiah says in his inaugural address: "Therefore the wrath of the LORD came on Judah and Jerusalem, and he has made them an object of horror, of astonishment, and of hissing. . . . For lo, our fathers have fallen by the sword and our sons and our daughters and our wives are in captivity for this" (29:8–9).

Hezekiah is ostensibly describing the fate visited upon Judah during the days of Ahaz (28:5–15). But through his word choice, he seems to be interpreting those events in light of the exile that is yet to come in his narrative. The expression "an object of horror . . . and of hissing" is a quotation from Jeremiah's prophecy regarding a seventy-year exile in Babylon, a prophecy to which the Chronicler will return at the end of his work (Jer. 25:9, 11–12, 18; also Deut. 28:25, 36–37, 41). In particular, he appears to be drawing from the letter that Jeremiah wrote to the first wave of exiles from Judah, those seized and deported to Babylon by Nebuchadnezzar in 597 BC (Jer. 29; see 2 Kgs. 24:8–17; 2 Chr. 36:9–10). In this letter, Jeremiah foretells a seventy-year "captivity" for the wives, sons, and daughters, of the people already in Babylon (Jer. 29:6). The prophet goes on to warn "the king who sits on the throne of David" and all the people remaining in Judah that they will fall by the sword and be made an object of horror and of hissing because they have failed to heed the divine word brought to them by the prophets (29:16, 18–19; also 15:2, 4).

The Chronicler will echo this condemnation in his penultimate verses, which record the final destruction of Judah and deportation of the population (2 Chr. 36:15–16). And in his narrative, Hezekiah shortly will address his own letter to an audience in similar circumstances to those whom Jeremiah was addressing. Issuing his invitation to the Passover celebration, Hezekiah will write not only to the people of the southern kingdom, but also to their kin who have escaped exile to Assyria and still remain in the land (30:6; cf. Jer. 29:17). Significantly, Hezekiah is the first king of Judah in the period after the overthrow of the northern kingdom by the Assyrians in 722 BC. While this traumatic event is recorded in detail elsewhere in the biblical record (2 Kgs. 17:1–23), it receives only glancing mention in the Chronicler's history. But these final pages of Chronicles, beginning with Hezekiah's reign, are suffused with an awareness of the exile and of the prophets' promise of restoration.

The sense of time is always portentous and fluid in the Chronicler's prophetic historiography, and never more than in these final chapters of his work. Here he is writing about the period after the fall and exile of the northern kingdom but before the fall and exile of the southern kingdom, which he will record in the final chapter of his work. He is writing to a contemporary audience for whom all of these events are a painful recent memory. As always, his purposes are as homiletic as they are historical: he wants his readers to see that their situation is not so very unlike that experienced by their forebears. Though many in his audience have returned to the land, he knows that many remain scattered abroad, from both the north and Judah. Hezekiah, like Josiah after him, is presented by the Chronicler as historically the last hope for the kingdom, the servant-kings that God had desired for his people. At the same time he is held up as a model leader for the postexilic community. The Chronicler urges his contemporaries to follow the priorities that Hezekiah establishes and the steps he takes to renew the kingdom.

Hezekiah's first desire is to reconsecrate the priests and the Levites and to purify the temple. These steps are prerequisites, means to his true end: to renew Israel's covenant with God "that his fierce anger may turn away from us" (2 Chr. 29:10). The making of this covenant is not explicitly recorded in Chronicles. Japhet believes that no formal covenant is intended by Hezekiah, that he is expressing simply his "absolute loyalty" to God (1993: 919). However, the liturgy enacted in the verses that follow Hezekiah's statement of intent (29:20–36) has a clear covenant-renewal quality about it, one that recalls the earlier covenant of Asa and the Sinai covenant. Hezekiah's exhortation to the Levites is made in the context of his desire to make a covenant. And the following atonement ritual seems to be a formal liturgical expression of Hezekiah and the people's humbling themselves in repentance according to the terms prescribed by Solomon in the dedication of the temple (6:24–25, 36–39; 7:14).

The liturgy is celebrated by the king and the "assembly" (*qāhāl*; 29:23–24) under the "command" of Hezekiah. The precedent for the king's presiding over the liturgy is Davidic and Solomonic, although no king since them has been presented as leading the people in worship (1 Chr. 16:40; 2 Chr. 8:14–15). This is also the first time since Solomon's dedication of the temple that the sacrificial liturgy is described as being celebrated by the *qāhāl* and the king (20:5, 14, 18; 23:3). With Hezekiah we see a unity of king and cult not seen since Solomon, when "the king and all the people offered sacrifice before the LORD" (7:4; cf. 1:5).

Kleinig argues forcefully that through his description of Hezekiah's atonement and renewal liturgy, the Chronicler wants to present his readers with a normative outline of the fixed sequence of sacrifices within the general order of temple worship (1993: 101–4). This is an attractive assertion, yet it is speculative: there are no surviving manuals of temple worship for us to compare, and historical reconstructions are notoriously tricky. But Kleinig rightly observes that the Chronicler's account is "remarkable for its unusual attention to the general order of the ritual as well as to significant details in its parts" (1993: 101). The question that cannot be answered, Kleinig notwithstanding, is to what extent the liturgy on this special occasion represents the regular pattern of "the service of the house of the LORD" (29:35).

From this episode we can nonetheless glean important insights into the Chronicler's idea of the proper worship of the kingdom. First, worship is ordered and overseen by the king. The priests and Levites sanctify themselves and prepare the liturgy "as the king had commanded, by the [authority of the] words of the LORD" (29:15). Hezekiah functions as master of ceremonies. He commands the performance of specific ritual acts and leads the *qāhāl* in worship (29:21, 24, 27, 29); he stations the Levites and cues their musical performance (29:25, 27, 30); and he exhorts and issues an altar call to the *qāhāl* (29:31).

The order of worship described is neatly divided between corporate and personal sacrifices. The ceremony begins with a corporate "sin offering" made by "the priests the sons of Aaron" on the "altar of the LORD," again using heptadic, covenantal symbolism: "seven bulls, seven rams, seven lambs, and seven he-goats." These animals are sacrificed as "a sin offering for the kingdom and for the sanctuary and for Judah," the Chronicler says. Atonement is being made, he emphasizes, for "all Israel." The bulls, rams, and lambs are killed, and with each the Chronicler repeats that "their blood was thrown against the altar." Then the he-goats are offered and their blood thrown against the altar (29:20–24).

Following the sin offering, the burnt offering is made, accompanied by Levites' playing "the instruments of David king of Israel"—cymbals, harps, and lyres—and priests blowing trumpets and singers singing "the song to the LORD." At the conclusion of the offering, the king and people bow and worship. The Levites then "sing praises to the LORD," using the psalms of David and Asaph, singing "with gladness"; again they bow and worship (29:25–30). In this description we see the ideal of temple worship envisioned by David's liturgical reforms and anticipated in Solomon's great liturgy of dedication. Again, the likes of this joyous celebration have not been seen since the days of Solomon.

Hezekiah then signals the end of the corporate sacrifices for the kingdom by calling the people to offer their individual sacrifices: "'You have now consecrated yourselves [*millē'tem yedkem*] to the LORD; come near [*nāgaš*], bring sacrifices [*zĕbāḥîm*] and thank offerings [*tôdôt*] to the house of the LORD.' And the assembly [*qāhāl*] brought sacrifices and thank offerings; and all who were of a willing heart [*nĕdîb lēb*] brought burnt offerings [*'ōlôt*]" (29:31).

Hezekiah's language here is highly unusual. He addresses the people as if they are priests, using an idiom associated almost exclusively with priestly ordination: *millē' 'et-yād* (lit., "filled the hand"; Exod. 28:41; 29:9, 29, 33, 35; 32:29; Lev. 8:33 [twice]; 16:32; 21:10; Num. 3:3; Williamson 1982: 359; Johnstone 1997: 2.198). He exhorts the people of the *qāhāl* to "come near," another expression reserved usually for priests who draw near to the altar in the performance of their cultic duties (Exod. 28:43; 30:20; Lev. 21:21, 23; cf. Ezek. 44:13; Exod. 19:22). The Chronicler is giving a beautiful image of the *qāhāl* as the reconstitution of the children of Israel in their original vocation given at Sinai to be a "kingdom of priests and a holy nation" (Exod. 19:6). Reconciled to God through the promise of his mercy and their humble seeking of his face in the temple, the people have had their sins forgiven and are once more able to worship the Lord and to praise him in his holy dwelling.

The radical newness of this restoration of the people's identity is stressed by the sheer enormity and spontaneity of the sacrifices: "seventy bulls, a hundred rams, two hundred lambs" brought by the *qāhāl*; and another "six hundred bulls and three thousand sheep" presented as "consecrated offerings." In a memorable image, the Chronicler says there were so many offerings that there were not enough priests to prepare them. In obvious respects, the scene recalls the earlier liturgies of David and Solomon with their extravagant sacrifices. But the sacrifices offered and the repetition of the expression "their blood was thrown against the altar" (2 Chr. 29:22–24) suggest that the Chronicler intends to evoke the precedent of the Sinaitic covenant. At Sinai, the young men also offered peace offerings and burnt offerings (29:35; Exod. 24:5), and Moses threw "the blood of the covenant" "against the altar" (Exod. 24:6, 8; Lev. 7:2).

There is an important difference. At Sinai the emphasis is on the gulf between Moses and the people. He alone can "come near" (*nāgaš*) the Lord (Exod. 24:2). By contrast, Hezekiah calls all the people to come near to worship God, and the entire episode stresses the cooperation of the king, not only with the priests and Levites, but also with the whole *qāhāl*. In making the sin offering, the king and the *qāhāl* lay hands upon the he-goats (2 Chr. 29:23). This again is highly unusual. It is likely that the Chronicler is referencing the Levitical scapegoat ritual (Lev. 16:20–22). In that ritual, the high priest laid both hands on the head of the sacrificial goat while confessing the sins of the people, thereby symbolically transferring those sins to the animal, which was then sent away into the wilderness in a gesture meant to represent Israel's forgiveness and atonement (Selman 1994b: 490). There is no biblical precedent for ordinary believers' participating in this rite; it is a sacrificial duty reserved for priests. Thus, in having the people under Hezekiah lay hands on the sin offerings, the Chronicler is again highlighting the renewal of Israel's royal priestly perogatives.

Throughout this liturgy of joy, the message seems to be that if sin abounded under Ahaz, the nadir of the monarchy, then God's grace and mercy abounds all the more under his son, the good King Hezekiah. Also at work here is a subtle reversal of the sin of Jeroboam, part of the original sin of the apostate northern kingdom. King Abijah's critique—that Jeroboam "made priests . . . like the peoples of other lands"—is of interest. He implies that it is an office of political patronage: "Whoever comes to consecrate himself [*lĕmallē' yādô*] with a young bull or seven rams becomes a priest of what are no gods" (2 Chr. 13:9). Jeroboam's ordinations are a hollow mockery of the priestly consecration intended by God. But though Jeroboam arrogated to himself those powers of consecration, it can avail him naught because his heart is not set on serving the true God (Johnstone 1997: 2.55).

In his farewell discourse to the *qāhāl*, King David had evoked Israel's vocation as a kingdom of priests. He stressed the need for the people to "willingly" (*nādab*) "consecrate" (*millē' 'et-yād*) their whole hearts to the Lord (1 Chr. 29:5, 6, 9, 14, 17; Williamson 1982: 359). The people of God are to have a priestly heart. This defines the central spiritual action of the Davidic covenant renewal led by Hezekiah. The people bring their offerings to the temple with "willing hearts," a sign that they have offered their whole lives, freely and willingly, to the Lord (2 Chr. 29:31). They have acknowledged that he is the king over all creation, the heavens and the earth; that the kingdom on earth is not theirs but his; and that it is his mighty arm alone that gives strength and can make them great. This recognition is what brings them to rejoicing and thanksgiving.

"Thus the service of the house of the Lord was restored" (29:35), the Chronicler concludes, with an echo of Solomon's finishing the work of the temple (8:16). Also following in Solomon's footsteps, Hezekiah reappoints the divisions of priests and Levites and reinstates the order of daily offerings in the temple and the regular celebration of Sabbaths, new moons, and feasts. He restores the practice of tithing and organized donations for the temple sacrifices and maintenance (2 Chr. 31). In addition, he is shown as defending the true God and his people against Assyrian invasion (2 Chr. 32). For his faithfulness, God "gave them rest on every side" and "exalted [Hezekiah] in the sight of all nations" (32:22–23).

### An Invitation to the Passover of All Israel

For Chronicles, the heart of Hezekiah's reign is his reinstatement of the Passover celebration, an episode that has no parallel in the other historical sources found in the Bible. Indeed, there is no biblical record of a Passover celebration by David, Solomon, or any other king before Hezekiah; many historical and cultic difficulties are raised by the Chronicler's account (Eves 1992: 108–33; Williamson 1982: 360–65). For our purposes, in the Chronicler's telling, Hezekiah is deeply convinced that God's people must "keep the passover to the Lord the God of Israel," and he believes it to be his solemn duty as king to ensure a faithful observance by all Israel (30:1). The questions that are more difficult to answer are why he feels this obligation and what he understands to be the meaning of the Passover, especially at this stage in the checkered history of the kingdom.

God instituted the Passover through Moses to commemorate the Israelites' exodus from Egypt; it was closely associated with a weeklong Feast of Unleavened Bread. The *pesah*, from a verb meaning "protect" or "rescue" (Isa. 31:5), was offered in remembrance of Israel's salvation from Egypt; the feast was inherently one of thanksgiving for the Lord's salvation of Israel. It recalled how God "passed over the houses of the people of Israel in Egypt, when he slew the Egyptians but spared our houses" and how "with a strong hand the Lord has brought you out of Egypt" (Exod. 12:27; 13:9). It was a sacrifice for the deliverance of the firstborn, linked especially to Israel's status as God's firstborn son and God's punishment of Egypt by a plague against the firstborn (4:22; 12:12–13). Passover was originally observed by families in their homes, but Deuteronomy envisions a time when families would bring their Passover sacrifice to be offered in the centralized sanctuary (Deut. 16:1–8; also Exod. 12:1–14, 43–51; 23:15; 34:18; Lev. 23:5–8; Ezek. 45:21–25; Eves 1992).

The Chronicler attaches great significance to the Passover. It is at the center of his portraits of both Hezekiah and Josiah, the final two good kings before the destruction of the kingdom and the exile of the people. The Passover is vital to Israel's national identity and corporate memory; there is no question that for the Chronicler the Passover is the feast of the kingdom par excellence, the feast in which the people experience intimate communion with God, who blesses them through his priest and accepts their prayers in his holy habitation (30:27).

Canonically speaking, the *qāhāl*, the liturgical assembly of all Israel, was first constituted on the night of the first Passover (Exod. 12:6). In the account of Hezekiah's Passover, the *qāhāl* figures prominently, mentioned nine times (2 Chr. 30:2, 4, 13, 17, 23, 24 [twice], 25 [twice]; Selman 1994b: 496). Indeed, the *qāhāl* is a distinctive feature of Hezekiah's reign (29:23, 28, 31, 32; 31:18; Japhet 1993: 928); he is the king who restores the *qāhāl* to the central place it was meant to occupy in the life of God's people. And Hezekiah's Passover is described in ways that call to mind Israel's origins in the exodus. Though Hezekiah is certainly portrayed as a new Solomon and a faithful son of David, there is a strong exodus subtext to the Passover episode and perhaps even some new-Moses typology at work.

Hezekiah's consultation with the *qāhāl* before the feast is patterned on David's consultation with the *qāhāl* before restoring the ark of the covenant. Like David, Hezekiah wants to send abroad to gather together brethren separated from the kingdom. David explained his intentions in terms of correcting the cultic failures of the previous royal administration ("for we did not seek [God] in the days of Saul"; 1 Chr. 13:3, my trans.). Hezekiah offers a similar rationale for restoring the Passover ("for they had not kept it in great numbers as prescribed"; 2 Chr. 30:5), although he adds a more urgent imperative: to avert God's covenant wrath (30:8). Both David's (1 Chr. 13:1–4) and Hezekiah's (2 Chr. 30:1–6) consultations concluded with the *qāhāl*'s deciding that the king's plan was the right thing to do.

As did David and Solomon, Hezekiah in this episode presumes to exercise spiritual authority and jurisdiction over all the tribes, over "all Israel and Judah" (30:1). The reunification of north and south as "all Israel" is the Chronicler's key theme in his account of Hezekiah's Passover. In effect, Israel cannot celebrate the Passover except as God's firstborn, which means as all the "sons of Israel." Thus he addresses his letter to the "sons of Israel" and sends it out "throughout all Israel, from Beer-sheba to Dan"—that is, from the southernmost region to the northernmost region of the kingdom as it was originally constituted under David (30:5; cf. 1 Chr. 21:2). This section of the Chronicler's account features a piling up of northern tribal names: Ephraim, Manasseh, Zebulun, Asher, and Issachar are all mentioned at various points, with some of these tribal names repeated (2 Chr. 30:10–11, 18; also Simeon and Naphtali in 34:6; Eves 1992: 94). To these northern tribes the Chronicler issues a heartfelt call to homecoming. Their true home, he wants them to know, is Jerusalem. Their true vocation is to worship the Lord in his temple.

The letter that Hezekiah publishes throughout the land is filled with inner-biblical quotations and echoes. His immediate sources are the promises made by God and Solomon during the dedication of the temple (6:18–42; 7:12–18). But there is a deeper stratum of biblical allusion at work as well. Hezekiah's form of address, "O sons of Israel,"[1] is used several times in the writings of the prophets to summon the exiled population to repentance and conversion (Isa. 27:12; 31:6; Amos 2:11; 3:1; 4:5; 9:7). In the context of his narrative, the Chronicler is writing primarily to the remnant of the people in the north who have escaped deportation by the Assyrians (2 Chr. 30:6). He is appealing to them in terms of their religious-national ancestry and identity; the designation "sons of Israel" originates in the exodus generation, at the inception of Israel's experience as God's chosen people (Exod. 3:9, 15, my trans.). And a close reading of Hezekiah's letter reveals that he has chosen his vocabulary carefully to evoke events from that first generation that came out of Egypt.

Hezekiah calls the people to remember "the Lord, the God of Abraham, Isaac, and Israel" (2 Chr. 30:6). This is not the ordinary way of referring to the God who made his covenant with his people at Sinai. The ordinary expression is "the God of Abraham, Isaac, and Jacob" and variants thereof. Hezekiah chooses a rare formulation found only once outside of Chronicles (1 Kgs. 18:36; cf. 1 Chr. 29:18), probably because he wants to allude to a critical juncture of Israel's journey out of Egypt: the golden-calf affair.

In the aftermath of the golden-calf affair, while Moses is still on Mount Sinai, receiving the tables of the law, God pointedly disowns his "firstborn" (Exod. 4:22). He says to Moses, "Go down; for *your* people, whom *you* brought up out of the land of Egypt, have corrupted themselves." God condemns the Israelites as a "stiff-necked" (*qĕšēh-ʿōrep*) people and describes how his "wrath glows hot" (*yiḥar-ʾappî*) against them; he threatens to destroy the people and make of Moses alone a great nation (32:7, 9–10).

Hezekiah picks up this language in his letter, seemingly to describe the experience of the people of the north. Their ancestors and relatives, he says, were "stiff-necked" and "faithless [*māʿal*] to the Lord God of their fathers" (2 Chr. 30:7–8). The expression "the Lord God of their fathers" is not used often outside of Chronicles. When it is, it is usually in the context of describing Israel's forsaking of the covenant that the Lord made with them "when he brought them out of the land of Egypt" (Deut. 29:25; Judg. 2:12; cf. Exod. 4:5). Hezekiah indicates that the "desolation" (*šammâ*) visited upon the north was a direct and deserved punishment for their sin. Hezekiah deliberately uses the

---

1. The RSV reads, "O people of Israel."

prophets' word for the condemnation of the exile in his address to the Levites (2 Chr. 29:8; cf. Jer. 25:9, 11, 18; Mic. 6:16). Several points of contact between Hezekiah's letter to the north and how he describes the southern kingdom in his address to the Levites are important to understanding the Chronicler's message (Selman 1994b: 493).

According to Hezekiah, both north and south have been "unfaithful" (*mā'al*; 2 Chr. 29:6; 30:7), provoking God to "anger" (*qeṣep* in 29:8; *'ap* in 30:8) and resulting in the "desolation" (*šammâ*; 29:8; 30:7) and "captivity" (29:9; 30:6, 9) of the people. Again using the vocabulary of the exodus, Hezekiah is calling both north and south to turn away God's "fierce anger" (*ḥărôn 'ap*) by humbling themselves, turning to the Lord, praying, and seeking his face. The covenant renewal he urges is to be consummated in the temple liturgy by hearts united in willing service to the Lord (29:10; 30:8). Chronicles is casting Hezekiah the king in a priestly and intercessory role. His model in this role is not only Solomon but also Moses at Sinai.

At Sinai, Moses appealed to God to remember his covenant oath sworn to "Abraham, Isaac, and Israel," and he implored God to "turn" (*šûb*) from his "fierce anger" (*ḥărôn 'ap*; Exod. 32:12–13). Now in his Passover invitation and in his speech to the Levites, Hezekiah is making the same argument from the other side. Moses begged God to be merciful for the sake of his covenant; Hezekiah is urging the people to produce the repentance necessary to receive God's mercy. Again, the language is drawn not only by analogy with Solomon, but also from the exodus tradition. Hezekiah implores the people not to be "stiff-necked" (*qāšeh 'ārep*) like their fathers and to "turn" (*šûb*) so that God's "fierce anger" (*ḥărôn 'ap*) may be turned away (*šûb*; 2 Chr. 30:8).

Such exact parallels in language can hardly be incidental. The Chronicler establishes a continuity between the original sin of the people at Sinai with the golden calf and the sins of the divided kingdom. The golden calf resulted in Israel's losing its covenant identity as a "kingdom of priests" and led to the Levites being established as a priestly caste. The incident also confirmed Moses's identity as a priestly intercessor for his people. Thus Hezekiah is renewing the priestly identity of the people and the Levitical prerogatives. But most significantly, the calf incident revealed that the basis for the people's survival in the face of their own sinfulness is God's covenant oath sworn to the patriarch Abraham on Mount Moriah (Gen. 22:18; Hahn 2009b: 240).

Hezekiah, like Moses before him (Exod. 32:13), appeals to that oath when he calls the people to remember "the LORD, the God of Abraham, Isaac, and Israel" (2 Chr. 30:6). Perhaps here the reader is meant to hear a confession of faith that God will honor his oath even when his people dishonor him. When Hezekiah tells the people not to be "stiff-necked" like their "fathers," he is establishing an analogy between the sins of the fathers of the divided kingdom and the sins of Israel's first-generation fathers with the golden calf. "Stiff-necked" is the repeated term of condemnation during the golden-calf affair and its aftermath (Exod. 32:9; 33:3, 5; 34:9). Jeroboam, the rebel-founder of the northern kingdom, was associated with golden calves (1 Kgs. 12:28–30), and his kingdom came to be characterized by its worship of strange gods. Idolatry remains a constant theme in the Chronicler's account of this period, as evidenced by the continued presence of altars, pillars, Asherim, and high places throughout Judah and Benjamin, even in Jerusalem on the eve of Hezekiah's Passover (2 Chr. 30:14; 31:1). The Chronicler's word for covenant infidelity, *mā'al*, is often understood in terms of idolatry (1 Chr. 5:25; 2 Chr. 28:19; 33:19).

For the Chronicler, the root sin of the people is their failure to set their hearts to seek God, and that sin is expressed in both idolatry and their failure to worship him in the place he has established for his name to dwell. Thus the king urges the people to come back to the "sanctuary, which he has sanctified for ever, and serve the LORD your God" (2 Chr. 30:8; cf. Exod. 10:8; 20:5; Deut. 10:12; 28:47). The good kings of the divided monarchy, especially Hezekiah and Josiah, do what God instructed Moses and the Israelites to do: they "tear down" (*nātaṣ*) and "break up" (*šābar*) altars, images, and pillars to false gods (2 Chr. 31:1; 34:4–7; Exod. 34:13–14). For the Chronicler, the temple is the source from which the living waters of God's blessings and mercy flow. The temple is the hope of all Israel. In his temple, Solomon had promised, God will hear the prayers of his people and forgive their sins, "for there is no man who does not sin" (2 Chr. 6:36).

### Release for the Captives in a Land Far or Near

Solomon's great prayer made provisions for a time when Israel would sin and find themselves punished by captivity in "a land far or near" (2 Chr. 6:36–39). If the people find themselves in exile, he said, they must "turn back" to God with their whole heart and pray toward the temple and the land given by God to their fathers. That is why, when Hezekiah concludes his letter to the exiles, he appeals to Solomon's promise. He builds his final argument on a fourfold use and wordplay on *šûb* (to turn, return). Again a clear connection is intended between his concluding argument and Solomon's prayer: God's "anger" at the people's covenant infidelities, the punishment of captivity, the land, and their fathers. As Solomon did, so also Hezekiah promises that if the people "return" to God and worship him in the temple, God will "turn away" his anger from them (30:6–9).

Hezekiah also uses exodus imagery, again drawn from the golden-calf episode. He promises, "The LORD your God is gracious and merciful, and will not turn away his face from you, if you return to him" (30:9). This echoes the revelation of the divine name to Moses in the covenant renewal after the golden calf. God passes before Moses's "face" and repeats his divine name: "The LORD! The LORD!" He then describes his attributes as being a "God merciful and gracious" (Exod. 34:6). Hezekiah appeals to God's name and nature in making an extraordinary promise: if the people turn back to God, not only will they find forgiveness for their infidelities, but their relatives in exile will be shown mercy in their captivity and will be returned to the land.

This promise is vividly if partially fulfilled in Hezekiah's Passover. Although many in the north mocked and scoffed at his invitation, many "humbled themselves" and came to Jerusalem, joining many in Judah to form "a very great assembly [qāhāl]" (2 Chr. 30:10–13). Hezekiah had adopted an accommodationist provision in the Mosaic law that allows for celebrating the Passover one month late in cases where people are ritually unclean or on a journey (Num. 9:9–14). It was a pastoral gesture intended to signify God's mercy and his willingness to accommodate the people in their weakness (Eves 1992: 201–15). Still, many from the north came to the feast without having properly purified themselves.

Hezekiah's response is again to make intercession, to pray that "atonement be made" (kipper) by "the good LORD" for "every one who sets his heart to seek God, the LORD the God of his fathers" (2 Chr. 30:18–19; cf. Exod. 32:31). Hezekiah is acting as the faithful son of David, the new Solomon, putting into practice the "programmatic divine statement" (Williamson 1982: 225–26, 368, 370) concerning repentance and forgiveness quoted before: "If my people who are called by my name humble themselves, and pray and seek my face, and turn from their wicked ways, then I will hear from heaven, and will forgive their sin and heal their land" (2 Chr. 7:14). There is a deliberate quoting from this statement throughout the account of Hezekiah's Passover. And verbs of repentance figure prominently in the account. The king had urged the northerners to "turn" to God, and they had "humbled themselves" to come to the feast (30:6, 9, 11). Hezekiah "prayed" that those who "seek" God would find pardon (30:18–19). And remarkably, God "heard" Hezekiah's prayer and "healed" the people (30:20).

The result is a Passover the likes of which had not been seen in Jerusalem "since the time of Solomon, the son of David king of Israel" (30:26). The Chronicler presents Hezekiah's Passover as a kind of sacrament of the united kingdom intended by God. It is a sign of the unity of all the tribes under the Davidic king as well as the efficacious means or instrument by which that unity is brought about: "The whole assembly [kōl qāhāl] of Judah, and the priests and the Levites, and the whole assembly [kōl qāhāl] that came out of Israel, and the sojourners [gērîm] who came out of the land of Israel, and the sojourners [gērîm] who dwelt in Judah, rejoiced" (30:25).

In Hezekiah's Passover we see the healing of the land promised by God; it is an anticipation of a greater and definitive healing hoped for by the people of his day. In this moment the breach between north and south has been bridged. The sons of Israel are once more united in "service" ('ăbōdâ) to the Lord their God (30:8), which is their vocation as his firstborn, his chosen people, a kingdom of priests. The Chronicler is urging his contemporaries, divided from their children and brethren still in exile (30:9), to renew their own observance of the Passover and, like Hezekiah, to celebrate it in the spirit of "the law of Moses the man of God" (30:16).

In the temple their voice of humble prayer and seeking will be heard in God's "holy habitation in heaven" (30:27). In the Passover they will see unleashed the mighty power of God. In Hezekiah's Passover they are to see that the blood of the lamb sprinkled on the altar (30:16), offered in place of God's firstborn, can turn away God's fierce covenant anger, atone for sins, and bring them peace and a renewal of their covenant with God.

### Humility and Restoration: Unexpected Lessons of an Evil King

The imagery of sevens—seven thousand sheep for the offerings, the keeping of the seven-day feast, and the decision to keep it for a subsequent seven days—alerts us again to the cosmic or salvation-historical significance of Hezekiah's Passover. There is even an anticipation of the universal significance of the temple liturgy and the Passover. Israel and Judah are joined by "foreigners" (gērîm), a gesture toward Solomon's promise that the temple would be a house of prayer for all people (6:32–33) and an evocation of God's promise to bless the nations.

Again and again, even the good kings stumble, and for every new creation there is an almost immediate fall into unfaithfulness. This is true especially in the twilight of the Davidic kingdom. The Chronicler gives a twist on this theme in his final royal portraits. Although Hezekiah succumbs to a proud heart and brings wrath upon himself and the kingdom, he "humbles" himself and finds mercy (32:25–26). Again we see the Chronicler holding Hezekiah up as a model for the Chronicler's contemporaries.

This model of repentance is writ large in the Chronicler's account of Hezekiah's son and successor, Manasseh. The Chronicler's portrait of Manasseh may be his most startling reinterpretation of the historical record. In 2 Kgs. 21:1–18, Manasseh's fifty-five-year reign is one of unrelenting wickedness. His sins—sorcery, idolatry, and child sacrifice among them—are portrayed as the decisive factor in bringing destruction upon Israel and the trauma of the exile. In Chronicles, by contrast, Manasseh becomes almost a figure of the exiled people and a paradigm for their experience.

Manasseh is depicted following the restoration program envisioned in 2 Chr. 7:14: "When he was in distress he sought the face of the LORD his God[2] and humbled himself greatly before the God of his fathers. He prayed to God, and God received his entreaty and heard his supplication and brought him again to Jerusalem into his kingdom. Then Manasseh knew that the LORD was

---

2. The RSV has "entreated the favor of the LORD his God," but the Hebrew idiom here is the Chronicler's familiar "sought the face of the LORD his God."

God" (33:12–13). The message is as blunt as it is hopeful. Even the greatest of sinners—one who did more evil than the nations that Israel had conquered in the promised land—even this one could receive forgiveness, reconciliation, and restoration to the land (Endres 2007: 6–12; Abadie 2003). True to form, however, the pattern of repentance ends with Manasseh. His son Amon "did not humble himself before the LORD, as Manasseh his father had humbled himself." The result is guilt upon more guilt until his own people rise up to kill him (33:23–25).

### The Last Good King: Josiah the Reformer

Amon the wicked is followed by his son Josiah the good. As Hezekiah is described as a new Solomon, the Chronicler describes Josiah in a similar way. He is an authentic son of David. When he was "yet a boy, he began to seek [dāraš] the God of David his father," and he "walked in the ways of David his father" (34:2–3). As with his portrait of Hezekiah, the Chronicler's portrayal of Josiah is overwhelmingly cultic, focusing on Josiah as an authoritative religious and liturgical reformer. He is a "seeker" after God and is zealous for the temple and the organization of the Levitical ministry and liturgy. Josiah destroys the rival sites of idolatry "throughout all the land of Israel" (34:7)—a reference to the northern and southern tribal territories once united under David, Solomon, and Hezekiah (1 Chr. 22:2; 2 Chr. 2:17; 30:25; 34:33; Japhet 1993: 1023–24; Williamson 1977: 131).

Josiah's reign picks up where Hezekiah's left off and in many ways continues in the long shadow of Hezekiah. Comparing the Chronicler's account to that of Josiah found in 2 Kings, Williamson rightly concludes: "Josiah is not so significant a monarch overall for the Chronicler as he is for the earlier historian. Much that he records is now to be understood as recapitulation of Hezekiah's work, who stands out as the real innovator in Chronicles" (1982: 396).

The earlier biblical history explains Josiah's reform and renewal efforts as a response to finding "the book of the law" in the temple. But for the Chronicler, Josiah was a seeker after God from an early age. His reforms had already begun before the discovery was made. In fact, it was because he had commanded the restoration of the temple that the priest Hilkiah "found the book of the law of the LORD given through Moses" (2 Chr. 34:15). Scholars have long debated the contents of the book that Hilkiah found. Interpretive options range from the entire Pentateuch to a portion of Deuteronomy (Deut. 29:21; 30:10; 31:26; cf. Josh. 1:8; 8:31, 34; 23:6; 24:26). It is impossible to know with certainty (Williamson 1982: 402; Japhet 1993: 1030).

In any event, what is most important is Josiah's response. He receives this book as the word of God, and it leads him to repentance and to seek prophetic insight and guidance so as to better understand it and order the life of the kingdom by its precepts. *Tôrâ* is important in the Chronicler's account of the monarchy; here Josiah is held up as a model not only for Davidic kings but also for all the faithful of the Chronicler's generation.

He gathers "all the people both great and small" (2 Chr. 34:30) in the temple to hear the law read and to renew their covenant with God. The scene is decidedly reminiscent of Moses's gathering of the people to hear the law at Sinai. There too the elders are present, together with all the people (2 Chr. 34:29; Exod. 24:1). Moses "read . . . in the[ir] hearing" the "book of the covenant." So Josiah "read in their hearing all the words of the book of the covenant" (2 Chr. 34:30; Exod. 24:7). At both Sinai and Jerusalem, the people enter into a covenant "to do all the words" they have heard (2 Chr. 34:31; Exod. 24:3, 7). And the Chronicler tells us that "all . . . in Israel serve[d] the LORD their God" and did not depart from this covenant for as long as Josiah was king (2 Chr. 34:33).

With the covenant reestablished and the law once more enshrined as the heart of kingdom spirituality, morality, and community life, Chronicles jumps to Josiah's Passover, said to be held in the eighteenth year of his reign (35:19). This will be the final account of temple worship in Chronicles; indeed the temple will be destroyed in the very next chapter (36:19). The Passover is preceded by Josiah's address to the Levites.

Appropriately, Josiah's concerns are understated and focused on the liturgy. There is no valedictory tone, as in David's final speeches or in Solomon's dedication of the temple. The hour is too late for oratory. Josiah is depicted as encouraging the priests and refining the cultic duties of the Levites to ensure the faithful celebration of the feast. The scene on some level evokes Solomon's installation of the ark in the temple. Josiah refers to it as "the holy ark," an expression not found anywhere else in the Bible (35:3; Johnstone 1997: 2.247). The extraordinary number of animal sacrifices heightens the sense that this is the last true liturgy of the kingdom. And the Chronicler concludes: "No passover like it had been kept in Israel since the days of Samuel the prophet; none of the kings of Israel had kept such a passover as was kept by Josiah, and the priests and the Levites, and all Judah and Israel" (35:18).

Immediately following this glorious Passover, Josiah's faith is tested. Without provocation, Josiah decides to engage the Egyptian Pharaoh Neco in battle—despite assurances from Neco that he is not marching against Judah. The scene is filled with ironies. The pharaoh of Egypt, the original mortal enemy of Israel, here plays the part of God's messenger: "Cease opposing God, who is with me, lest he destroy [*šāḥat*] you" (35:21). Neco's warning deliberately evokes the night of the first Passover. Indeed, the Passover was intended to protect Israel from the "destroyer" (*mašḥît*) sent by God to slay all the firstborn in Egypt (Exod. 12:23). But Josiah does "not listen to the words of Neco from the mouth of God," and he is destroyed in the battle he had no reason to fight (2 Chr. 35:22).

It is a swift, anticlimactic, and disconcerting ending to the reign of a good king and true son of David. The king who more than any other is associated with the word of God and who was so zealous for its interpretation is struck down for failing to heed that word.

### From Babylon to Persia: Exile and Restoration

Josiah's death begins the final descent of the kingdom into ruin. Things unravel quickly and almost methodically from there in the Chronicler's narrative. Josiah will be the last Davidic king to be buried in Jerusalem. The final four, in short order, are carried off into exile. The exodus typology evident from the initial days of the divided kingdom continues on through the kingdom's destruction. As the first post-Solomonic king, Rehoboam, is described as a pharaoh-like figure, the last is described in terms that evoke not only the pharaoh of the exodus but also the unfaithfulness of the golden-calf generation. Zedekiah "stiffened his neck and hardened his heart"—a sad but fitting symbol of the people's abnegation of their status as God's firstborn and elect people and their return to the bondage of sin and idolatry (36:13–14).

The Chronicler issues his verdict on the kingdom in summary terms drawn in part from the prophecies of Jeremiah. The Lord had "persistently sent" them messengers, but the people had rejected his compassion, until there was now "no remedy" (lit., "no healing"; 36:15–16; cf. Jer. 7:25; 14:19; 25:3–4; 29:19). Judgment is swift and summary, in marked contrast to the more elaborate descriptions elsewhere in the biblical record (2 Kgs. 24–25; Jer. 39:1–10; 52:3–30; Kalimi 2005: 117–18). But the Chronicler does not fail to convey the utter destruction: young and old are killed indiscriminately, the holy vessels and temple treasures are looted, the temple is burned, and the people are carried into exile. In the same breath that he mentions the exile, the Chronicler hints at restoration and what it all means in the divine plan for Israel: "He took [the people] into exile in Babylon . . . until the establishment of the kingdom of Persia, to fulfil the word of the LORD by the mouth of Jeremiah, until the land had enjoyed its sabbaths. All the days that it lay desolate it kept sabbath, to fulfil seventy years" (2 Chr. 36:20–21).

The exile and restoration are here almost telescoped into a single movement. According to this theological interpretation, Judah's destruction and the carrying off of the people into exile were the fulfillment of one of Jeremiah's prophecies. Jeremiah had foretold that the "whole land" would be laid waste and that the people would serve the king of Babylon for seventy years, until Babylon was overthrown and the people were brought back home (Jer. 25:11–12; 29:10). The Chronicler links this prophecy with a warning text found in Leviticus that also envisions the people's punishment by exile for violating the law of the Sabbath. To "execute vengeance for the covenant," God would cause the people to be "scatter[ed] . . . among the nations." This

makes the land a "desolation," so that the land would finally "enjoy its sabbaths." In this way the people make amends for their iniquity in not following
the Sabbath provisions of the law (Lev. 26:25, 32–35, 43). Thus the Chronicler
suggests that the exile was not only a punishment for Israel's sin, but also a
time of divinely imposed Sabbath rest for the land.

Despite the Chronicler's inner-biblical reference points, his meaning in
this enigmatic pronouncement remains vigorously contested (De Vries 1986;
Applegate 1997: 97–100; Jonker 2008). Much of the scholarly discussion centers
on possible chronologies and timetables. The return from exile began in 538
BC, only forty-eight years after the fall of Jerusalem. It is possible that the
Chronicler is counting seventy years from the initial conquest of Judah in 605
BC to the return of 538 BC. Or he may be measuring the duration between the
destruction of Solomon's temple in 586 BC and the dedication of the second
temple in 515 BC. Williamson suggests that adding up the reigns of the kings
in Chronicles from David to Zedekiah gives a total of 474 years; allowing for
some uncertainty in the length of the reign of Saul, Israel's first king, "it will
be seen that the figures could coincide almost exactly" (1982: 418).

Plausible and intriguing speculations merit further reflection. Yet at the end
of the Chronicler's work, as throughout, he is writing not only chronology but
also prophetic historiography; he is not only documenting Israel's antiquity but
also illuminating that history with a theological interpretation. Thus it seems
unlikely that his point here, at the very climax of his work, is to advance some
numerological symbolism. All that we know about the Chronicler suggests
that for him the lessons of history and the ways of God cannot be reduced
in this way. Indeed, Jeremiah's original "seventy years" (Jer. 25:11) may have
been simply a metaphor for the lifetime of a person (Ps. 90:10) or two or three
generations (Job 42:16).

The meaning of "seventy years" lies in the assertion that the historical
events of the monarchy—including the destruction of the kingdom and the
exile—unfolded to "fulfil the word of the LORD." The Chronicler emphasizes
this in his very next verse, repeating that the "proclamation" of King Cyrus
of Persia was made in order "that the word of the LORD by the mouth of Jeremiah might be accomplished" (2 Chr. 36:22). The word "proclamation" here
is the same used to describe Hezekiah's invitation for the scattered tribes to
come home and celebrate the Passover at Jerusalem (30:5). What word from
Jeremiah does he refer to here? Presumably, the prophecy of the seventy years
and the end of the exile. How does Cyrus's proclamation "accomplish" that
word? To answer these questions requires understanding better what exactly
Jeremiah prophesied concerning the exile.

Jeremiah's promise to the house of Judah and the house of Israel is actually
twofold. First is the promise concerning the exile, which sounds remarkably
like the divine assurances resounded throughout the Chronicler's history: if the
people pray to the Lord and seek him with all their heart, they will be found

by him, and he will gather them from all the nations and bring them home
(Jer. 29:10–14; cf. 1 Chr. 28:9; 2 Chr. 7:14; 15:2). However, there is much more
to Jeremiah's promise that is rooted in God's concern for his covenant with
David. Jeremiah announces that the return from exile will be accompanied
by the raising up of a "righteous Branch" for David, a new son of David to
reign as king (Jer. 23:3–6; 33:14–16). This aspect of the promise is associated
with a new exodus motif:

> Therefore, behold, the days are coming, says the LORD, when men shall no longer
> say, "As the LORD lives who brought up the people of Israel out of the land of
> Egypt," but "As the LORD lives who brought up and led the descendants of the
> house of Israel out of the north country and out of all the countries where he
> had driven them." Then they shall dwell in their own land. (Jer. 23:7–8)

The Davidic-covenant dimension of Jeremiah's prophecy is closely associated
with Judah, Jerusalem, and the temple. Jeremiah foresees the day when the
"desolate" streets of Jerusalem will once again be filled with the voices of those
who sing and bring their "sacrifices of praises / thanksgiving" the *tôdât*, to the
house of the Lord. And he foresees them singing the song that is so important
to the Chronicler's understanding of the temple liturgy: "Give thanks to the
LORD of hosts, for the LORD is good, for his steadfast love endures for ever!"
(Jer. 33:10–11; cf. 1 Chr. 16:34, 41; 2 Chr. 5:13; 7:3, 6; 20:21).

The word of the Lord to Jeremiah concerning the exile included the promise
of a new temple, a new "house" at Jerusalem in Judah. This is the immediate
subject of Cyrus's edict, and it suggests that the Chronicler must have had this
larger vision of Jeremiah's prophecy in mind in saying that Cyrus's proclamation was to "accomplish" the word spoken to Jeremiah. Much is made of the
Chronicler's concluding his work with an abbreviated version of Cyrus's edict
as found in the opening verses of Ezra (1:2–4). But he has done more than
append Cyrus's words to make a neat ending to his book. The Chronicler's
editing here, as throughout his work, is deliberate. His editing focuses Cyrus's
words on the key promise of the Davidic covenant—the building of a house
for God in Jerusalem—and the imperative that the people join themselves to
this effort (1 Chr. 17:10–12; 22:6, 10, 19; 28:6, 10; 2 Chr. 6:9–10).

The promise to David was, however, about more than the temple. God
promised that David's son would build him a house. But God also promised
that he himself would build a "house" (*bayit*) for David, a royal dynasty that
would be established forever (1 Chr. 17:10–14). In the divine word given to
Jeremiah, the "Branch" to spring forth from David is to fulfill God's promise
to build David a house. God tells Jeremiah that there will always be a son of
David to reign on his throne over the house of Israel. In addition, God's word
to Jeremiah takes the covenant promises to the house of David and links them
with his covenant establishing the Levitical priesthood. This is presumably a

reference to the incidents after the golden calf (Exod. 32:25–29) and at Baal-peor (Num. 25:10–12). What is more, God equates these covenant promises with his covenant in creation, an image that not only implies the permanence of his covenant, but also its centrality to his plan for history and creation:

> The word of the LORD came to Jeremiah: . . . "Behold, the days are coming, says the LORD, when I will fulfil the promise I made to the house of Israel and the house of Judah. In those days and at that time I will cause a righteous Branch to spring forth for David; and he shall execute justice and righteousness in the land. In those days Judah will be saved and Jerusalem will dwell securely. . . .
> "For thus says the LORD: David shall never lack a man to sit on the throne of the house of Israel, and the Levitical priests shall never lack a man in my presence to offer burnt offerings, to burn cereal offerings, and to make sacrifices for ever."
> The word of the LORD came to Jeremiah: "Thus says the LORD: If you can break my covenant with the day and my covenant with the night, so that day and night will not come at their appointed time, then also my covenant with David my servant may be broken, so that he shall not have a son to reign on his throne, and my covenant with the Levitical priests my ministers. As the host of heaven cannot be numbered and the sands of the sea cannot be measured, so I will multiply the descendants of David my servant, and the Levitical priests who minister to me."
> The word of the LORD came to Jeremiah: . . . "Thus says the LORD: If I have not established my covenant with day and night and the ordinances of heaven and earth, then I will reject the descendants of Jacob and David my servant and will not choose one of his descendants to rule over the seed of Abraham, Isaac, and Jacob. For I will restore their fortunes, and will have mercy upon them." (Jer. 33:1, 14–23, 25–26)

Given the Chronicler's profound concern for the Davidic covenant and the Levitical priesthood and ministry, it is hard to imagine that he did not have these words of Jeremiah in mind when he was composing the final verses of his work (but see Murray 1993: 75–79). Perhaps this partly explains his preoccupation with the Levites during the reign of his last good king, Josiah. In any event, what is beyond dispute is that "the word of the LORD by the mouth of Jeremiah" includes far more than the people's returning to the land. It means the fulfillment of a complex of promises associated with the Davidic covenant and the kingdom founded on that covenant.

The deeper meaning and implications of his edict perhaps escaped the great Cyrus, although the Persian king appears to understand that he is playing a part in salvation history. He does invoke Israel's God as "the God of heaven" and recognizes God's sovereignty not only over creation but also over "all the kingdoms of the earth" (2 Chr. 36:23). The Chronicler abridged Ezra's account of Cyrus's edict in order to stress God's lordship over all creation and history. In Ezra 1:3, Cyrus speaks of "the LORD, the God of Israel—he is the God who is in Jerusalem." Kalimi recognizes that the effect of this language in

Ezra is to reduce the Israelites' God to be a "*local* deity rather than a universal one" (2005: 152–53).

For the original readers or hearers of the Chronicler's prophetic historiography, Cyrus's call to rebuild "the house at Jerusalem" would have elicited expectations going far beyond the building of a new temple. Isaiah evidenced this when he wrote of Cyrus in Davidic and messianic terms as God's "anointed" and his "shepherd" (Isa. 44:28–45:7; Braun 2003). The Chronicler does not present Cyrus as a messiah. He is sketched briefly as an instrument, as the appointed servant of God's covenant will. Cyrus is God's messenger, the latest of a series of foreign kings and queens who have recognized Israel's God as the true God and come to serve him. The Cyrus vignette is a reminder of the Creator's dominion over nations and individuals. As he was able to harden the heart of Pharaoh, so also the Lord is able to open the heart of Cyrus to the stirrings of his Spirit.

It is appropriate, then, that this work ends with the words of a non-Israelite's acting as God's agent in bringing about God's plans for his chosen people and for history: "The LORD, the God of heaven, . . . has charged me to build him a house at Jerusalem, which is in Judah. Whoever is among you of all his people, may the LORD his God be with him. Let him go up" (2 Chr. 36:23).

Cyrus has the last word in Chronicles, but his word indicates that it is God who has the last word in history. Cyrus's edict marks a new day dawning for God's chosen people. The land has been healed, as God had promised it would be. The exile has been revealed as a chastisement for the people's unfaithfulness to their covenant with the God of their fathers. The exile marked the purgation and purification of the people and the land, which had suffered pollution and abominations at the hands of kings, priests, and people who had been "exceedingly unfaithful" (36:14). In its desolation, the land was finally set at rest. The exile marked a new Sabbath, heralding the dawn of a new creation. With the restoration of the people, their going up to Judah and Jerusalem, God is once more filling the world, placing his people in his new creation, the children of Abraham, whom he has promised will be multiplied past all numbering.

From Adam to the end of the exile, the Chronicler has shown that history is governed by God according to his mercy and justice and guided by his faithfulness to his covenants, first with Abraham, again with Moses and Israel, and finally with David. The exile has been part of a larger divine pedagogy, a pattern by which God has been fathering his firstborn since the days of the exodus. The message for his first audience is that God continues, through the exile and the frustrations of the partial restoration, to test his people through their adversity, through all the inevitable wounds they inflict upon themselves by their weakness and unfaithfulness.

Chronicles ends on a message of profound hope—that God can draw good out of evil (Gen. 50:20; Japhet 1993: 656), that his mercy can be found in the temple. Beneath the passing of monarchs and empires, God remains in charge of history. The future is in his hands (Dirksen 1999: 50). The guarantee of Israel's future is God's faithfulness to his covenant, sworn to Abraham on Mount Moriah and renewed in his promise to David. The nature of God in Chronicles is that he is gracious and merciful, "keeping covenant and showing steadfast love," as Solomon put it in his great temple prayer (2 Chr. 6:14). That prayer ended with a solemn appeal for God to stay true to the covenant he had made with David: "O LORD God, do not turn away the face of thy anointed one! Remember thy steadfast love for David thy servant!" (6:42).

God's steadfast love for David, *ḥasdê dāwîd*, is shown by the Chronicler to be the true meaning of history (21:7; Newsome 1975: 208). This expression of covenant faithfulness, *ḥasdê dāwîd*, is found in only one other place in the Bible, in a prophecy in which Isaiah calls the exiles to return to the Lord and to seek him while he still may be found. For Isaiah, God's everlasting covenant, his *ḥasdê dāwîd*, is not only for David and his royal line, but also for all Israel (Isa. 55:3–7).

God's steadfast love for David is an invitation and a vocation to the people—to join him in his mighty work of salvation and blessing, his great plan for history (Selman 1999: 46; but see Kalimi 2005: 148–49n17). The children of Abraham, under the Davidic king, are to be his witnesses to the nations, for the sake of his covenant purposes, which is to bless the nations.

In the final pages of Chronicles there is a sense that God's promised deliverance, this new exodus and new creation, has already begun with the ascension of King Cyrus of Persia. Chronicles ends on the same note as Genesis, with the promise of a divine restoration from exile. Genesis ends with the people Israel, represented by Israel's son Joseph, stranded in Egypt, far from the land promised to Abraham. On his deathbed, Joseph promises that God "will visit" (*pqd*) his people. The Chronicler puts similar language into the mouth of Cyrus, who proclaims that God has "charged" (*pqd*) him to rebuild the temple. As Joseph asks the Israelites to "carry up" (*'lh*) his bones from Egypt when they are delivered into the promised land (Gen. 50:25), Cyrus calls upon God's people to "go up" (*'lh*) from Babylon to Jerusalem (Johnstone 1998: 64). There is no mistaking the air of expectation at the conclusion of Chronicles, an air of confident hope for the fulfillment of God's covenant promises to Abraham, renewed in the everlasting covenant made with David. The Chronicler knows the history he has written is ongoing, that God's creation is *in statu viae*, in a state of journeying toward the perfection and fulfillment for which it was created.

## Christian Interpretation

In many ways the authors of the New Testament lived under conditions similar to those in the Chronicler's audience—trying to keep the faith while living in "exile" as believers in the true God, yet under the domination of a foreign power and its gods. The Chronicler helps us to grasp the meaning of the New Testament, especially the Apocalypse of John, which shows the church in its essence—as a divine mystery and not just an institution, as a heavenly kingdom and not only an earthly body. The Chronicler's liturgical worldview, which builds to the dedication of the temple and concludes with a Passover celebration in the renewed Davidic kingdom, also anticipates the New Testament, where the church, through its participation in the heavenly liturgy, will be delivered from a succession of earthly empires that persecute it.

There is still much that we can learn from Chronicles about the church as it was understood by Christ and the New Testament. Brueggemann says: "The most consistently *ecclesiological* presentation of Davidic hope in the Old Testament is that of the Chronicler" (1985: 99). Brown sees quite clearly the close relationship between the Davidic kingdom and the church: "The Kingdom established by David was a political institution to be sure, but one with enormous religious attachments (priesthood, Temple, sacrifice, prophecy). . . . It is the closest parallel to the Church" (1992: 5–6).

In addition, the renewal of the Davidic kingdom in Chronicles is symbolized by the reconstitutions of the *qāhāl* under kings Hezekiah and Josiah and their celebration of the Passover (2 Chr. 30, 35), as the climax of the new covenant is the institution of the new Passover, the Eucharist.

The Chronicler advances a kingdom ecclesiology in which the kingdom on earth is a sacrament of the kingdom of God. This message is intended to speak to his audience in the years after the exile. Although there is no Davidic king seated on an earthly throne, the kingdom is nonetheless real. In the restored temple liturgy, the people have the divine kingdom made manifest on earth in its sacramental and liturgical expression. Whether there is an earthly ruler who is Jewish and Davidic, or whether the world is governed by a Gentile, such as King Cyrus, nevertheless in the rebuilt and rededicated Jerusalem temple, Israel will glimpse on earth its true king, who reigns in heaven. Living in a land occupied by an external foe, the task is to trust in the promises of God to David and to apply themselves to right worship and to giving glory to the God of Israel, in the new house they are to build in Jerusalem (36:23).

In all of this, we have the seeds of an alternative biblical theology of empire, one that intends to instruct Israel on how to live in the new postexilic environment, how to worship the true God while still living under the domination of a foreign power. Schniedewind observes that the prophetic speeches in Chronicles, while ostensibly speaking to the historical events being recounted, are also addressed homiletically to the Chronicler's audience (1997: 222–23). Thus, the prophet Shemaiah explains to Rehoboam why God permitted Israel's subjugation to King Shishak in terms that could apply to the entire exilic generation: "so that they may know the difference between serving me and serving the kingdoms of the world" (12:7–8, trans. from Schniedewind 1997: 222).

The Chronicler's prophetic historiography teaches a morality of exile and reflects what E. Sanders calls "restoration eschatology" (1985: 77; also N. Wright 1992: 269–72). The Chronicler's audience is, in a very real sense, still in exile, even though the people have been freed from Babylon and have returned to the land. They need to learn how to keep faith in exile, how to serve God while still in captivity to the kingdoms of the world, awaiting the restoration of the kingdom of David and the temple.

The Chronicler's prophetic historiography thus points to its own fulfillment; the story that the Chronicler tells is not yet complete. This sense of a history awaiting its own fulfillment is what makes Chronicles such fertile ground for New Testament studies. To date, the work has not received the kind of attention from New Testament scholars that it deserves. Indeed, it is no mere coincidence that the Christian canon begins with the genealogy of Matthew 1:1–17, just as Chronicles began with a genealogy; what better way for the first editors of the Christian canon to emphasize the continuity between the Old and New Testaments and the unity of the economy of salvation from Adam to Jesus. The Chronicler also seems to be behind Luke's tracing of Christ's human lineage back to "Adam, the son of God" (Luke 3:38; W. Davies and Allison 1988: 167–88; Fitzmyer 1981: 499–504).

Careful study of certain aspects of Chronicles—the Chronicler's vision of salvation history rooted in creation, his covenantal typology, his treatment of the kingdom of God as a *qāhāl/ekklēsia* and a liturgical empire—can shed great light on Jesus's teaching about kingdom, church, and sacramental liturgy. Indeed, in these and other areas the Chronicler offers us a blueprint that the New Testament church actualizes. With his liturgical and sacramental vision of history, the Chronicler wants to lead his audience to see the "signs of the times," the divine purposes being unfolded in everyday reality. He is preparing his readers, those who have returned to Jerusalem and those still in the Diaspora, to recognize these signs and to prepare their hearts to live as a royal and priestly people, the agents through whom God will bless all nations.

# Works Cited

Abadie, Philippe. 2003. "From the Impious Manasseh (2 Kings 21) to the Convert Manasseh (2 Chronicles 33): Theological Rewriting by Chronicler." Pp. 89–104 in *The Chronicler as Theologian: Essays in Honor of Ralph W. Klein.* Edited by M. Patrick Graham, Steven L. McKenzie, and Gary N. Knoppers. Journal for the Study of the Old Testament Supplement 371. New York: T&T Clark.

Ackroyd, Peter R. 1991. *The Chronicler in His Age.* Journal for the Study of the Old Testament Supplement 101. Sheffield: JSOT Press.

Allen, Leslie C. 1988. "Kerygmatic Units in 1 and 2 Chronicles." *Journal for the Study of the Old Testament* 41:21–36.

———. 2003. "Aspects of Generational Commitment and Challenge in Chronicles." Pp. 123–32 in *The Chronicler as Theologian: Essays in Honor of Ralph W. Klein.* Edited by M. Patrick Graham, Steven L. McKenzie, and Gary N. Knoppers. Journal for the Study of the Old Testament Supplement 371. New York: T&T Clark.

Allison, Dale C. 1993. *The New Moses: A Matthean Typology.* Minneapolis: Fortress.

Anderson, Gary A. 1991. "The Praise of God as a Cultic Event." Pp. 15–33 in *Priesthood and Cult in Ancient Israel.* Edited by Gary A. Anderson and Saul M. Olyan. Journal for the Study of the Old Testament Supplement 125. Sheffield: JSOT Press.

———. 2001. *The Genesis of Perfection: Adam and Eve in Jewish and Christian Imagination.* Louisville: Westminster John Knox.

Andreasen, Niels-Erik. 1983. "The Role of the Queen Mother in Israelite Society." *Catholic Biblical Quarterly* 45:179–94.

Applegate, John. 1997. "Jeremiah and the Seventy Years in the Hebrew Bible: Inner-Biblical Reflections on the Prophet and His Prophecy." Pp. 91–110 in *The Book of Jeremiah and Its Reception.* Edited by A. H. W. Curtis and T. Römer. Leuven: Leuven University Press.

ArtScroll. 1987. *1 Chronicles: A New Translation with a Commentary Anthologized from Talmudic, Midrashic, and Rabbinic Sources.* Translated by Moshe Eisemann. ArtScroll Tanach Series. Brooklyn, NY: Mesorah.

Balentine, Samuel E. 1999. *The Torah's Vision of Worship.* Minneapolis: Fortress.

193

Barber, Michael. 2001. *Singing in the Reign: The Psalms and the Liturgy of God's Kingdom*. Steubenville, OH: Emmaus Road.

Batto, Bernard F. 2004. "The Divine Sovereign: The Image of God in the Priestly Creation Account." Pp. 143–63 in *David and Zion: Biblical Studies in Honor of J. J. M. Roberts*. Edited by Bernard F. Batto and Kathryn L. Roberts. Winona Lake, IN: Eisenbrauns.

Beale, G. K. 1999. *The Book of Revelation: A Commentary on the Greek Text*. New International Greek Testament Commentary. Grand Rapids: Eerdmans.

———. 2004. *The Temple and the Church's Mission: A Biblical Theology of the Dwelling of God*. New Studies in Biblical Theology 17. Downers Grove, IL: InterVarsity.

Beecher, Willis. 1975. *The Prophets and the Promise*. Reprinted, Grand Rapids: Baker (orig., 1905).

Beentjes, Pancratius C. 2001. "Prophets in the Book of Chronicles." Pp. 45–53 in *The Elusive Prophet: The Prophet as a Historical Person, Literary Character, and Anonymous Artist*. Edited by Johannes C. de Moor. Oudtestamentische Studiën 45. Leiden: Brill.

———. 2006. "Israel's Earlier History as Presented in the Book of Chronicles." Pp. 57–76 in *Deuterocanonical and Cognate Literature Yearbook 2006: History and Identity; How Israel's Later Authors Viewed Its Earlier History*. Edited by Núria Calduch-Benages and Jan Liesen. New York: de Gruyter.

Begg, Christopher T. 1982. "'Seeking Yahweh' and the Purpose of Chronicles." *Louvain Studies* 9:128–41.

———. 2003. "The Ark in Chronicles." Pp. 133–45 in *The Chronicler as Theologian: Essays in Honor of Ralph W. Klein*. Edited by M. Patrick Graham, Steven L. McKenzie, and Gary N. Knoppers. Journal for the Study of the Old Testament Supplement 371. New York: T&T Clark.

Berger, Yitzhak, ed. 2007. *The Commentary of Rabbi David Kimhi* [Kimchi] *to Chronicles: A Translation with Introduction and Supercommentary*. Brown Judaic Studies 345. Providence: Brown University Press.

Bergsma, John S. 2009. "The Persian Period as Penitential Era: The 'Exegetical Logic' of Daniel 9:1–27." Pp. 50–64 in *Exile and Restoration Revisited: Essays on the Babylonian and Persian Period in Memory of Peter R. Ackroyd*. Edited by Gary N. Knoppers, Lester L. Grabbe, and Deirdre N. Fulton. Library of Second Temple Studies 73. London: T&T Clark.

Berlin, Adele, and Marc Zvi Brettler, eds. 2004. *The Jewish Study Bible: Jewish Publication Society Tanakh Translation*. New York: Oxford University Press.

Blenkinsopp, Joseph. 1976. "The Structure of P." *Catholic Biblical Quarterly* 28:275–92.

Braun, Roddy L. 1976. "Solomon, the Chosen Temple Builder: The Significance of 1 Chronicles 22, 28, and 29 for the Theology of Chronicles." *Journal of Biblical Literature* 95:581–90.

———. 2003. "Cyrus in Second and Third Isaiah, Chronicles, Ezra and Nehemiah." Pp. 146–64 in *The Chronicler as Theologian: Essays in Honor of Ralph W. Klein*. Edited by M. Patrick Graham, Steven L. McKenzie, and Gary N. Knoppers. Journal for the Study of the Old Testament Supplement 371. New York: T&T Clark.

Brooks, Simcha Shalom. 2005. "From Gibeon to Gibeah: High Place of the Kingdom." Pp. 40–59 in *Temple and Worship in Biblical Israel*. Edited by John Day. Library of Hebrew Bible/Old Testament Studies 422. London: T&T Clark.

Brown, Raymond L. 1992. "Communicating the Divine and Human in Scripture."
  *Origins* 22.1 (May 14): 5–6.
Brueggemann, Walter. 1970. "Of the Same Flesh and Bone (Gn 2,23a)." *Catholic
  Biblical Quarterly* 32:532–42.
———. 1985. *David's Truth in Israel's Imagination and Memory*. Philadelphia: Fortress.
Bultmann, Rudolf. 1951–55. *Theology of the New Testament*. 2 vols. Translated by
  Kendrick Grobel. New York: Scribner.
Callender, Dexter E., Jr. 2000. *Adam in Myth and History: Ancient Israelite Perspec-
  tives on the Primal Human*. Winona Lake, IN: Eisenbrauns.
Cassuto, Umberto. 1973. *Bible*. Vol. 1 of *Biblical and Oriental Studies*. Jerusalem:
  Magnes.
Chae, Young S. 2006. *Jesus as the Eschatological Davidic Shepherd: Studies in the
  Old Testament, Second Temple Judaism, and in the Gospel of Matthew*. Wissen-
  schaftliche Untersuchungen zum Neuen Testament 2/216. Tübingen: Mohr-Siebeck.
Clements, R. E. 1967. *Abraham and David: Genesis XV and Its Meaning for Israelite
  Tradition*. Naperville, IL: Allenson.
Clifford, Richard J. 1972. *The Cosmic Mountain in Canaan and the Old Testament*.
  Harvard Semitic Monograph 4. Cambridge, MA: Harvard University Press.
Clines, David J. A. 1998. "Humanity as the Image of God." Pp. 447–97 in vol. 2 of
  *On the Way to the Postmodern: Old Testament Essays, 1967–1998*. Journal for the
  Study of the Old Testament Supplement 293. Sheffield: Sheffield Academic Press.
Cohen, Jeremy. 1989. *"Be Fertile and Increase, Fill the Earth and Master It": The An-
  cient and Medieval Career of a Biblical Text*. Ithaca, NY: Cornell University Press.
Congar, Yves. 1962. *The Mystery of the Temple: The Manner of God's Presence to
  His Creatures from Genesis to the Apocalypse*. Westminster, MD: Newman.
Cross, Frank Moore. 1998. *From Epic to Canon: History and Literature in Ancient
  Israel*. Baltimore: Johns Hopkins University Press.
Dahl, Nils A. 1966. "The Story of Abraham in Luke-Acts." Pp. 139–58 in *Studies in
  Luke-Acts: Essays Presented in Honor of Paul Schubert*. Edited by Leander E. Keck
  and J. Louis Martyn. Nashville: Abingdon.
Damrosch, David. 1987. *The Narrative Covenant: Transformations in the Growth of
  Biblical Literature*. San Francisco: Harper & Row.
Daniélou, Jean. 1960. *From Shadows to Reality: Studies in the Biblical Typology of
  the Fathers*. Westminster, MD: Newman.
Davies, John A. 2004. *A Royal Priesthood: Literary and Intertextual Perspectives on
  an Image of Israel in Exodus 19:6*. Journal for the Study of the Old Testament
  Supplement 395. London: T&T Clark.
Davies, W. D., and Dale C. Allison Jr. 1988. *Introduction and Commentary on Mat-
  thew i–vii*. Vol. 1 of *A Critical and Exegetical Commentary on the Gospel accord-
  ing to St. Matthew*. International Critical Commentary. Edinburgh: T&T Clark.
Day, Peggy L. 1988. *An Adversary in Heaven: Śāṭān in the Hebrew Bible*. Harvard
  Semitic Monographs 43. Atlanta: Scholars Press.
De Vries, Simon J. 1986. "The Land's Sabbath in 2 Chronicles 36:21." *Proceedings of
  the Eastern Great Lakes and Midwest Biblical Societies* 4:96–103.
———. 1988. "Moses and David as Cult Founders in Chronicles." *Journal of Biblical
  Literature* 107:619–39.

———. 1997. "Festival Ideology in Chronicles." Pp. 104–24 in *Problems in Biblical Theology: Essays in Honor of Rolf Knierim*. Edited by Henry T. C. Sun and Keith L. Eades. Grand Rapids: Eerdmans.

Dillard, Raymond G. 1985. "David's Census: Perspectives on II Samuel 24 and I Chronicles 21." Pp. 94–107 in *Through Christ's Word: A Festschrift for Dr. Philip E. Hughes*. Edited by W. Robert Godfrey and Jesse L. Boyd. Phillipsburg, NJ: P&R.

Dirksen, Piet B. 1999. "The Future in the Book of Chronicles." Pp. 37–51 in *New Heaven and New Earth: Prophecy in the Millennium: Essays in Honor of Anthony Gelston*. Edited by P. J. Harland and C. T. R. Hayward. Vetus Testamentum Supplement 27. Leiden: Brill.

Driscoll, Jeremy. 2009. "Worship in the Spirit of *Logos*: Romans 12:1–2 and the Source and Summit of Christian Life." *Letter and Spirit* 5:77–101.

Duke, Rodney K. 1990. *The Persuasive Appeal of the Chronicler: A Rhetorical Analysis*. Journal for the Study of the Old Testament Supplement 88. Sheffield: Almond.

Dyck, Jonathan E. 1988. *The Theocratic Ideology of the Chronicler*. Leiden: Brill.

Endres, John C. 2007. "The Spiritual Vision of Chronicles: Wholehearted, Joy-Filled Worship of God." *Catholic Biblical Quarterly* 69:1–21.

Eves, Terry L. 1992. "The Role of the Passover in the Book of Chronicles: A Study of 2 Chronicles 30 and 35." PhD diss., Annenberg Research Institute, Philadelphia.

Fensham, F. Charles. 1971. "Father and Son as Terminology for Treaty and Covenant." Pp. 121–35 in *Near Eastern Studies in Honor of William Foxwell Albright*. Edited by Hans Goedicke. Baltimore: Johns Hopkins University Press.

Fishbane, Michael. 1979. *Text and Texture: Close Readings of Selected Biblical Texts*. New York: Schocken.

———. 1985. *Biblical Interpretation in Ancient Israel*. Oxford: Clarendon.

———. 1989. *Garments of the Torah: Essays in Biblical Interpretation*. Bloomington: Indiana University Press.

Fitzmyer, Joseph A. 1981. *The Gospel according to Luke (i–ix)*. Anchor Bible 28. Garden City, NY: Doubleday.

———. 1998. *The Acts of the Apostles*. Anchor Bible 31. New York: Doubleday.

Freedman, David Noel. 1961. "The Chronicler's Purpose." *Catholic Biblical Quarterly* 23:436–42.

Frei, Hans. 1974. *The Eclipse of Biblical Narrative: A Study in Eighteenth and Nineteenth Century Hermeneutics*. New Haven: Yale University Press.

Friedman, Richard E. 1980. "The Tabernacle in the Temple." *Biblical Archeologist* 43:241–48.

Frisch, Amos. 2000. "Jeroboam and the Division of the Kingdom: Mapping Contrasting Biblical Accounts." *Journal of the Ancient Near Eastern Society* 27:15–29.

Gerhardsson, Birger. 1966. *The Testing of God's Son (Matt. 4:1–11 and par.): An Analysis of an Early Christian Midrash*. Coniectanea Biblica New Testament 2. Lund: Gleerup.

Gerleman, Gillis. 1997. "נסה *nsh* Piel 'to test.'" Pp. 741–42 in vol. 2 of *Theological Lexicon of the Old Testament*. Edited by Ernst Jenni and Claus Westermann. Translated by Mark E. Biddle. Peabody, MA: Hendrickson.

Gese, Hartmut. 1981. *Essays on Biblical Theology*. Translated by Keith Crim. Minneapolis: Augsburg.

Gorman, Frank H. 1990. *The Ideology of Ritual: Space, Time, and Status in the Priestly Ritual*. Journal for the Study of the Old Testament Supplement 91. Sheffield: JSOT Press.

Goulder, M. D., and M. L. Sanderson. 1957. "St. Luke's Genesis." *Journal of Theological Studies* 8:12–30.

Grossfeld, Bernard. 1977. "The Targum to Lamentations 2:10." *Journal of Jewish Studies* 28:60–64.

Gunkel, Hermann. 1998. *An Introduction to the Psalms: The Genres of the Religious Lyric of Israel*. Edited by J. Begrich. Translated by J. D. Nogalski. Macon, GA: Mercer University Press.

Guthrie, Harvey H., Jr. 1981. *Theology as Thanksgiving: From Israel's Psalms to the Church's Eucharist*. New York: Seabury.

Hahn, Scott W. 2001. *Hail Holy Queen: The Mother of God in the Word of God*. New York: Doubleday.

———. 2004. *Swear to God: The Promise and Power of the Sacraments*. New York: Doubleday.

———. 2005a. "Covenant in the Old and New Testaments: Some Current Research (1994–2004)." *Currents in Biblical Research* 3:263–92.

———. 2005b. "Kingdom and Church in Luke–Acts: From Davidic Christology to Kingdom Ecclesiology." Pp. 294–326 in *Reading Luke: Interpretation, Reflections, Formation*. Edited by Craig Bartholomew, Joel Green, and Anthony Thiselton. Scripture and Hermeneutics Series 6. Grand Rapids: Zondervan.

———. 2005c. *Letter and Spirit: From Written Text to Living Word in the Liturgy*. New York: Doubleday.

———. 2005d. "Worship in the Word: Toward a Liturgical Hermeneutic." *Letter and Spirit* 1:101–36.

———. 2009a. *Covenant and Communion: The Biblical Theology of Pope Benedict XVI*. Grand Rapids: Brazos.

———. 2009b. *Kinship by Covenant: A Canonical Approach to the Fulfillment of God's Saving Promises*. Anchor Yale Bible Reference Library. New Haven: Yale University Press.

Hahn, Scott W., and Curtis Mitch. 2001. *The Gospel of Luke, with Introduction, Commentary, and Notes*. Ignatius Catholic Study Bible. San Francisco: Ignatius.

Hayward, C. T. R., ed. 1996. *The Jewish Temple: A Non-Biblical Sourcebook*. New York: Routledge.

Hurowitz, Victor Avigdor. 2005. "Yhwh's Exalted House—Aspects of the Design and Symbolism of Solomon's Temple." Pp. 63–110 in *Temple and Worship in Biblical Israel*. Edited by John Day. Library of Hebrew Bible/Old Testament Studies 422. London: T&T Clark.

Ishida, Tomoo. 1977. *The Royal Dynasties in Ancient Israel: A Study on the Formation and Development of Royal-Dynastic Ideology*. Beiheft zur Zeitschrift für die alttestamentliche Wissenschaft 142. New York: de Gruyter.

Japhet, Sara. 1979. "Conquest and Settlement in Chronicles." *Journal of Biblical Literature* 98:205–18.

———. 1993. *I and II Chronicles: A Commentary*. Old Testament Library. Louisville: Westminster John Knox.

————. 1997. *The Ideology of the Book of Chronicles and Its Place in Biblical Thought.* 2nd ed. Beiträge zur Erforschung des Alten Testaments und des antiken Judentums 9. New York: Lang.

Johnson, Marshall D. 1969. *The Purpose of the Biblical Genealogies, with Special Reference to the Setting of the Genealogies of Jesus.* Cambridge: Cambridge University Press.

Johnstone, William. 1997. *1–2 Chronicles.* 2 vols. Journal for the Study of the Old Testament Supplement 253. New York: T&T Clark.

————. 1998. *Chronicles and Exodus: An Analogy and Its Application.* Journal for the Study of the Old Testament Supplement 275. Sheffield: Sheffield Academic Press.

Jonker, Louis. 2008. "The Exile as Sabbath Rest: The Chronicler's Interpretation of the Exile." Pp. 213–28 in *Exile and Suffering: A Selection of Papers Read at the 50th Anniversary Meeting of the Old Testament Society of South Africa.* Edited by Bob Becking and Dirk Human. Oudtestamentische Studiën 50. Leiden: Brill.

Kaiser, Walter C. 1974. "The Blessing of David: The Charter for Humanity." Pp. 298–318 in *The Law and the Prophets: Old Testament Studies Prepared in Honor of Oswald Thompson Allis.* Edited by John H. Skilton. Nutley, NJ: P&R.

Kalimi, Isaac. 2002. *Early Jewish Exegesis and Theological Controversy: Studies in Scriptures in the Shadow of Internal and External Controversies.* Assen: Van Gorcum.

————. 2003. "Jerusalem—The Divine City: The Representation of Jerusalem in Chronicles Compared with Earlier and Later Jewish Compositions." Pp. 189–205 in *The Chronicler as Theologian: Essays in Honor of Ralph W. Klein.* Edited by M. Patrick Graham, Steven L. McKenzie, and Gary N. Knoppers. Journal for the Study of the Old Testament Supplement 371. New York: T&T Clark.

————. 2005. *An Ancient Israelite Historian: Studies in the Chronicler, His Time, Place, and Writing.* Studia semitica neerlandica 46. Assen: Van Gorcum.

————. 2009. *The Retelling of Chronicles in Jewish Tradition and Literature: A Historical Journey.* Winona Lake, IN: Eisenbrauns.

Kaminsky, Joel S. 2000. "Paradise Regained: Rabbinic Reflections on Israel at Sinai." Pp. 15–43 in *Jews, Christians, and the Theology of the Hebrew Scriptures.* Edited by Alice Ogden Bellis and Joel S. Kaminsky. Atlanta: Society of Biblical Literature.

Kearney, Peter J. 1977. "Creation and Liturgy: The P Redaction of Ex. 25–40." *Zeitschrift für die alttestamentliche Wissenschaft* 89:375–87.

Kelly, Brian E. 1996. *Retribution and Eschatology in Chronicles.* Journal for the Study of the Old Testament Supplement 211. Sheffield: Sheffield Academic Press.

————. 1998. "David's Disqualification in 1 Chronicles 22:8: A Response to Piet B. Dirksen." *Journal for the Study of the Old Testament* 80:53–61.

————. 2003. "'Retribution' Revisited: Covenant, Grace, and Restoration." Pp. 206–27 in *The Chronicler as Theologian: Essays in Honor of Ralph W. Klein.* Edited by M. Patrick Graham, Steven L. McKenzie, and Gary N. Knoppers. Journal for the Study of the Old Testament Supplement 371. New York: T&T Clark.

Klein, Ralph W. 1983. *1 Samuel.* Word Biblical Commentary 10. Waco: Word.

————. 2006. *1 Chronicles: A Commentary.* Hermeneia. Minneapolis: Fortress.

Kleinig, John W. 1993. *The Lord's Song: The Basis, Function, and Significance of Choral Music in Chronicles.* Journal for the Study of the Old Testament Supplement 156. Sheffield, JSOT Press.

Knoppers, Gary N. 1990. "Rehoboam in Chronicles: Villain or Victim?" *Journal of Biblical Literature* 109:423–40.

———. 1995. "Images of David in Early Judaism: David as Repentant Sinner in Chronicles." *Biblica* 76:449–70.

———. 1999. "Hierodules, Priests, or Janitors? The Levites in Chronicles and the History of the Israelite Priesthood." *Journal of Biblical Literature* 118:49–72.

———. 2000. "'Great among His Brothers,' But Who Is He? Heterogeneity in the Composition of Judah." *Journal of Hebrew Scriptures* 3/4. www.jhsonline.org.

———. 2001. "Intermarriage, Social Complexity, and Ethnic Diversity in the Genealogy of Judah." *Journal of Biblical Literature* 120:15–30.

———. 2003a. "The Relationship of the Priestly Genealogies to the History of the High Priesthood in Jerusalem." Pp. 109–33 in *Judah and the Judeans in the Neo-Babylonian Period*. Edited by Oded Lipschits and Joseph Blenkinsopp. Winona Lake, IN: Eisenbrauns.

———. 2003b. "Shem, Ham, and Japheth: The Universal and the Particular in the Genealogy of Nations." Pp. 13–31 in *The Chronicler as Theologian: Essays in Honor of Ralph W. Klein*. Edited by M. Patrick Graham, Steven L. McKenzie, and Gary N. Knoppers. Journal for the Study of the Old Testament Supplement 371. New York: T&T Clark.

———. 2004. *1 Chronicles*. 2 vols. Anchor Bible 12–12A. New York: Doubleday.

Knoppers, Gary N., and Paul B. Harvey Jr. 2002. "Omitted and Remaining Matters: On the Names Given to the Book of Chronicles in Antiquity." *Journal of Biblical Literature* 121:227–43.

Kreitzer, Larry J. 2007. "The Messianic Man of Peace as Temple Builder: Solomonic Imagery in Ephesians 2:13–22." Pp. 484–512 in *Temple and Worship in Biblical Israel*. Edited by John Day. New York: Continuum.

Kugel, James L. 1986. "Topics in the History of the Spirituality of the Psalms." Pp. 113–41 in *Jewish Spirituality: From the Bible through the Middle Ages*. Edited by Arthur Green. World Spirituality: An Encyclopedic History of the Religious Quest 13. New York: Crossroad.

Lane, William L. 1991. *Hebrews 1–8*. Word Biblical Commentary 47A. Dallas: Word.

Leithart, Peter J. 2003. *From Silence to Song: The Davidic Liturgical Revolution*. Moscow, ID: Canon.

Levenson, Jon. 1976. *Theology of the Program of Restoration of Ezekiel 40–48*. Harvard Semitic Monograph 10. Missoula, MT: Scholars Press.

———. 1979. "The Davidic Covenant and Its Modern Interpreters." *Catholic Biblical Quarterly* 41:205–19.

———. 1984. "The Temple and the World." *Journal of Religion* 64:275–98.

———. 1985. *Sinai and Zion: An Entry into the Jewish Bible*. San Francisco: HarperOne.

———. 1986. "The Jerusalem Temple in Devotional and Visionary Experience." Pp. 32–61 in *Jewish Spirituality: From the Bible through the Middle Ages*. Edited by Arthur Green. World Spirituality: An Encyclopedic History of the Religious Quest 13. New York: Crossroad.

———. 1988. *Creation and the Persistence of Evil: The Jewish Drama of Divine Omnipotence*. New York: Harper & Row.

Maher, Michael, ed. 1992. *Targum Pseudo-Jonathan: Genesis*. Aramaic Bible 1B. Collegeville, MN: Liturgical Press.

Marcus, Joel. 2003. "Son of Man as Son of Adam." *Revue biblique* 110:38–61, 370–86.

May, Herbert G. 1962. "The King in the Garden of Eden: A Study of Ezekiel 28:12–19." Pp. 166–76 in *Israel's Prophetic Heritage: Essays in Honor of James Muilenberg*. Edited by Bernhard W. Anderson and Walter Harrelson. New York: Harper.

Mayer, Günter, et al. 1986. "ידה *ydh*; תּוֹדָה *tôḏâ*." Pp. 427–43 in vol. 5 of *Theological Dictionary of the Old Testament*. Edited by G. Johannes Botterweck and Helmer Ringgren. Translated by David E. Green. Grand Rapids: Eerdmans.

McCarthy, Dennis J. 1971. "An Institution Genre?" *Journal of Biblical Literature* 90:31–41.

———. 1982. "Covenant and Law in Chronicles–Nehemiah." *Catholic Biblical Quarterly* 44:25–44.

McCartney, Dan. 1994. "*Ecce Homo*: The Coming of the Kingdom as the Restoration of Human Viceregency." *Westminster Theological Journal* 56:1–21.

McIvor, J. Stanley, ed. 1994. *The Targums of Ruth and Chronicles*. Aramaic Bible 19. Collegeville, MN: Liturgical Press.

McNamara, Martin J., ed. 1992. *Targum Neofiti 1: Genesis*. Aramaic Bible 1A. Collegeville, MN: Liturgical Press.

Milgrom, Jacob. 1976. "The Concept of *Ma'al* in the Bible and the Ancient Near East." *Journal of the American Oriental Society* 96:236–47.

———. 1989. *Numbers: The Traditional Hebrew Text with the New JPS Translation*. New York: Jewish Publication Society.

Morris, Paul. 1992. "Exiled from Eden: Jewish Interpretations of Eden." Pp. 117–66 in *A Walk in the Garden: Biblical, Iconographical, and Literary Images of Eden*. Edited by Paul Morris and Deborah Sawyer. Journal for the Study of the Old Testament Supplement 136. Sheffield: Sheffield Academic Press.

Murray, Donald F. 1993. "Dynasty, People, and the Future: The Message of Chronicles." *Journal for the Study of the Old Testament* 58:71–92.

———. 2001. "Under Yʜwʜ's Veto: David as Shedder of Blood in Chronicles." *Biblica* 82:457–76.

Neusner, Jacob. 1988. *The Mishnah: A New Translation*. New Haven: Yale University Press.

———. 2004. *Making God's Word Work*. New York: Continuum.

Newsome, James D. 1975. "Toward a New Understanding of the Chronicler and His Purposes." *Journal of Biblical Literature* 94:201–17.

Pagolu, Augustine. 1998. *The Religion of the Patriarchs*. Journal for the Study of the Old Testament Supplement 277. Sheffield: Sheffield Academic Press.

Pao, David W. 2002. *Thanksgiving: An Investigation of a Pauline Theme*. New Studies in Biblical Theology 13. Downers Grove, IL: InterVarsity.

Pitre, Brant. 2003. "Rewritten Bible." Pp. 413–14 in *The Westminster Dictionary of Early Christian Literature and Rhetoric*. Edited by David E. Aune. Louisville: Westminster John Knox.

Rad, Gerhard von. 1961. *Genesis: A Commentary*. Translated by John Marks. Old Testament Library. Philadelphia: Westminster.

———. 1962–65. *Old Testament Theology*. 2 vols. Translated by D. M. G. Stalker. New York: Harper & Row.

———. 1966. *The Problem of the Hexateuch and Other Essays*. Translated by E. W. Trueman Dicken. New York: McGraw-Hill.

Raney, Donald C., II. 2003. *History as Narrative in the Deuteronomistic History and Chronicles*. Studies in the Bible and Early Christianity 56. Lewiston, NY: Mellen.

Rashi. 1992. *1 Chronicles: A New English Translation*. Translated by A. J. Rosenberg. New York: Judaica.

Ratzinger, Joseph. 1983. *Daughter Zion: Meditations on the Church's Marian Belief*. San Francisco: Ignatius.

Reif, Stefan C. 2006. "The Function of History in Early Rabbinic Liturgy." Pp. 321–33 in *Deuterocanonical and Cognate Literature Yearbook 2006: History and Identity; How Israel's Later Authors Viewed Its Earlier History*. Edited by Núria Calduch-Benages and Jan Liesen. New York: de Gruyter.

Riley, William. 1993. *King and Cultus in Chronicles: Worship and the Reinterpretation of History*. Journal for the Study of the Old Testament Supplement 160. Sheffield: JSOT Press.

Roberts, J. J. M. 2002. *The Bible and the Ancient Near East: Collected Essays*. Winona Lake, IN: Eisenbrauns.

Rooke, Deborah W. 1998. "Kingship as Priesthood: The Relationship between the High Priesthood and the Monarchy." Pp. 187–208 in *King and Messiah in Israel and the Ancient Near East: Proceedings of the Oxford Old Testament Seminar*. Edited by John Day. Sheffield: Sheffield Academic Press.

———. 2000. *Zadok's Heirs: The Role and Development of the High Priesthood in Israel*. New York: Oxford University Press.

Runnalls, Donna R. 1983. "The King as Temple Builder: A Messianic Typology." Pp. 15–37 in *Spirit within Structure: Essays in Honor of George Johnston on the Occasion of His Seventieth Birthday*. Edited by E. J. Furcha. Allison Park, PA: Pickwick.

Saebo, Magne. 1980. "Messianism in Chronicles? Some Remarks to the Old Testament Background to the New Testament Christology." *Horizons in Biblical Literature* 2:85–109.

Sanders, E. P. 1977. *Paul and Palestinian Judaism: A Comparison of Patterns of Religion*. Philadelphia: Fortress.

———. 1985. *Jesus and Judaism*. Philadelphia: Fortress.

Sanders, James A. 1955. *Suffering as Divine Discipline in the Old Testament and Post-Biblical Judaism*. Rochester: Colgate Rochester Divinity School.

Sarna, Nahum M. 1986. *Exploring Exodus: The Heritage of Biblical Israel*. New York: Schocken.

———. 1989. *Genesis: The Traditional Hebrew Text with the New JPS Translation*. New York: Jewish Publication Society.

Schniedewind, William M. 1994. "King and Priest in the Book of Chronicles and the Duality of Qumran Messianism." *Journal of Jewish Studies* 45:71–78.

———. 1995. *The Word of God in Transition: From Prophet to Exegete in the Second Temple Period*. Journal for the Study of the Old Testament Supplement 197. Sheffield: Sheffield Academic Press.

———. 1997. "Prophets and Prophecy in the Books of Chronicles." Pp. 204–24 in *The Chronicler as Historian*. Edited by M. Patrick Graham, Kenneth G. Hoglund, and Steven L. McKenzie. Journal for the Study of the Old Testament Supplement 238. Sheffield: Sheffield Academic Press.

————. 2003. "The Evolution of Name Theology." Pp. 228–39 in *The Chronicler as Theologian: Essays in Honor of Ralph W. Klein*. Edited by M. Patrick Graham, Steven L. McKenzie, and Gary N. Knoppers. Journal for the Study of the Old Testament Supplement 371. New York: T&T Clark.

Schweitzer, Steven James. 2003. "The High Priest in Chronicles: An Anomaly in a Detailed Description of the Temple Cult." *Biblica* 84:388–402.

————. 2007. *Reading Utopia in Chronicles*. New York: T&T Clark.

Selman, Martin J. 1989. "The Kingdom of God in the Old Testament." *Tyndale Bulletin* 40/2:161–83.

————. 1994a. *1 Chronicles: An Introduction and Commentary*. Tyndale Old Testament Commentaries 10A. Downers Grove, IL: InterVarsity.

————. 1994b. *2 Chronicles: A Commentary*. Tyndale Old Testament Commentaries 10B. Downers Grove, IL: InterVarsity.

————. 1999. "Jerusalem in Chronicles." Pp. 43–56 in *Zion, City of Our God*. Edited by Richard J. Hess and Gordon J. Wenham. Grand Rapids: Eerdmans.

Shaver, Judson R. 1989. *Torah and the Chronicler's History Work: An Inquiry into the Chronicler's References to Laws, Festivals, and Cultic Institutions in Relationship to Pentateuchal Legislation*. Brown Judaic Studies 196. Providence: Brown University Press.

Smith, Carol. 1998. "'Queenship' in Israel? The Cases of Bathsheba, Jezebel, and Athaliah." Pp. 142–62 in *King and Messiah in Israel and the Ancient Near East: Proceedings of the Oxford Old Testament Seminar*. Edited by John Day. Sheffield: Sheffield Academic Press.

Smolar, Leivy, and Moses Aberbach. 1968. "The Golden Calf Episode in Postbiblical Literature." *Hebrew Union College Annual* 39:91–116.

Sparks, James T. 2008. *The Chronicler's Genealogies: Towards an Understanding of 1 Chronicles 1–9*. Academia biblica 28. Atlanta: Society of Biblical Literature.

Spencer, F. Scott. 1984. "2 Chronicles 28:5–15 and the Parable of the Good Samaritan." *Westminster Theological Journal* 46:317–49.

Sri, Edward. 2005. *Queen Mother: A Biblical Theology of Mary's Queenship*. Steubenville, OH: Emmaus Road.

Steins, Georg. 1995. *Die Chronik als kanonisches Abschlussphänomen: Studien zur Entstehung und Theologie von 1/2 Chronik*. Weinhelm, Germany: Beltz Athenäum.

Steussy, Marti J. 1999. *David: Biblical Portraits of Power*. Columbia: University of South Carolina Press.

Stinespring, William F. 1961. "Eschatology in Chronicles." *Journal of Biblical Literature* 80:209–19.

Stuhlmueller, Carroll. 1983. *Psalms 2*. Wilmington, DE: Michael Glazier.

Tanner, Beth. 2004. "King Yahweh as the Good Shepherd: Taking Another Look at the Image of God in Psalm 23." Pp. 267–84 in *David and Zion: Biblical Studies in Honor of J. J. M. Roberts*. Edited by Bernard F. Batto and Kathryn L. Roberts. Winona Lake, IN: Eisenbrauns.

Timmer, Daniel C. 2009. *Creation, Tabernacle, and Sabbath: The Sabbath Frame of Exodus 31:12–17; 35:1–3 in Exegetical and Theological Perspective*. Forschungen zur Religion und Literatur des Alten und Neuen Testaments 227. Göttingen: Vandenhoeck & Ruprecht.

Trompf, G. W. 1979. "Notions of Historical Recurrence in Classical Hebrew Historiography." Pp. 213–29 in *Studies in the Historical Books of the Old Testament*. Edited by J. A. Emerton. Vetus Testamentum Supplement 30. Leiden: Brill.

Tucker, Gene M. 1965. "Covenant Forms and Contract Forms." *Vetus Testamentum* 15:487–503.

Tuell, Steven S. 2001. *First and Second Chronicles*. Louisville: Westminster John Knox.

Van Seters, John. 1989. "The Creation of Man and the Creation of the King." *Zeitschrift für die Alttestamentliche Wissenschaft* 101:333–42.

Vawter, Bruce. 1977. *Genesis: A New Reading*. Garden City, NY: Doubleday.

Wanke, Gunther. 1997. "שָׂטָן *śāṭān*, Adversary." Pp. 1268–69 in vol. 3 of *Theological Lexicon of the Old Testament*. Edited by Ernst Jenni and Claus Westermann. Translated by Mark E. Biddle. Peabody, MA: Hendrickson.

Weinfeld, Moshe. 1970. "The Covenant of Grant in the Old Testament and in the Ancient Near East." *Journal of the American Oriental Society* 90:184–204.

———. 1981. "Sabbath, Temple, and the Enthronement of the Lord: The Problem of the Sitz im Leben of Genesis 1:1–2:3." Pp. 501–12 in *Mélanges biblique et orientaux en l'honneur de M. Henri Cazelles*. Edited by A. Caquot and M. Delcor. Alter Orient und Altes Testament 212. Kevelaer: Butzon & Bercker/Neukirchen-Vluyn: Neukirchener Verlag.

Wellhausen, Julius. 1994. *Prolegomena to the History of Ancient Israel*. Translated by J. S. Sutherland and Allan Menzie. Reprinted, Atlanta: Scholars Press (orig. 1885).

Wells, Jo Bailey. 2000. *God's Holy People: A Theme in Biblical Theology*. Journal for the Study of the Old Testament Supplement 305. Sheffield: Sheffield Academic Press.

Wenham, Gordon J. 1986. "Sanctuary Symbolism in the Garden of Eden Story." Pp. 19–25 in *Proceedings of the Ninth Congress of Jewish Studies*. Jerusalem: World Union of Jewish Studies.

———. 1995. "The Akedah: A Paradigm of Sacrifice." Pp. 93–102 in *Pomegranates and Golden Bells: Studies in Biblical, Jewish, and Near Eastern Ritual, Law, and Literature in Honor of Jacob Milgrom*. Edited by David P. Wright, David Noel Freedman, and Avi Hurvitz. Winona Lake, IN: Eisenbrauns.

Westermann, Claus. 1981. *Praise and Lament in the Psalms*. Translated by Keith R. Crim and Richard N. Soulen. Atlanta: John Knox.

Williamson, H. G. M. 1977. *Israel in the Books of Chronicles*. London: Cambridge University Press.

———. 1982. *1 and 2 Chronicles*. New Century Bible Commentary. Grand Rapids: Eerdmans.

———. 1991. "The Temple in the Books of Chronicles." Pp. 15–31 in *Templum Amicitiae: Essays on the Second Temple Presented to Ernst Bammel*. Edited by William Horbury. Journal for the Study of the New Testament Supplement 48. Sheffield: JSOT Press. Reprinted in Williamson 2004: 150–61.

———. 2004. *Studies in Persian Period History and Historiography*. Forschungen zum Alten Testament 38. Tübingen: Mohr-Siebeck.

Wilson, Ian. 1995. *Out of the Midst of the Fire: Divine Presence in Deuteronomy*. Society of Biblical Literature Dissertation Series 151. Atlanta: Scholars Press.

Wright, G. E. 1962. "Cult and History: A Study of a Current Problem in Old Testament Interpretation." *Interpretation* 16:3–20.

Wright, John W. 2006. "Remapping Yehud: The Borders of Yehud and the Genealogies of Chronicles." Pp. 67–90 in *Judah and the Judeans in the Persian Period*. Edited by Oded Lipschits and Manfred Oeming. Winona Lake, IN: Eisenbrauns.

Wright, N. T. 1992. *The New Testament and the People of God*. Minneapolis: Augsburg-Fortress.

Zlotnick, Helena. 2001. "From Jezebel to Esther: Fashioning Images of Queenship in the Hebrew Bible." *Biblica* 82:477–95.

Zvi, Ehud Ben. 2006. *History, Literature, and Theology in the Book of Chronicles*. London: Equinox.

# Subject Index

# Scripture Index